MEDITATION DIFFERENTLY

MEDITATION DIFFERENTLY

Phenomenological-psychological Aspects of Tibetan Buddhist (Mahāmudrā and sNying-thig) Practices from Original Tibetan Sources

HERBERT GUENTHER

MOTILAL BANARSIDASS PUBLISHERS
PRIVATE LIMITED • DELHI

First Edition: 1992

ISBN: 81-208-0870-3

Also available at:
MOTILAL BANARSIDASS
41 U.A., Bungalow Road, Jawahar Nagar, Delhi 110 007
120 Royapettah High Road, Mylapore, Madras 600 004
16 St. Mark's Road, Bangalore 560 001
Ashok Rajpath, Patna 800 004
Chowk, Varanasi 221 001

PRINTED IN INDIA
BY JAINENDRA PRAKASH JAIN AT SHRI JAINENDRA PRESS, A-45 NARAINA INDUSTRIAL AREA, PHASE I, NEW DELHI 110 028 AND PUBLISHED BY NARENDRA PRAKASH JAIN FOR MOTILAL BANARSIDASS PUBLISHERS PVT. LTD., BUNGALOW ROAD, JAWAHAR NAGAR, DELHI 110 007

For

Ilse, Candace, Jeanette, and Mariana

CONTENTS

ACKNOWLEDGEMENTS

IT IS IMPOSSIBLE to mention the names of all the scientists, philosophers, artists, and friends who have helped me in formulating my ideas in stimulating discussions and by critical comments on earlier drafts of the material presented in this book. However, special thanks are due to Candace Schuler for drawing the diagrams, Mariana Neves for the lovely frontispiece entitled "Intensities", Kent Johnson for invaluable editorial suggestions and, together with my wife Ilse, the preparation of the indices.

INTRODUCTION

Over the last few decades meditation has captured the imagination of many people, especially the younger, as a means to guide them in their personal development. This is both a rediscovery of one's innate potential and a rectification of the unbalanced attitude to which Western man under the impact of a dehumanizing technology has succumbed and from which he on and off has attempted to escape by usually ill-fated ego-trips. However, the concept of meditation is not precise and eventually will have to be replaced by others more fully descriptive and elucidative of the processes involved.

Within the Indo-Tibetan cultural milieu at least three closely related, though highly differentiated concepts are available: *dhyāna* (*bsam-gtan*), *bhāvanā* (*sgom-pa*), and *yoga* (*rnal-'byor*). But it is in the Tibetan context that all these concepts have been deeply probed as to the subtleties in lived through experience which they attempt to convey. Two approaches or modes of inquiry are detectable. The one, which is the older (*rnying-ma*) one and living on in rDzogs-chen thinking, is hermeneutical and offers an interpretation which understands through an inner-standing, because it has its origin in the lighting of Being (to use a Heideggerian phrase) as one's primordial ontological potential. The other approach belongs to the newer (*gsar-ma*) tradition of the Mahāmudrā teaching and reflects the strictly Indian preoccupation with objectification in which the 'lighting of Being' is dimmed and its luminous field put in abeyance in order to have a tighter hold on the object. Nowhere are these two approaches more conspicuous than in the assessment of what to understand by the concept of *bsam-gtan* which is probably the most complex one amongst the three above-mentioned ones. Its general use in connection with what we would call 'concentration' or a 'focusing of the mind on something objectively given', in other words, an imaginative dealing with an objective reference, is only one of its meanings. The important and divergent aspects noted by the Tibetans, have been mostly ignored in Western presentations that reflect a depressingly sad state of affairs: psychologists, as a rule, have no knowledge of the original texts (be they in Sanskrit or Tibetan) and have to depend on haphazard translations by linguists who, steeped in 19th century mechanism and reductionism, either have little or no knowledge of what thinking as a creative process means and involves, or conceive of thinking as a problem-solving activity and, where it becomes a matter of divergent Tibetan and Indian patterns of thought, suffer from a severe case of 'Sanskrit-only' glaucoma which makes them blind to Tibetan hermeneutical thinking so that they are content with a mechanical transposition of words from one language into another, desperately trying to suppress any traces of experience and understanding.

As the Tibetans noted concentrative processes (*bsam-gtan*) are primarily referential (*rten-can*) in the sense that they contain a referent which is both a 'world-frame' (to use a term coined by E. Casey), an external phenomenologically present domain (*phyi snang-ba'i yul*) specified as sense-specific colored shapes, sounds, fragrances, flavors, and tactility, and a 'noematic nucleus' (a Husserlian term) of the concentrative-imaginative process whose 'presence' tends to become more or less reified in the imaged gestalt of a felt presence termed a god (*lha'i sku*), its emblems (*phyag-mtshan*) as symbolic expressions of its function, or, continuing an earlier naive realism that stood at the beginning of Buddhist thought (and by implication, meditation-concentration), a so-called 'real', 'physically' existing wooden stick (*shing-bu*) or a pebble (*rde'u*)[1].

There is still another referential aspect which is lacking the externalization and reification of the noematic nucleus and remains purely 'imaginative'. Its characterization as 'non-referential' (*rten-med*)[2] is to be understood as 'non-externalizable' and 'non-reifiable', not in the sense of there being no reference whatsoever, as a 'literal' (uncomprehendingly mechanical) translation would suggest. The referent in this concentrative-imaginative process is the imaginary, yet strongly felt, presence (*snang-bcas*) of the organism's dynamics described in terms of its chreods (standing-wave patterns, *rtsa*), the currents moving along these patterns (*rlung*), and the overall organizing dynamics (*thig-le*), claimed to be a non-dichotomic, conceptually undisturbed and undivided (*mi-rtog-pa*) experience, as well as audibly imaged gnosemes (*yi-ge*), visibly imaged globes of pure light (*'od-kyi gong-bu*), feelingly imaged rotary movements within and constituted by the chreods (*rtsa'i 'khor-lo*) and an inner fire (*gtum-mo'i me*). Lastly, there is, however paradoxically it may sound, a referent or sensum with no noticeable reference (*snang-med*), a kind of 'pure sensation' or 'staring' into some non-dichotomic (*mi-rtog-pa*) dimension. In whatever nuances this concentrative activity may appear it remains in the service of an egological subjectivity (*sems-'dzin-pa*) with its inveterate grasping and holding to what it has grasped (*'dzin-pa*)[3]. Since it prescinds from the ecstasy of visionary non-egological Being (*rig-pa*)[4], it is counted to be of a low-level activity in which those who do not know better, who still have not outgrown their childhood (*byis-pa*)[5], engage. Or, to put it even more bluntly, such concentrative activity is an affectation (*bcos-ma*)[6], deliberately initiated by the intellect (*blo*)[7] which operates on the metaphysical assumption that the intellectual order it imposes on reality is representative of the world which it presumes to be reducible to unchanging structures of universal validity.

Strictly speaking, such rational and egological concentrative activity, geared to the reinforcement of the notion of a static cosmos, has little to do with concentration as a process of centering. Rather, it is a de-centering of psychic activity, a channelling of its stream into the backwater of dichotomic thought that inevitably leads to stagnation. From a dynamic perspective, concentration means that the divergent trends of psychic life *con*-verge into a single point such that the process becomes *centered* in itself and thereby leads to an extraordinary intensification of itself and of life in general. As against the 'artificiality' of the intellect's concentrative activity, this self-centering (*rang-babs*)[8] and self-abiding (*rang-gnas*)[9] concentration is the most natural (*rang-bzhin*)[10] activity of one's cognitive potential that in its ec-static intensity (*rig-pa*) is an utter openness and undimmed radiance.

This important distinction between an object-oriented and a self-centering process is met with again in what is described as 'one-pointedness' (*rtse-gcig*) or as a 'one-pointed in-depth appraisal' (*rtse-gcig ting-nge-'dzin*)[11], implying by the term *'dzin* that the mind's 'grasping' of what it set down before it, is still operative, though in a highly attenuated form. In object-oriented concentration this one-pointedness simply means focal attention to something that has been isolated and abstracted from its environing world and, by implication, is exclusive and unresponsive to the connective tissue of the matrix of one's seeing. The appeal this kind of concentrative meditation has, lies in the fact that everything remains as it is, because essentially it is but a reconfirmation of the rational mind's tendency to dominate and control.[12]

As against this reductionist aspect of concentrative (object-oriented) meditation there is another more dynamic and process-oriented aspect that marks a withdrawal from the engagement with these dispersive tendencies and a gathering of the energy getting lost in them into a 'point' that in its restful motion (*gnas-'gyu*)[13] is the level where mind as we ordinarily understand it is poised to either pass beyond itself into the wholeness of Being or revert to its 'normal' dichotomic functioning. Inasmuch as this process of a gathering, of becoming increasingly centered in itself, does not know of any fixation, the older concept of *bsam-gtan* with its predominantly static connotation has been replaced by the more dynamic one of *rnal-'byor*, which describes the individual's tuning in to or linking up with (*'byor*) Being's dynamic genuineness (*rnal*)[14] or, as we might say with reference to what is called one-pointedness, its stillpoint, involving four vector feelings of different intensities that cannot be torn apart without mutual destruction. Summed up under the code term "The Fourfold Tuning-in" (*rnal-'byor bzhi*)[15], they are the cornerstone of the Mahāmudrā teaching which is the hallmark of the various bKa'-brgyud-pa schools that once flourished in Tibet.

NOTES

1. *Chos-dbyings*, pp. 191f.
2. *ibid.*
3. *Theg-mchog* II, pp. 75f.
4. rDzogs-chen texts distinguish very clearly between *sems* 'mind/mentation' as a low intensity operation and *rig-pa* (which I render by 'ec-static (cognitive) intensity') as the highest intensity of wholeness whose dynamics expresses itself in a 'pristine awareness' and its multifaceted nuances (*ye-shes*). Images to illustrate this intensity that also is its autonomy which comes into full play when it has become 'ec-static', 'broken out' of what has held it confined, are a lion cub that has come

out of its mother's womb or the mythological garuda bird that has broken the egg in which it had been hatched and immediately soars into the sky. As we shall have occasion to note, rDzogs-chen teaching distinguishes between three levels of psychic life. The lowest level is that of ordinary persons whose 'concentration/meditation' (*bsam-gtan*) consists in what comes dangerously close to developing a fixation; the intermediary level is that of the person who by tuning in (*rnal-'byor*) to the forces working in and through him approximates wholeness; and the highest level is wholeness itself whose 'intelligence' exceeding all limits is referred to as *dgongs-pa* suggesting some 'superintelligence' or 'superthought' or 'supermind' that is irreducible to any lower level, be this called *bsam-gtan* or *rnal-'byor*.

In *Chos-dbyings*, p. 68, Klong-chen rab-'byams-pa gives a concise account of the above:

The self-existing pristine awareness (*rang-byung-gi ye-shes*), undivided by concepts dealing with objects, is a self-abiding 'concentration' (*rang-gnas-kyi bsam-gtan*); its uncreated spontaneity is a yogi's concentration (*rnal-'byor-pa'i bsam-gtan*); the inner calm and 'out-of-the-ordinary' perception (*zhi-lhag*, short for *zhi-gnas* and *lhag-mthong*) that comes by 'staring' one-pointedly at an object (*yul rtse-gcig-tu yid-la byed-pa*) is the concentration of worldly people who do not know better (*'jig-rten byis-pa'i bsam-gtan*). The difference (between the two kinds of concentration) is that the latter continues building up the tendencies (that hold a person prisoner in the world), the former does not. The self-abiding dynamics of the ec-static intensity (*rig-pa*) is (one's) mind intending and suffused by (the whole's) pellucidity and consummation (*byang-chub-kyi sems*) and it is called 'the superthought of Being's possibilizing dynamics' (*chos-nyid-kyi dgongs-pa*). One's cognitive capacity (*shes-pa*) that manifests itself in its concern with objects is called 'sǎmsaric mind'; it arises in the dichotomic pattern of subject and object.

5. See also preceding note.
6. *Theg-mchog* II, p. 163.
7. *ibid.*
8. *Chos-dbyings*, p. 93. On p. 194 Klong-chen rab-'byams-pa succinctly states:

   In brief, the mind's (concentrative) preoccupation with what is before it, clings to the peg of the subject-object dichotomy; the self-centered concentration of the ec-static cognitive intensity is the dynamic movement of Being's possibilizing dynamics that is self-centered. Their difference is that the former initiates the (material) world or samsara as well as higher levels of sensibility in the mind, while the latter links (the experiencer) with the releasement (from all worldliness) or nirvana and (lastly,) as the 'superthought of Buddhahood' it abides in what is its legitimate dwelling.
9. *ibid.*, pp. 68; 93.
10. *ibid.*, p. 238; *Tshig-don*, pp. 316, 318, *Theg-mchog* II, p. 163.
11. *Rig-pa rang-shar*, pp. 392 and 530 respectively. In *Man-ngag*, p. 99. Klong-chen rab-'byams-pa poetically speaks of the inseparability of a

composure state (*mnyam-gzhag*) and post-composure state (*rjes-thob*) by comparing their unity with a cold breeze (the stirring of a thought) in the air (the calmness of the psyche):

(Being's, that is, one's) pristine awareness that in its brilliance and translucency is like the sky's reach
Must be sensuously experienced in its own limpidity (which is such that a thought's) stirring dissolves in translucency and dynamic freedom:
This is the sensuously felt experience of the insubstantiality (of one's, that is, Being's 'intelligence') to be without any egocentric grasping (*'dzin-med*).
Not knowing it so, (one's) single-pointedness in-depth appraisal (*rtse-gcig ting-'dzin*)
Is like a flame shaken by the wind—it cannot withstand any adverse conditions.

Note the contrast between *'dzin-med* (the non-egological) and *'dzin* (the egocentric).

12. For further details see my *From Reductionism to Creativity*, pp. 77, 78, 82, 83.
13. See Chapter Two for a more detailed discussion.
14. *rnal-ma*. In both *Bi-ma* I, p. 79 and *Vairo*, vol. 7, p. 123 this term is explained as 'uncontrived', 'genuine' (*ma-bcos*).
15. With the followers of the Mahāmudrā teaching this 'code term' refers to the four vector feelings described and 'epistemologically objectified' as *rtse-gcig* 'one-pointedness', *spros-bral* 'dissociation from conceptual-propositional proliferations and overshadowings, *ro-gcig* 'one-flavoredness' and *bsgom-med* 'no model-building'; with the rDzogs chen thinkers it refers to the lived through continuity of (an existential) vision, its development through creative imagination, its acting out in one's life, and their integration.

Chapter One

THE MAHĀMUDRĀ APPROACH: THE FOUR TUNING-IN PHASES

The earliest, rather concise but nonetheless systematic, statements concerning four tuning-in phases seem to have been made by sGam-po-pa (1079-1153),[1] one of the most important and favored students of Mi-la ras-pa (1040-1123) who is famous for his often sarcastic songs in which he expressed his spiritual experiences.

Here are a few quotations from sGam-po-pa as recorded by his students:

(1) The single-pointedness (*rtse-gcig*) tuning-in phase is a time- and space-binding psychic energy (*shes-pa*) that in its brilliance is a ceaseless opening-up.[2]

The conceptualization-free (*spros-bral*) tuning-in phase is such that by seeing the 'stuff' one's mind in its ec-static intensity (*rig-pa*) is made of as being not something that comes into existence (like some thing or notion), one does not anticipate a state of spiritual wakefulness as an upper limit, nor is one afraid of (erring into) samsara as a lower limit, nor does one (egocentrically) hold to what lights up (as one's phenomenal world), nor can one's (perception of reality) be changed by some other (ideological claim).[3]

The single-piquancy (*ro-gcig*) tuning-in phase is the deeply felt understanding that the phenomenal ('that which lights up', *snang*) and the noumenal ('that which is dynamically open, nothing', *stong*) are indivisible.

The no-more-model-building (*bsgom-med*) tuning-in phase is such that, since whatever lights up (as the phenomenal world) and whatever has become a concrete phenomenon has arisen as (presenting) the same 'stuff' (that Being or the whole is made of), the totality (of one's reality) turns out, on closer inspection, to be a (finished) model.[4]

(*Collected Works*, vol. *tha*, fol. 16b)

(2) When the 'stuff' one's mind (*sems*) is made of abides in a

state of brilliance that is a ceaseless opening-up, a shimmering and glittering, not exteriorizing itself, this (state) is said to be the single-pointedness tuning-in phase. The indication that it has come to pass in one's psyche is that one's interest in worldly matters grows less. The fluctuations in its sensation are very great. Sometimes one has the impression that there is nothing beyond this state; sometimes one has the impression that there has never been anything that one might have had to develop imaginatively after one's psychic energy (*shes-pa*) has lost its fluidity. (According to sGam-po-pa) these (impressions) are concentrative modes marked by an ambivalence concerning what lights up.

When one has familiarized oneself with this (single-pointedness tuning-in phase) in a disinterested manner, the deeply felt understanding that the 'stuff' one's psychic energy (*shes-pa*) is made of is in its brilliance without divisive concepts (and as such) dissociated from the limitations set up by (the intellect's) categories of existence and non-existence, eternity and nihility, is (as) the mind's (*sems*) 'stuff', itself without origination and cessation (the whole's) meaning-(saturated) gestalt, is the conceptualization-free (*spros-bral*) tuning-in phase. (The indication that this phasc) has come to pass within one's psyche is that all the entities of one's reality formerly encountered are (experienced as being but) an outer shell, that the proliferation of the notions pertaining to representational thinking has stopped, and that (one feels) like a pauper having found a treasure.

When one has, furthermore, familiarized oneself with this (conceptualization tuning-in phase) in a disinterested manner, the spontaneous deeply felt understanding that all that lights up as the concrete objects of one's experience, be they bright or dark, are what one's mind is in its ownmostness that is without origination, is the single-piquancy (*ro-gcig*) tuning-in phase. The indication that (this phase) has come to pass within one's psyche is that the subject-object dichotomy has completely subsided. (According to sGam-po-pa) even if there is the coming-to-presence of (the phenomenal world's) multiplicity, it has done so out of the 'stuff' one's psychic energy (*shes-pa*) is made of which is cognate with mind (as such, *sems*).

When one has familiarized oneself with this (single-piquancy tuning-in phase), one stands free of the notions of there being something that has to be built imaginatively and of someone imaginatively building (a model), which means that one deeply understands that (both) the 'stuff' one's psychic energy (*shes-pa*) is made of and all the concrete objects of one's experience are of the same single-piquancy in their not being something that comes-into-existence (like some thing). The uninterrupted flow of (the unity of) the composure and post-composure ('states') is (according to sGam-po-pa) the no-more-model-building (*bsgom-med*) tuning-in phase.

(*Collected Works*, vol. *dza*, fol. 17a)

(3) Thus when through imaginatively attending to the shimmering brilliance the evil in one's self has run its course and come to an end, a flawless single-pointedness (*rtse-gcig*) tuning-in phase comes to pass within one's psyche from within it. In the absence of a basis for one's psychic energy (*shes-pa*) one cannot come into contact with it anywhere and, in its being dissociated from all conceptual-propositional adumbrations, the 'stuff' one's ec-static intensity is made of is (laid bare) as if the bark of a tree) had been peeled off, or as if its matter 'stuff' had been energized. At this time one attains what one had not attained (before), one comes to know what one has not known (before), and like in the case of a pauper having laid his hand on some treasure a feeling of lasting joy spreads so that one's mind (*sems*) is completely happy and cheerful.

By attending seriously to this (tuning-in phase) the mistaken notions (about one's phenomenal reality) disappear and, dissociated from laborious practising, one's ec-static intensity (*rig-pa*) becomes free from any conceptual-propositional adumbrations, and this is the conceptualization-free (*spros-bral*) tuning-in phase. Without dismissing the phenomenal from one's intellect (*blo*) the phenomenal (presents itself) dissociated from (the intellect's) negations and affirmations; the totality of the phenomenal assumes a morally neutral character.

When through imaginatively attending to this (tuning-in

phase) it persists for a long time the single-piquancy of the multiple (*ro-gcig*) tuning-in phase rises from within (one's psyche). Without there being the need to cut off the positive and negative imputations concerning the phenomenal by one's ec-static intensity (*rig-pa*) the totality (of one's notions about the phenomenal) is determined as being (the working of the) mind (*sems*).

At that time there also comes a feeling of independence. One's intellect (*blo*) is raised to higher levels and the psychic energy (*shes-pa*) that the phenomenal is one's mind's (*rang-gi sems*) projections, is about to come to pass. Without there being any need for model-building the phenomenal is sometimes seen as some enchantment, sometimes it is seen as being nothing, sometimes (one wonders) how the mind (*sems*) engages (in its model-building). Through the crucial (psychic energy) charge in the encounter of one's ec-static intensity (*rig-pa*) with nothingness (*stong-pa*) the 'stuff' (one's psychic life consists of) is fused with one's intellect (*blo*) and all dichotomies disappear without leaving a trace. When one stays on in this shimmering (light) for a long time, the no-more-model-building (*bsgom-med*) tuning-in phase comes to pass: the totality of (one's) phenomenal (world) rises as the sheer lucency of (Being's) possibilizing dynamics.

(*Collected Works*, vol. *da*, fols. 5ab)

From these few quotations that could easily be multiplied and to whose specific terminology we shall return later on, it is evident that for sGam-po-pa these four tuning-in processes or, more precisely, vector feelings were seen as constituting a single, multilevel co-ordinated process with varying degrees in intensity. It is the inability of language to express the complexity of this unity that has given rise to the notion of their seriality as when 'single-pointedness' (*rtse-gcig*) is said to be the first vector feeling, followed by the other three in a seemingly granular manner. Also, from sGam-po-pa's account it follows that, psychologically speaking, this single-pointedness compares to what is called the absolute (or detection) threshold, not a referential point in an allegedly objective universe. Its later description as restful motion is essentially a phenomenological account of a vivid experience as may be gleaned from what Padma dkar-po (1526-92) says about this initial and initiatory phase:[5]

> When the interface between quiescence (*gnas*) and agitation ('*gyu*) comes tumbling down
> By recognizing what agitation means in quiescence being uppermost
> And by holding on to quiescence in agitation being uppermost
> The single-pointedness tuning-in phase has been understood as what it is in itself.

And a modern author, David Michael Levin, writing four hundred years after Padma dkar-po virtually says the same and, in addition, has clearly brought out the difference between the older notion of *bsam-gtan* as fixation and the newer, dynamic notion of *rnal-'byor* as restful aliveness by stating:[6]

> There was less need for painful staring, less need to stare the forms into fixity, because the greater tranquillity of my gaze effortlessly stabilized the inevitable display of moving, changing forms. There was less visual jumping and darting about, because the gaze was not so readily seduced by the play of light into forming attachments to its transformations that would disturb my becalmed presence. And there was less compulsion to withdraw into conceptual interpretation, because the gaze, more inwardly quiet, could let me begin to enjoy simply being in and with the lighting of the dark.

More poetically the same sentiment has been voiced by Johann Wolfgang von Goethe:[7]

> No slumber now! Oh let me ponder
> Those peerless apparitions yonder
> My eye envisions. To the core
> How wondrously I am affected!

Lastly, in this context of an interpenetrating togetherness the words of Medard Boss may be quoted:[8]

> Another major emotional mode is composed, joyous serenity. It can give human existence the kind of receptivity that allows it to see in the *brightest light* the meaningfulness and connections of every phenomenon that *reveals itself*. Such a serenity is a *clearness and openness* in which a human

> being is emotionally connected to everything he meets, wanting not to have things in his own power but content to let them be and *develop on their own*. Because this composed, joyous serenity opens a human being to the broadest possible responsiveness, it constitutes *happiness* as well. (Italics added)

sGam-po-pa's statements contain a number of terms that deserve special attention even if, generally speaking, they all refer to what we may call the 'mental-spiritual'. This compound itself is far from satisfactory. In the most general sense 'mental' is that which pertains to mind whose 'nature' has been a topic of bitter dispute in Western philosophy and psychology so that the adjectival term 'mental', too, has become extremely hazy. The word 'spiritual' is absent in modern psychological dictionaries where it has been replaced by 'psychic' used as a synonym with 'psychological' in its narrower sense of 'pertaining to that which is mental in origin'. In a wider sense it is also used as pertaining to various aspects of parapsychology—'a more or less (with the emphasis on the *less*) accepted branch of psychology'.[9]

Central to sGam-po-pa's thinking (and Buddhist thought in general) is the recognition of the cognitive character of any life-form. This cognitive character (*shes-pa*) is, in the terminology of Carl Gustav Jung an 'unextended intensity'[10] that can be experienced feelingly. As Gilles Deleuze and Félix Guattari[11] have pointed out, this intensity allows intensities to come to pass and be distributed over a *spatium* that is neither space nor in space, but a dimension corresponding to the intensity that set it up. As such it equals what Carl Gustav Jung called 'psychic energy'[12] that allows itself to be interpreted according to its manifest presence. As the raw material of possible structures this psychic energy—to use this Jungian term as the most appropriate rendering of the Tibetan *shes-pa*—is specified by sGam-po-pa variously as 'primary' (*dang-po*[13]), 'ordinary', 'plain', 'unsophisticated' (*tha-mal*[14]), 'uncontrived' (*ma-bcos-pa*[15]), and 'genuine' (*gnyug-ma*[16]).

There are two distinct 'structuration' aspects or transformations of this psychic energy (*shes-pa*). The one is termed *ye-shes* and it operates in such a manner that the primordiality of the whole—a primordiality that points back to a 'time before time' (*ye*)—still reverberates in it and in this way approximates the original energy. Hence, in an attempt to capture this quality I render (and have rendered) this term as 'pristine', 'primordial', 'originary' (from the French *originaire,* itself a translation of the German *ursprünglich*) awareness. That of which it is or becomes aware is a whole, a gestalt (*sku*) such that the gestalt is both the expression and the expressed of this primordial psychic energy.[17] The other aspect is termed *rnam-(par) shes-(pa)* and corresponds to our 'perception' or an 'awareness of observable qualities presented to the senses' of which there are in Buddhist psychology six, our five sensory perceptions (*sgo-lnga,* in Tibetan) to which is added a conceptual perception (*yid-kyi rnam-par shes-pa* or *yid* as its shorthand term), for the Buddhist knew all the time that the concept, say, 'tree' is not derived from the data proffered by the senses but brought to them. Because of its 'thought' character this 'sixth' sense is more or less synonymous with *sems,* designating a feed-forward and feed-backward 'mechanism' and customarily rendered as 'mind/mentation'.[18] Slightly wider in scope than *yid, sems* resembles a person's fore-structure of thought that has decided in advance how something is to be 'thought of' or interpreted. It does not deal with wholes, but with isolatable objects (*yul*), and it insists on the separation between the observed (*gzung,* 'that which is to be grasped') and the observer (*'dzin,* 'the one who grasps'):[19] The above can be diagrammed as follows:

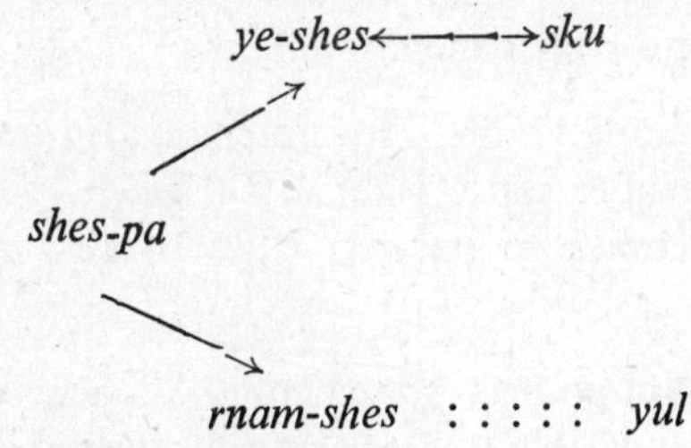

Here ←——→ means 'inseparability'; : : : : : 'separation'.

Figure 1

How does *rig-pa* enter into this schema? Let us begin with what seems to be its exact opposite *ma-rig-pa*. Certainly, *ma-rig-*

pa has never been understood as a negation of *rig-pa*, but rather as an as-yet-unevolved *rig-pa* that as 'zero intensity' is the matrix of intensities whose intensity degrees are commensurate with and correspond to the experiencer's understanding (*rtogs*) or lack of understanding (*ma-rtogs*) of them. We have seen that sGam-po-pa likes to speak of psychic energy as 'ordinary', 'plain' or 'unsophisticated' (*tha-mal-gi shes-pa*) and elaborates on it in the following words:[20]

> Since it is the root of the totality of the entities (that make up our reality, *chos thams-cad-kyi rtsa-ba*) one has to recognize this ordinary psychic energy for what it is (and does). This ordinary psychic energy is such that itself it cannot ruin this energy by any notions (it may entertain about it), it cannot be muddied by perceptions pertaining to worldliness, and without ever becoming caught in moods of elation and depression it holds its own. When one recognizes it for what it is, it is the pristine awareness in an ec-static intensity that is known by itself (*rang-gi rig-pa'i ye-shes*). If one does not understand what it is it becomes (one's) simultaneity-spontaneity zero intensity (*lhan-cig skyes-pa'i ma-rig-pa*). If one understands what it is, it is called 'ec-static intensity' (*rig-pa*), 'intensity-energy-stuff' (*ngo-bo*), 'simultaneity-spontaneity pristine awareness (*lhan-cig skyes-pa'i ye-shes*), 'plain psychic energy' (*tha-mal-gyi shes-pa*), 'the genuine' (*gnyug-ma*), '(the) conceptualization-free (*spros-bral*), and '(a) sheer lucency' (*'od-gsal*).

Elsewhere[21] sGam-po-pa pertinently remarks:

> By having encountered the zero intensity (in one's self, *ma-rig-pa*) as (one's) ec-static intensity (*rig-pa*) perception (*rnam-par shes-pa*) comes to pass as (the working of) sheer lucency (*'od-gsal*).

If in the light of sGam-po-pa's statement we conceive of perception as a 'making visible', the words of David Michael Levin[22] gain added significance:

> We are beings of light, not only because we belong to the light and are, as visionary beings, essentially dependent on it, but also because our 'substance' is light—luminous energy. Being ourselves made of light, we are capable of making visible.

Lastly sGam-po-pa's terse statement may be adduced:[23]

> The (fluctuation between the) zero intensity (*ma-rig-pa*) and the simultaneity-spontaneity pristine awareness (*lhan-cig skyes-pa'i ye-shes*) is like turning one's hand (palm or back up, as the case may be).

In this passage, as in many others in his writings as recorded by his disciples, we notice one of sGam-po-pa's key terms and ideas—*lhan-cig skyes-pa* 'simultaneity-spontaneity'.[24] In his famous dictum[25]

> *sems-nyid lhan-cig skyes-pa chos-kyi sku*
> *snang-ba lhan-cig skyes-pa chos-sku'i 'od*

> Simultaneous with (one's) spirituality comes the spontaneous gestalt (experience of Being's/life's) meaningfulness;
>
> Simultaneous with the lighting-up (of what becomes one's phenomenal world) comes the spontaneous light of (what is the) gestalt of (Being's/life's) meaningfulness

this simultaneity-spontaneity idea has found its highest expression. However, sGam-po-pa's profound insights are constantly marred by an often 'sloppy' diction that reflects the impact the Indian epistemology—and structure-oriented mentalism has had on Tibetan thinking that was primarily hermeneutical and continued to exert its influence. After all, sGam-po-pa came from a family that was steeped in the 'older' Tibetan way of thought. This tension between the 'older' and the 'newer' approaches to the life of the spirit may be gleaned from the distinction between *sems* and *sems-nyid* of which the followers of the Mahāmudrā teaching that owes so much to sGam-po-pa, were well aware, but which they in the wake of Indian-Buddhist mind/mentation-only (*cittamātra*, *sems-tsam*) reductionism and the traps set up by language—*sems* and *sems-nyid* not only sound and look deceptively similar, they may even in their operation fool an unwatchful person[26]—tended to blur by using them indiscriminately.[27]

In all fairness to sGam-po-pa it must be stated that as often as he was 'sloppy' he also was extremely meticulous. Elaborating on the difference between the purely intellectualistic (Pāramitāyāna) and the sensuously (aesthetic) experiential (Mantrayāna) approach, he declares:[28]

Once you have encountered and recognized the fact that (the triune dynamics of) bliss, lucency, and undividedness (*bde gsal mi-rtog-pa*) is your own experiencing (nature, *rang-gi sems-nyid*) in its ec-static intensity (*rig-pa*), you will by attending to it not overevaluate either bliss or lucency or undividedness, but be certain in the cognitive (quality of) this very intensity.

Elsewhere he states:[29]

By knowing that the phenomenal (*snang-ba*) is (the working of) mind (*sems*), one does not glide off into (the assumption that the phenomenal and the mind form a) duality; by knowing the experiencing dynamics, *sems-nyid*) to be an ec-static intensity (*rig-pa*), one does not glide off into insensate materiality; by knowing this ec-static intensity to be nothing (*stong-pa*) one does not glide off into (the belief that like a thing it has) attributes; by knowing this nothingness to be bliss (*bde-ba*) one does not glide off into misery; and since bliss is one's own disposition (or mind, *rang-sems*) one does not glide off into (the assumption that it is some) alien phenomenon. Since this mind cannot be objectified nor non-objectified because it cannot be grasped (as some thing) it is (referred to as) Mahāmudrā.

Nonetheless, it is Klong-chen rab-'byams-pa who succinctly states:[30]

By speaking of *sems-nyid* one speaks of the foundation (of psychic life, Being's) ec-static intensity (*rig-pa*), the level at which *sems* has ended, not of *sems*,

rDzogs-chen thinkers have always insisted on this distinction in all their writings (no 'sloppiness').

Although, as we have seen, sGam-po-pa was aware of the difference between *sems* and *sems-nyid*, his mentalistic fore-structure prevented him from fully realizing the ontological difference involved. While one-pointedness (*rtse-gcig*) and dissociation from conceptual-propositional proliferations and overshadowing (*spros-bral*) are aspects of mind/mentation (*sems*) on its way to no longer assertively re-presenting that which simply is as an object, the 'feeling' of the singular and unique piquancy, the single-piquancy (*ro-gcig*) of all that is and the 'feeling' that there is no longer a need for model-building (*sbgom-med*) are facets of pure experiencing (*sems-nyid*) in its ec-static cognitive intensity (*rig-pa*). By lumping these two ontologically different levels, different in the sense that neither can be reduced to nor derived from the other (which does not contradict their remaining co-ordinated), into a 'fourfold' which by definition was geared to mind/mentation (*sems*), together with the often indiscriminate use of the terms *sems* and *sems-nyid*, the followers of the Mahāmudrā teaching laid themselves open to the charge that their approach was essentially rationalistic-speculative, rather than experiential-existential. Though valid to a certain degree this charge reflects the limited awareness of staunch reductionists (of whom there obviously were as many in Tibet as they still are with us in the West and dominate our intellectual climate).

The above critical remarks are not intended to detract from sGam-po-pa's importance for Tibetan thought. What he had to offer was a challenge to further probings. This becomes evident from a comparison of how sGam-po-pa and Padma dkar-po—these most profound thinkers in the bKa'-bryud-pa tradition—assessed the four tuning-in phases in terms of what we now-a-days would call vector feeling-tones. For sGam-po-pa,[31] favoring a more static view, the 'single-pointedness' (*rtse-gcig*) tuning-in phase is 'in its brilliance a ceaseless opening-up' (*gsal-la ma-'gags-pa*); the 'conceptualization-free' (*spros-bral*) tuning-in phase is the fact that it is 'without birth' (*skye-med*), that is, it is not something that has come or does come into existence like a mental construct; the 'single-piquancy' (*ro-gcig*) tuning-in phase is the indivisibility of the phenomenal from the noumenal (the openness/nothingness of the whole, *snang-stong*); and the 'no-more-model-building' (*bsgom-med*) tuning-in phase is its oneness with the whole's intensity-'stuff' (*ngo-bo gcig*). By contrast, Padma dkar-po,[32] favoring a more dynamic view that is in accord with the feeling-tone of these tuning-in phases, offers the following 'equations' in the above sequence: the paradox of there being a feeling of bliss while yet there is nothing (*bde-stong*); the paradox of there being a brilliance while yet there is nothing (*gsal-stong*); the paradox of there being a lighting-up as the phenomenal while yet there is nothing (*snang-stong*); and the paradox of there being an ec-static intensity while yet there is nothing (*rig-stong*). Retaining the Tibetan terms for brevity's sake the above can be diagrammed as follows:

		sGam-po-pa	Padma dkar-po
rtse-gcig	:	*gsal-la ma-'gags-pa*	*bde-stong*
spros-bral	:	*skye-med*	*gsal-stong*
ro-gcig	:	*snang-stong*	*snang-stong*
bsgom-med	:	*ngo-bo gcig*	*rig-stong*

Figure 2

NOTES

1. *Collected Works*, vols. *Tha* 16b; *Da* 5ab; *Dza* 17a; *Wa* 4a; *'A* 6a; *La* 7a, *Ki* 17a, 21a.
2. *gsal-la ma-'gags-pa*, short for *gsal-la go ma-'gags-pa* as in *Dza*, fol. 17a.
3. This paraphrase of an extremely concise diction is based on *Tha*, fol. 31a.
4. The otherwise identical passage in *'A*, fol. 6a has *mnyam-gzhag* instead of *bsgoms-pa*. In *Ca*, fol. 6b sGam-po-pa says that in the composure state the totality of one's phenomenal reality is experienced to be like the open sky, and in *Ca*, fol. 16a he declares this state to be the imaginative unfoldment of a profound dynamic openness/nothingness.
5. *gnas-'gyu*. In the rendering of this term by 'rest and motion' the 'and' is not to be understood in an additive sense. Rather, what this term wants to convey is the paradox of there being an abiding (*gnas*) restfulness and yet a subtly flickering (*'gyu*) motion or a subtly flickering motion and yet an abiding restfulness. This fusion of two contrary notions into a single dynamic one is characteristic of process-oriented thinking which does not know of any sharp separation between contrary aspects of reality.
6. David Michael Levin, *The Opening of Vision*, p. 480.
7. *Faust*, part 2, lines 7271f.
8. Medard Boss, *Existential Foundations of Medicine and Psychology*, p. 112.
9. Arthur S. Reber, Dictionary of Psychology, p. 516.
10. C.G. Jung, *On the Nature of the Psyche*, p. 143.
11. Gilles Deleuze and Félix Guattari, *A Thousand Plateaus*, p. 153.
12. C.G. Jung, *Symbols of Transformation*, p. 135f. See also Marie-Louise von Franz, *On Dreams and Death*, p. 83; Walter A. Shelburne, *Mythos and Logos in the Thought of Carl Jung*, pp. 44-45.
13. *Nga*, fol. 7b; *Tha*, fol. 31a.
14. *Cha*, fol. 13a.
15. *Nya*, fol. 13a.
16. *Tha*, fol. 31a=*Ki*, fol. 18b.
17. The standard term for this inseparability, frequently occurring with Klong-chen rab-'byams-pa, is *sku dang ye-shes 'du-'bral med-pa* '(a) ges-

talt and (its) awareness can neither be added one to the other nor be detracted one from the other'. *Chos-dbyings*, pp. 53, 54, 66, 315, *Tshig-don*; p. 515; Theg-mchog I, p. 124, II, p. 38.

18. For further details see my *From Reductionism to Creativity*, pp. 15-40.
19. In this context C.G. Jung's remarks (*Symbols of Transformation*, p. 141) may be quoted:

    The "conception" (*Auffassung*) gives us a "handle" (*Griff*) by which to "grasp hold" of things (*fassen, begreifen*), and the resultant "concept" (*Begriff*) enables us to take possession of them.

    Buddhist thinkers would not speak of a 'resultant', they conceive of *gzung* and *'dzin* as constitutive elements in the principle of complementarity: none can be without the other.
20. *Nya*, fol. 13a.
21. *Cha*, fol. 8a=*Tha*, fol. 39b.
22. *loc. cit.*, p. 469.
23. *Ta*, fol. 4a.
24. See for instance *Ca*, fols. 26b, 27a; *Tha*, fol. 33a in connection with *'od-gsal*; *'A*, fol. 2b in connection with *tha-mal-gyi shes-pa*.
25. *Nga*, fol. 11a.
26. The *Kun-tu bzang-po Klong-drug-pa* (in *Ati*, vol. 2, pp. 111-214), p. 141 explicitly states:

    One's own mind (*rang-sems*) in which there is no muddiness (*rnyog-pa med*) and
    One's ec-static cognitive intensity (*rang-rig*) in which there is no conceptualization (*rtog-pa med*)
    May, indeed, be similar, but it would be a big mistake (to mix and confuse them, *'dra'o 'dra'o nor-ra-re*).

    See also the lengthy discussion in *Chos-dbyings*, p. 193f.
27. See for instance *Cha*, fol. 6b: *thams-cad sems-kyi rnam-'phrul* 'all that is (the totality of one's phenomenal reality) is the magic of the mind', and *Sha*, fol. 2b: *chos thams-cad sems-nyid yin-pas* 'since all the entities (of one's phenomenal reality) are mind-as-such'.
28. *Cha*, fol. 6b.
29. *Da*, fol. 25a.
30. *Bla-yang* II, p. 13.
31. *Tha*, fol. 16b and *'A*, fol. 6a.
32. *Collected Works*, vol. 21, p. 447.

CHAPTER TWO

PADMA DKAR-PO'S 'DEFINITIVE INVESTIGATION OF THE FOUR TUNING-IN PHASES'

PADMA DKAR-PO (1527-92) was one of the rare monks who was more interested in serious studies than in politics which at his time was already as partisan and crooked as it has been ever since all over the world with its inordinate greed for wealth and insatiable hunger for power. The high esteem in which he was held by the followers of the 'Brug-pa bka'-brgyud tradition, dating back to gTsang-pa rGya-ras ye-shes rdo-rje (1161-1211), is attested by the fact that he is referred to as *kun-mkhyen* 'omniscient', an epithet reserved for outstanding scholars in the tradition. As a matter of fact, he is for the bKa'-brgyud-pa tradition what Klong-chen rab-'byams-pa (1308-1363/64), also spoken of as *kun-mkhyen*, is for the rNying-ma-pa tradition with the difference that whatever Klong-chen rab-'byams-pa touches is turned into poetry. All those who came after these two luminaries were mere epigones and few among them ever rose above average.

Although the 'Four Tuning-in Phases' (*rnal-'byor bzhi*) are the leitmotif of the Mahāmudrā—'all beings are marked by Being', as Heidegger in modern times has pointed out—teaching in its experiential aspect and are mentioned in all works dealing with this doctrine, Padma dkar-po seems to have been the only one who has made an independent in-depth study of these tuning-in phases.

In an unusually small work that nonetheless bears the long title 'The definitive investigation of the four tuning-in phases: the quintessence of all discussions concerning the Mahāmudrā' (*rnal-'byor bzhi'i nges-pa rab-tu dbye-ba phyag-rgya chen-po'i bshad-pa thams-cad-kyi bla-ma*), he gives an outline that in its intricacy becomes itself a 'meditation' text.[1] In the traditional manner of presenting a chosen subject-matter the text begins with a double invocation, a short one and a longer one that intimates the author's point of departure, in this case, the complementarity of the female and male aspects of Being, symbolized by the gnosemes *E* and *VAṂ*,[2] formulated energies that in anthropomorphic shape are experienced as the *rdo-rje rnal-'byor-ma*, the Vajrayoginī, *alias* Vajravarāhī and Heruka/Hevajra respectively. This invocation is followed by a brief statement of content with a further emphasis on the interconnectedness of all the aspects that make up the tuning-in process. The sense of the following investigation of the tuning-in phases is in this that a result is reached which had not been known explicitly at the outset. While the starting point and the result are formally identical, thinking or the 'way' does in the end arrive at something different in content than what it had started with. This circularity resolves the earlier static linearity of thought and remains dynamic through and through.

In the traditional manner this essay concludes with an apology to the reader for any shortcomings of the author.

THE DEFINITIVE INVESTIGATION OF THE FOUR TUNING-IN PHASES: THE QUINTESSENCE OF ALL DISCUSSIONS CONCERNING THE MAHĀMUDRĀ

1. Homage to the precious bKa'-brgyud.

2. I bow to the feet of the august teacher supreme
   Who forever joyfully plays
   In the supreme mystery of Being's certainty
   As the (gnosemic) *VAṂ* in the center of Being's spaciousness as the (gnosemic) *E*.

3. The starting point, the taking up its challenge, the delight deriving from it,
   The exposure of the indicators (of the progress on the path such as) the warmth (one feels),[3] and the goal realization
   (With each of these five points involving four tuning-in phases) have here been presented as a definitive summary of the path.

4. The assessment of the starting point as well as
   The taking up of its challenge and
   The delight that derives from doing so as well as
   The goal realization by having travelled the path as it behoves, are all interconnected.

I

5. Because it cannot be ruined (*mi-bslad*); because it is not localized (*mi-gnas*);
Because it is not contradictory (*mi-'gal*); and because it is not objectifiable (*mi-dmigs*)—
These four (facets) are declared to be the four (tuning-in phases termed) single-pointedness (*rtse-gcig*),
Dissociation from conceptualization (*spros-bral*), single-piquancy (*ro-gcig*), and no-more-model-building (*sgom-med*), respectively.

6. It cannot be ruined because (in it) there is not the slightest trace of
What would have to be removed or installed (referred to as)
Polluting factors and, different from them,
Cleansing factors.

7. Not localized is said so
Because the dual grouping of
The interconnected (entities of one's reality) in terms of their existence or non-existence and so on, is not itself something so existing
And also does not reside in an in-between (or middle).

8. Not contradictory (is said so)
Because all the entities (of one's reality) in their interconnectedness
Are not different from their (starting point) and the latter (pervasively) enters
The observable qualities of these entities in their interconnectedness.

9. Not objectifiable (is said so)
Because not being an object of (one's) representational thinking it cannot be illustrated by analogies and
Even the Omniscient One, if he were to speak about it,
Would run out of words.

II

10. Taking up the challenge of the starting point
As the path, also, is fourfold because it places us into (Being's) dynamics:

Conceptually undivided (*mi-rtog*); ontically without origination (*skye-med*);
Non-dual (*gnyis-su med*); and not lying within the scope of representational thought (*bsam-mi-khyab*).

11. As long as there is the belief in substantive particular existents)
So long one is fettered in the prison of one's fictions.
Therefore, one has to completely dismiss this belief in substantive particular existents,
But also must not entertain the divisive fiction of non-substantive particular existents.

12. Since one does not find (a place) from which (the entities of one's reality) have originated, or in which they reside,
Or into which they fade away,
Their identity with that which has no roots (allowing them to grow) is (what is meant by) ontically without origination.

13. Because as long as there is a proliferation into conceptual-propositional specifications
This (proliferation) is precisely what mentation is about;
Become composed in that (state) in which (such specifications as)
'Thingness' and 'nothingness' do not obtain as a duality.

14. Since, indeed, there is no model-building activity (as such)
There also is no model (as such) to be built;
Know that what is beyond the model-building activity and the model so to be built
Does not lie within the scope of representational thought.

III

15. This set of four tuning-in phases—
Single-pointedness, dissociation from conceptualization,
Single-piquancy, and no-more-model-building—
Is said to be the opening up (of the potential in the starting point) by the razor of the delight (in taking up the challenge of the starting point).[4]

16. When the interface between quiescence and agitation (*gnas 'qyu'i bar-lag*) comes tumbling down

By recognizing what agitation means in quiescence being uppermost
And by holding on to quiescence in agitation being uppermost,
The single-pointedness tuning-in phase has been understood as what it is in itself.[5]

17. When the conceptual proliferations initiated
By (such predications as) origination, cessation, eternalism, nihility,
Coming and going, one and many, have come to rest,
The felt understanding of being free from (a mere judgmental) dissociation from conceptualization is the (real) dissociation from conceptualization.[6]

18. Of all the substantival particular existents the most prominent one is the 'stuff' of (one's) mind in itself.
By understanding it properly
Everything turns out to be this ('stuff') and one
Does not find anything else but this ('stuff'). This is (what is meant by) single-piquancy.[7]

19. When totality of one's entitative reality has become a holistic (pattern) in Being's field-(like) expanse such that
Simultaneously that which has to be eliminated and that which aids its elimination have become exhausted
Like the fire and its fuel,
This is the no-more-model-building tuning-in phase.[8]

IV

20. Since the differences in the individuals' capacities
Is clearly threefold—
Having an instantaneous grasp (of the subject-matter), having an (occasional) dawning of it, and advancing toward it step by step—
The manner of understanding is said to be threefold.

21. The (four tuning-in phases) are (furthermore) said to be divisible into twelve varieties,
Each being of a low, medium, or high intensity
According to (their qualifications as) stability as yet not gained,
Gained, and thoroughly gained.

22. Inasmuch as these four tuning-in phases, just discussed,
Follow (and include the last) intensity (in the preceding one),[9]
Each of these four phases
Is present as a four times four, that is, sixteenfold intensification process.

23. These (tuning-in phases) are (furthermore) subdivided according to whether Being's 'stuff' is seen (or not) and whether one's divisive and disruptive thought processes turn into (creative) model-building[10] (or not);
Whether the creative dynamics in them is fully present (or not) and whether their potentialities have come into being (or not);
Whether the enticement (to return) to the conventionally accepted ('lower order') reality still prevails (or not) and
Whether the seed for (the realization of) the experience of Being in its manifest gestalt has been planted (or not)

24. Those who have seen the 'higher order' reality have stated that
The single-pointedness tuning-in phase is the linkage stage[11] on the Path; that the dissociation from conceptualization tuning-in phase
Is the stage of vision[12] on the Path; that the single-piquancy tuning-in phase is the model-building stage[13] on the Path; and
The no-more-model-building tuning-in phase is the stage of no-more-learning[14] on the Path.

25. In the same manner as there are twelve intensity degrees to the break-through facets
So also the single-pointedness (tuning-in phase has twelve aspects).
In the four break-through facets that are of an out-of-the-ordinary quality
The four tuning-in phases are included.

V

26. The Fully Awakened One has elaborated on
A fourfold division (pertaining to the circumstances of)

Whether (the higher levels in one's spiritual development) have been reached or not and,
Even if they have been reached, whether they are demarcated (from each other) by low, medium, or high intensities.

27. The tuning-in process is said to exhibit four characteristic qualities such that
Never parting from the experience of Being as (presenting a) meaning-rich gestalt
Is the single-pointedness tuning-in phase; this,
When it is free from all obscurations,

28. Is the dissociation from conceptualization tuning-in phase; from this comes
The active concern for others which is the single-piquancy tuning-in phase; and
Since this has neither a beginning nor an end
It is the no-more-model-building tuning-in phase which is (the potential in the starting point) manifested as the goal.

29. Please bear with me if there is any flaw in
What I have said by way of an outline only,
Though I have received this profound message
By the kindness of the teacher supreme.

Notes

1. This text is contained in vol. 21, pp. 423-429 of his *Collected Works,* reproduced photographically from prints from the 1920-1928 gNam 'Brug Se-ba Byang-chub-gling blocks. Darjeeling 1973. Padma dkar-po wrote two commentaries on this short treatise: the *Phyag-rgya chen-po rnal-'byor bzhi'i bshad-pa nges-don lta-ba'i mig* (*loc. cit.*, pp. 431-463) of a general nature and the *rRnal-'byor bzhi'i bshad-pa don-dam mdzub-tshugs-su bstan-pa* (*ibid.*, pp. 465-497) of a highly scholastic nature. His *Phyag-chen-gyi zin-bris* (ibid., pp. 372-391) deals with the four tuning-in phases in the general context of the Mahāmudrā (*phyag-rgya chen-po*) teaching. In the following these three works will be quoted as *A*, *B* and *C*, followed by the page number, respectively.
2. Lengthy hermeneutical interpretations of this 'code'-term are given in the *dPal Kye'i rdo-rje zhes-bya-ba'i rgyud-kyi rgyal-po'i 'grel-pa legs-bshad nyi-ma'i 'od-zer*, pp. 51-60, by Dvags-po Pan-chen bKra-shis rnam-rgyal (1512/13-1587), the *rGyud-kyi rgyal-po dpal brtag-pa gnyis-pa'i spyi-don legs-par bshad-pa gsang-ba bla-na-med-pa rdo-rje drwa-ba'i rgyan*, pp. 91-92, by 'Jam-mgon Kong-sprul Blo-gros mtha'-yas (1813-1899), and the *Doha skor gsum-gyi ti-ka ('bring-po) sems-kyi rnam-thar*

ston-pa'i me-long by Karma Phrin-las-pa (1456-1539). On this work see my *The Royal Song of Saraha*, pp. 165-167.

3. For a detailed discussion of the 'indicators' marking the increase in intensity in the probability of a breakthrough phase on the Buddhist Path see my *From Reductionism to Creativity*, pp. 161-165.
4. According to *C*, p. 375, the experience of these four tuning-in phases marks a progression over two distinct levels in a person's psychosomatic organization. The first two phases belong to the 'ordinary' (*thun-mong*) level which is the one most people stay on all their life. Inasmuch as mentation (*sems*) is an integral aspect of a person's life, on this particular level, it has a decidedly 'epistemological' character comprising two hierarchical organized levels that remain co-ordinated and reflect the 'ordinary' person's ego-logical control and dominance psychology. The one I shall call, following Erich Jantsch, *The Self-Organizing Universe*, pp. 162, 240), 'organismic' as it is primarily behavioral—(this term is used without implying a specific behaviorist theory). The other is the person's 'rational' mentation "which corresponds to the lowest level of the everyday I" (Jantsch, *loc. cit.*, p. 296). These levels are commonly known as 'inner calm' (*zhi-gnas*) and 'wider perspective' (*lhag-mthong*). However valuable these two features may be in the person's psychic growth they do not, as their specification as 'ordinary' indicates, pass beyond the person's ego-centric gaze.

   The following two tuning-in phases belong to the 'out-of-the-ordinary' (*thun-mong-ma-yin-pa*) level which ordinary persons rarely reach. This level has a decidedly 'ontological' character. Its two tuning-in phases may be said to be 'cosmic' in scale and ultimately 'holistic'.
5. See also *A*, p. 440; *B*, pp. 466-481; *C*, pp. 375, 378-385. The single-pointedness tuning-in phase is, strictly speaking, the outcome of the search for 'inner calm'. This involves three major steps:

   1. The first step is to suppress any thought that might arise (*thol-skyes rbad-gcod*) and not to allow oneself to be caught in the maelstrom the emergence of thought initiates, but rather to watch dispassionately this rushing along of one's mind that is like 'water tumbling over a cliff' (*ri-gzar-kyi chu 'bab*). However, any such suppressive action is counter-productive; one can only hope that the practitioner learns from this exercise in futility and proceeds to the

   2. second step which is not to interfere with the 'life-stream' (*gang-shar bzo-med*) so that it is allowed to flow quietly (*chu-klung dal-gyis 'bab*). This then leads to

   3. the third step or the consolidation (*gzhag-thabs*) of what is deeply felt as an inner calm (*zhi-gnas*), so evocatively illustrated by the image of a lake in which no waves stir (*rgya-mtsho rlabs dang bral-ba*). Its consolidation is summed up by four images that tell us more than words could ever convey:

   (a) a Brahmin twining his sacrificial cord (not too loose and not too tight);

   (b) cutting the rope that holds a bundle of hay together (tension release);

(c) a child visiting a shrine (wonder and awe); and
(d) pricking an elephant with a thorn (unconcern).

The realization of this inner calm is no end in itself; rather it the point that marks and facilitates the transition from the instinctive-organismic level of psychic life to the reflexive level that scrutinizes the single-pointedness, the paradox of the simultaneity of rest (quiescence) and motion (agitation), intuitively-*inner*spectively (*kha-nang-du bltas-pa'i rang-rig*), rather than merely discursive. This, as *C*, p. 384 points out, imperceptively leads to an understanding of what is meant by 'wider perspective' (*lhag-mthong*) which marks the irruption of Being's openness/nothingness into the individual's closedness and expresses itself in the experiencer's heightened (*lhag*) sense of feeling with and for others (compassion) without this feeling turning into some sentimentality that always exhibits a lack of understanding or *inner*standing.

6. *B*, pp. 466 and 481-489 speaks of this tuning-in phase as the 'tumbling down of the interface between errancy and freedom' (*'khrul-grol-gyi bar-lag 'gyel-ba*). While the word 'errancy' has retained its verbal character of a going astray (into the categories of representational thinking), the word 'freedom' is unable to convey what the Buddhist understood by *grol*. Both *'khrul* and *grol* are vector feeling-tones of a process: we 'feel' how we become involved with the 'arrow of time', how we are enslaved by the tyranny of the concrete, and how we are caught in the dilemma of identity and difference, but we also 'feel' how this stranglehold dissolves and makes us feel 'free'. Thus, the demolition of 'time' (present, future, *dus-gsum*), of the antithesis between 'the concrete and the non-concrete' (*dngos-po—dngos-med*), and of the dilemma of identity and difference (*gcig tha-dad*) is the concern of this tuning-in-phase.
7. *B*, pp. 466 and 489-496 speaks of this tuning-in phase as the 'tumbling down of the interface between the coming-to-presence of the phenomenal world and the mind (*snang-sems-kyi bar-lag 'gyel-ba*), and *C*, p. 387 states that this phase pertains to the 'out-of-the-ordinary' (*thun-mong-ma-yin-pa*) level. On this ontological level 'mind/mentation' (*sems*) is both individual/local ('one's mind') and cosmic/nonlocal, that is, it is an utter openness/nothingness (*stong-pa/stong-pa-nyid*) that in its dynamics is the matrix of all that comes-to-presence (*snang-ba*). From a mechanistic point of view the phenomenal world is a projection of mind and as such of the same nature as the projecting agency; from a dynamic point of view the phenomenal world is self-manifestation of (Being's) openness/nothingness and in so being a structured nothingness it can only have the flavour of the latter's openness. *C*, pp. 387-389 illustrates this tuning-in phase that dissolves the rigidity of the preceding phases into one of fluidity by the images of sleeping and dreaming (*gnyid dang rmi-lam*, the phenomenal is recognized to be the working of mentation just as a dream is the activity of one's sleep), of water and ice (*chu dang khyag-rom*, the phenomenal entering into unity with nothingness), and of water and waves (*chu dang rlabs*, the totality of one's reality having one and the same piquancy).
8. *B*, pp. 466 and 496-498 speaks of this tuning-in phase as the 'tumbling

down of the interface between the composure and the post-composure states (*mnyam-rjes-kyi bar-lag 'gyel-ba*), and *C*, p. 389 declares:

> Once one has come to the conclusion that the totality of one's (phenomenal reality) is the gestalt (through which Being's) meaningfulness (is experienced by one's self) as simultaneous with (Being's) genuineness (*gnyug-ma lhan-cig-skyes-pa chos-kyi sku*) the experience of the no-more-model-building tuning-in phase is such that, in view of the fact that the emotions as pollutants to be discarded are no more and consequently there is also no more an agent to discard them, the way has come to an end. From here one cannot go anywhere else; any involvement has come to an end and there is no place higher than this. This is the nonlocalized (and nonlocalizable) nirvāṇa, Mahāmudrā, the attainment of the supreme realization.

While these words describe the 'composure' state (*mnyam-gzhag*), the 'post-composure' state (*rjes-thob*) involves three operations:

1. the 'recognition' of Mahāmudrā as being one's existential 'program';
2. the scrutiny of possible hindrances and pitfalls; and
3. the co-ordination of the (at first intellectual) understanding (*go-ba*) of what is involved, the felt awareness (*nyams*) of what is involved, and the real understanding (*rtogs*).

9. That is to say, the highest intensity in the first tuning-in phase is the lowest intensity in the second phase, and so on.

10. I have added 'creative' in order to emphasize that *sgom* never aims at fixation but as an imaginative activity is an unfolding of possibilities whose vision prompts us to give them forms. This is what is meant by model-building.

11. For further details see my *From Reductionism to Creativity*, p. 151.

12. *ibid.*

13. *ibid.*

14. *ibid.*

CHAPTER THREE

THE rDZOGS-CHEN APPROACH: SYMMETRY TRANSFORMATIONS: THE REALMS OF POTENTIA AND ACTUALITY

RDZOGS-CHEN TEXTS, especially those of the sNying-thig persuasion, address the question which concerns the human individual most—the question of 'Being'. This is not an abstract speculation but the close attention to how is it that we are here. rDzogs-chen thinking starts from and ends with the immediacy of existence and experience, where not only linear and irreversible time becomes suspended but where also images fuse with one another without the clear demarcations that our language geared to the project of survival tries to legislate into ultimate norms. The Tibetan term for our word 'Being' is *gzhi* which literally means both 'ground' and 'reason'. What is the ground of our being and what is the reason for our being here? rDzogs-chen thinkers emphatically state that this 'ground' is not grounded anywhere: it is 'without a ground and has no root to grow from'. It is, in modern diction, pure dynamics, and as such it has neither a beginning nor an end—those fateful traps into which reason has over and again led mankind astray.

rDzogs-chen thinkers refer to the triune dynamics of Being by three substantival terms *ngo-bo*←——→*rang-bzhin*←——→*thugs-rje* to which a twofold set of three adjectival terms *ka-dag*←——→*lhun-grub*←——→*kun-khyab* and *stong*←——→*gsal*←——→*rig-pa* corresponds, the former triad indicating Being's ontological character, the latter the dynamics involved, as shown in Figure 3.

ngo-bo←——→	*rang-bzhin*←——→	*thugs-rje*
ka-dag	*lhun-grub*	*kun-khyab*
stong-(pa)	*gsal-(ba)*	*rig-pa*

FIGURE 3

Elsewhere[1] I have already pointed out the difficulty in rendering rDzogs-chen terms adequately; here it suffices to note that the rendering of the term *ngo-bo* by 'facticity' is intended to avoid any concretistic reductionism while at the same time intimating a certain similarity with the use of this term by Martin Heidegger.[2] Facticity is furthermore such that it allows intensities to 'occupy' it without being a support upon which this occupying can come to pass. It is, so to say, the 'stuff' the universe including ourselves is made of, but it is not matter, at least not as commonly or popularly understood, it is 'intense matter, the matrix of intensity, intensity=0'.[3] It also goes without saying that it is not an absolute, for if it were, no relation to or connection with us would be possible. Facticity is specified as both 'diaphanous' (*ka-dag*), the 'static' counterpart to the 'dynamic' aspect 'nothing' (*stong-pa*) that, far from being empty or void, is a void*ing*. Though we may speak of it by using a or a combination of nouns such as 'nothingness/openness', because our language presupposes a noun-verb structure, we must bear in mind that there is nothing negative about it. There are no negative intensities. Only through its association with the Sanskrit word *śūnya*, which is an adjective, the Tibetan word *stong-pa*, which is a verb, has the wide-spread misconception of this word in Western presentations occurred.[4] As a dynamic intensity it, already in its virtual, purely potential state, undergoes a symmetry transformation. Dissolving (old) intensities while at the same time weaving (new) intensities, even in its *potentia* it becomes it 'ownmost' intensity or actuality (*rang-bzhin*)—nothingness/openness becomes its own luminosity/radiance (*gsal-ba*) and because of its dynamic not only breaks the original symmetry but also reaches into our being and makes us luminous beings.

The second term in the description of Being's triune dynamics, *rang-bzhin*, is made up of two terms, *rang* meaning 'own' and 'itself', though not in the sense of an egological self, and *bzhin* having the double connotation of 'continuance' and 'face' so that this highly technical term can be paraphrased by saying that Being continues showing *its* face (not some counterfeit mask or somebody else's face). This 'showing its face' is Being's nothingness/openness 'lighting-up' (*gzhi snang*). It is a holomovement such that Being's diaphaneity and (dynamic) nothingness become Being's spontaneity (*lhun-grub*) and radiance (*gsal-ba*) in its actuality or ownmost intensity (*rang-bzhin*). This lighting-up is a phase halfway between Heisenberg's[5] world of potentia and world of actuality. It is a 'becoming-an-actuality' and in this becoming presents a variety of options.

To 'whom' does Being presents itself as options? To itself, to its own intelligence (which must not be confused with one's narrow egocentricity), to its own capability of resonating with itself (*thugs-rje*). Since without intelligence and resonance nothing pertinent could be said about Being in its facticity or actuality, intelligence as the experiencer's ever-active (and for his ego ever-unsettling) spirituality (*thugs*) can be said to be lording (*rje*) it over the whole. It is for this reason that I have rendered this multivalent third term in the description of Being's triune dynamics by 'resonance'. As K.C. Cole aptly remarks:[6]

> Resonance gives things character; the difference between the music of a violin and a flute, the difference between the voices of a man and a woman, the difference between the clatter of a tennis racket and the plop of the ball, are subtly shaped by sympathetic vibrations.

Resonance *thugs-rje* is recording to rDzogs-chen thinkers 'all-encompassing' (*kun-khyab*) and 'excitatory' (*rig-pa*) which, in the context of the experiencer becomes his/her ec-static intensity. In this its very intensity it is an ongoing going 'out-of' (*ec-*) all limits set by the prevalent 'unexcited' state of one's everydayness, as intimated by Heidegger's statement that 'the ecstatic essence of man consists in ek-sistence'[7], not just some altered state of consciousness.

rDzogs-chen text never tire of emphasizing the inseparability of these three 'aspect' of Being's dynamics. In aesthetically appealing images Klong-chen rab-'byams-pa speaks of this inseparability with reference to its being experienced by us through 'primordial awareness modes' (*ye-shes*), of which more will be said in another chapter, as follows[8]:

> Being's facticity (*ngo-bo*) is the inseparability of nothingness and radiance (*stong-gsal dbyer-med*); its actuality (*rang-bzhin*) is the inseparability of radiance and nothingness (*gsal-stong dbyer-med*); and its resonance (*thugs-rje*) is the inseparability of ec-static intensity and nothingness (*rig-stong*

dbyer-med). How can (Being's) presence (in us) be illustrated by similes? Being's facticity, a diaphanous (*ka-dag*) primordial awareness, is present like the clear sky; Being's actuality, a spontaneous (*lhun-grub*) primordial awareness, is present like a shimmering lake; and Being's resonance, an all-encompassing (*kun-khyab*) primordial awareness, is present like a flawless jewel.

These images to illustrate the 'fine-structure' of Being's dynamics are more than mere images or metaphorical expressions, they are symbols disclosing dimensions of existence and at the same time engaging the experiencer in his or her quest for the meaning of life. All of these images (or by whichever name we want to refer to them) have a luminous quality that refers back to Being's lucency and lighting-up as it becomes our own innermost being and ownmost intensity that in its 'ownmostness' loses nothing of its connectedness with the 'wider ownmostness' of Being. The experiential character of this triune dynamics is well described by Klong-chen rab-'byams-pa:[9]

> These three (facticity, actuality, resonance) exist as an inner glow, not as an outwardly visible effulgence, like the luster in a crystal or a flame in a container. The inseparability of (their) lucency and nothingness (*gsal-stong dbyer-med*) is adorned by the vitalizing energy of (Being's) ec-static intensity (*rig-pa'i snying-po*) (which gives the whole the opalescence of a) peacock's egg. Within Being's facticity that in its gestalt 'embodying' Being's meaningfulness (*chos-sku*) becomes the precious envelope of its spontaneity (felt as a) presence (in us), there abides Being's actuality that in its sheer lucency by virtue of being an inner glow presents a panorama of gestalts and their (respective) primordial awareness modes; and in this actuality (of Being) there resides Being's resonance as the vitalizing energy of its ec-static intensity. By the simile of a blazing turquoise one can understand (the significance of the above).

Although much more will be said about the gestaltism of Being as a process of 'embodying' the meaningfulness of Being in its multiple nuances, here it suffices to point out that *chos-sku* is the expression of an ontological experience as explicated by David Michael Levin:[10]

> The experience of our natural luminosity, our radiance as bodies of light, is an *ontological* experience, an ek-static experience of human being that takes in our ontological dimensionality, our primordial inherence in a field of light.

Long before Heidegger pointed to one's attunement (*Gestimmtheit*) to one's *ontological understanding of being*, Klong-chen rab-'byams-pa had poetically expressed this sentiment as follows[11]:

> Since into the precious mansion [that is our live body] adorned by sun and moon [our actional and appreciative comportments]
> Being's sheer lucency, the superb vitalizing energy (of) its indestructibility has entered,
> Its very triune dynamics of facticity, actuality, and resonance (*ngo-bo rang-bzhin thugs-rje gsum-nyid de*)
> Is spontaneously (and holistically there in us) in its vitalizing energy of nothingness, luminosity, and ec-static intensity (*stong gsal rig-pa'i snying-por lhun-gyis grub*).

This experience is 'prompted', not caused, by Being's pervasive 'intelligence' that in its ec-static intensity is resonating in primordial awareness modes (*ye-shes*). The shapes these vibrations assume are gestalts (*sku*) which we describe in terms of the felt sense of our corporeal existence.

It is important to bear in mind that Being's triune dynamics, becoming the 'fine-structure of our being', is already operative before there can be said to be a beginning. In this respect it is similar to Heisenberg's world of potentia which in some ways is much more 'real' because in it a multitude of contradictory qualities and tendency can coexist, which they cannot do in the 'real' world of actuality. The transition from the world of potentia to the world of actuality is made possible through the unsettling presence of the whole's ec-static intensity that prevents it from ever becoming static and constantly seems to push it over the instability threshold into the world of actuality. Still, in rDzogs-chen thought, this world of actuality is not yet lowered into the concrete determinism of our everyday 'real' world. There are options and the transition phase in this process comes as a challenge. We can recognize this our ownmost being and link ourselves back to the source (*grol-ba*)—this linking backward, in the language of symmetry, becoming an approximation symmetry transformation. Or we can fail recognizing our ownmost being and go farther and farther astray (*'khrul-pa*). There is no culpability involved, rather it is a self-inflicted alineation. We alienate ourselves from ourselves and by according superiority to an ego-logical and egocentric point of view we cannot but continue breaking the unity and symmetry of Being. In the language of symmetry, our egocentric way of existing is a displacement symmetry transformation.

Being (*gzhi*)
(Similar to Heisenberg's world of potential):

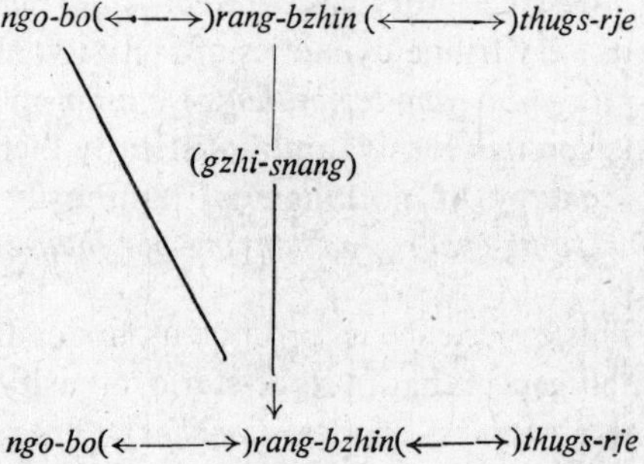

Being's lighting-up or holomovement (Similar to Heisenberg's world of potentia in its strangeness of somehow being in between possibility and reality):

Being's ethereal reality:

sku←→*'od/dbyings*←→*ye-shes/rig-pa*

Being's errancy mode (*'khrul-pa*) (Similar to von Neumann's consciousness-created reality):

lus←→*yul*(←→ *sems*

Here←→means 'connectedness'; ←'collapse of connectedness'.

FIGURE 4

With Being's lighting-up (*gzhi-snang*), its holomovement—that magic moment when what has been virtual becomes actual, the experiencer is 'confronted' with two alternatives: either he can continue in the rich world of heightened (nirvāṇic) sensibilities or slide into the drab (samsaric) world of misplaced concreteness and mistaken identities:[12]

> By seeing Being's gestalt (*sku*) (within a) field-like expanse (*dbyings*) (through its) ec-static intensity (*rig-pa*) as presencing themselves as something other (than what they are and becoming involved in mistaken identifications) one goes from the gestalt into the (concreteness of one's) physical body (*lus*); from the experience of (Being's) field-like expanse into (the domain of granular an juxtaposed) objects (*yul*); and from ec-static intensity into mind/mentation (*sems*).

All of the above can be diagrammed as shown in page 30.

Notes

1. *From Reductionism to Creativity*, pp. 184ff.
2. *Basic Problems of Phenomenology*, p. 356.
3. Gilles Deleuze and Félix Guattari, *A Thousand Plateaus*, p. 153.
4. *From Reductionism to Creativity*, p. 190.
5. There are startling similarities between rDzogs-chen thought and modern science. See, for instance, Guenther, (1981, 1989). It is not without interest that more and more scientists recognize that the spiritual or consciousness is an integral aspect of the universe. Unfortunately the terms 'spiritual' and 'consciousness' have too many unwarranted connotation as to be very useful for further research: 'spiritual' opens the door to all kinds of idiosyncrasies and 'consciousness' narrows the vast field of reality to mere egocentricity. For understanding rDzogs-chen thought the ideas of John von Neumann and Werner Heisenberg are invaluable. Concerning von Neumann's consciousness-created reality the quantum physist Eugene Wigner (also a Nobel prizewinner) made the comment: 'It is not possible to formulate the laws of quantum mechanics in a fully consistent way without reference to consciousness...' (quoted from Nick Herbert, *Quantum Reality*, pp. 25f.) and the implications of Heisenberg's duplex world were summed up by Sir James Jeans in the words: 'The universe begins to look more like a great thought than a great machine' (quoted from Willis Harman and Howard Rheingold, *Higher Creativity*, p. 130). Sir James Jeans' 'great thought' seems to intimate what rDzogs-chen thinkers understand by *dgongs-pa* which I render as 'superthought'

or 'superintelligence' in order to emphasize that this term implies *more* than mere thought or intelligence.

6. *Sympathetic Vibrations*, p. 268.
7. *Letter on Humanism*, p. 205.
8. *Tshig-don*, p. 178.
9. *mKka'-yang* II, p. 71.
10. *Opening of Vision*, p. 452.
11. *Zab-yang* I, p. 289.
12. *Bi-ma* II, p. 339.

Chapter Four

THE GESTALT EXPERIENCE OF BEING AND THE CLOSED SYSTEM POTENTIAL

The importance of recognizing the alternatives available to the experiencer either to continue the cycle of mistaken identifications and emotional blunderings or re-discover the fullness of Being is reflected in the rDzogs-chen distinction between *kun-gzhi* and *chos-sku.* The common rendering of the term *kun-gzhi* by 'all-ground' or 'universal ground', though literally correct, it fails to convey the richness of ideas encoded in this term and to take into account its thoroughly dynamic character. A few quotations may underscore this point. Klong-chen rab-'byams-pa, summing up the various hermeneutical assessments in the rNying-ma Tantras, declares:[1]

> It is the first and foremost site (*rten*) of all those (entities spoken of in terms of) mind/mentation and mental events/operators, specificities set up by a drop in the whole's (Being's) ec-static cognitive intensity (*ma-rig-pa*); in between (their onset and fading-out) it is their 'playground' (*gnas*), and lastly it is their home (*khyim*, to which they return). Having turned into a vessel of inveterate tendencies (programs, *bag-chags*) it is like a pool,

and:[2]

> Since, in substance, it is set up by mind/mentation and mental events/operators it has become the site of all activities and programs related to samsara and nirvāṇa; it is the (as yet) undifferentiated level of what is (spoken of as) the drop in the whole's ec-static cognitive intensity;

and:[3]

> Since, in precise terms, it is the basis for multiple programs it is called the basis (or ground, *gzhi*) for all and everything (that can be thought of and pragmatically dealt with, *kun*).

The important point to note is that the *kun-gzhi* presents a low-level (cognitive) intensity which, tending to run its full course, 'results' in what is an individual's structural model of the mind as well as the programs that come with this model and which the experiencer is going to execute. In other words, it is a put-up phenomenon—put up by the dynamics of Being that in so closing in onto itself constitutes itself as a closed system with respect to its internal (logical) organization serving as the experiencer's ontical foundation. In its operation the *kun-gzhi* resembles what Manfred Eigen[4] has called a hypercycle which is a closed circle of transformatory processes in which one or more participants act as autocatalysts. Hence, for brevity's sake we may speak of the *kun-gzhi* as closed system potential. But in view of the fact that the *kun-gzhi* in a certain sense is the experiencer himself it is possible to speak of it in philosophical terms as the experiencer's 'ontic ground'. Its implicit complexity is summarized by Klong-chen rab-'byams-pa as follows:[5]

> In substance, it is a 'put-up' (*'dus-byas*) phenomenon that has become the vessel for what constitutes (the system's or individual's) striving for wholesomeness as well as the multitudinous entities that make up samsara together with the programs for it;
>
> In precise terms, 'all' (each and everything, *kun* means plenty; 'ground' (*gzhi*) means the duration of the site where the various patterns gather;

and:[6]

> In substance, the *kun-gzhi* is that which has become the vessel for programs; in precise terms, it is what makes up samsara or, rather, is the rationale behind it.

Four significant distinctions in what has been given the codename *kun-gzhi* and to which I shall refer as closed system potential have been made. Since these have been detailed in their historical-philosophical perspective elsewhere (Guenther, 1989) it here suffices to point out their salient features:

1. *ye-don-gyi kun-gzhi*—'the closed system potential that is the experiencer's primordiality-(constituted) existentiality', de-

notes the orientational zero-point from which the experiencer becomes aware of particular projects-at-hand. On this level that marks a drop in the whole's ec-static cognitive intensity, they are the programs of a becoming enworlded, the *kun-gzhi* proper, and the program of a 'dissipative structuration', *sangs-rgyas*,[7] the samsaric and the nirvāṇic respectively.

2. *sbyor-ba* (*ye-*)*don-gyi kun-gzhi*, 'the closed system potential of what is one's primordiality-(constituted) existentiality as a linking' emphasizes the functional aspect of the former in the sense that the experiencer becomes thoroughly involved in the various programs.

3. *bag-chags lus-kyi kun-gzhi* 'the closed system potential that (expresses itself) in an animate organism (such that its) body is (the expression of a process of embodying levels of mental life that act as) programs for it'. While the previous closed system potential may be said to determine or generate the space for the unfolding of the programs of mental-spiritual life, with this closed system potential the level of the 'body-proper', to use Merleau-Ponty's diction, has been reached. It is, as the Buddhist thinkers note, a program that continuously renews itself and regulates this process in such a manner that the integrity of its structure remains intact.

4. *bag-chags sna-tshogs-pa'i kun-gzhi* 'the closed system potential that operates as the sundry programs for conscious life'. While the 'body program' may be said to be the primal condition for the existence of the physico-cultural environment in which the embodied experiencer is embedded, this closed system potential sums up the way of how the experiencer deals with his environment by way of his (usually) inconsiderate actions (*las*) and affective vagaries (*nyon-mongs*) that are latently present as sedimented experiences that very much influence subsequent experiences in what becomes a vicious circle in the individual's cybernetic existence.

Inasmuch as the *kun-gzhi* is one of two possible alternatives through which Being in undergoing a symmetry transformation expresses and presents itself to its inherent 'resonance-intelligence' (*thugs-rje*), it retains the original triune dynamics of Being, each facet reflecting the principle of complementarity, metaphorically described in terms of 'resting' and 'surging'. This 'basic' complementarity entails a 'derivative' complementarity that is of utmost importance for the domain of the living as it prevents stagnation. This 'derivative' complementarity is described in terms of a becoming ever more enworlded and of an *Entweltlichung*, the system's self-transcendence. Thus Klong-chen rab-'byams-pa states:[8]

Being's intensity-'stuff' (facticity, *ngo-bo*), when resting on its bed (that is nothing else but Being's intensity-'stuff' itself, *rang-mal*), becomes the grounding of its gestaltism (*sku=chos-sku*) and its (commensurate) pristine awareness mode (*ye-shes*); when surging, as it does ceaselessly, it becomes the closed system potential of one's primordiality-(constituted) existentiality (*ye-don-gyi kun-gzhi*) because it relates to what has become the basis of an indeterminate cognitive intensity that 'takes in' the whole of samsara and nirvāṇa.

Being's ownmost intensity (actuality, *rang-bzhin*), when resting on its bed (that is nothing else but Being's ownmost intensity itself), becomes Being's holomovement (*gzhi-snang*), spontaneously present as a blueprint for five pristine awareness modes (of Being's contextualized horizon of meaning, *longs-sku*); when surging, as it does ceaselessly, it becomes the closed system potential of sundry programs (*bag-chags sna-tshogs-kyi kun-gzhi*) which either end up with the five poisons initiated by inconsiderate actions and their (affective) pre-programs or stay with the five pristine awareness modes in their ceaseless creativity.

Being's resonance (*thugs-rje*), when resting on its bed (that is nothing else but Being's resonance itself), provides the [evolutionary] predisposition for the (two) vividly experienced gestalt patterns of Being (*gzugs-sku=longs-sku* and *sprul-sku*) in the projective glow of Being's ec-static intensity; when surging, as it does ceaselessly, it becomes the closed system potential in its linking function (*sbyor-ba (ye-) don-gyi kun-gzhi*), because if one recognizes the intrinsic creativity in Being's resonance (that is) inseparable (from Being's intensity-'stuff' and ownmost intensity) for what it is, its pristine awareness blends with Being's field-like vastness (from which meanings are born) and one passes into nirvāṇa; if one does not recognize it for what it is, it blends with the mistaken identifications a sentient being (becomes involved) and becomes the predisposition for the eight perceptual patterns that become engrossed in the pleasures and plains of samsara.

This lengthy quotation introduces the gestalt character and experience (*sku*) of Being which is discussed in terms of Being's meaningfulness (*chos-sku*), of Being's coming-to-presence as a 'world'-engagement (*longs-sku*), and of Being's presencing as cultural guiding images (*sprul-sku*). In spite of the importance these terms have in Buddhist thinking, Western writers have either passed over them hastily, referring to them as 'Buddha bodies', or listed their Sanskrit equivalents (no more questions please). This superciliousness is all the more objectionable in the present context since these terms were intended to be experientially relevant to the individual who is attempting to see for himself what the Buddhist texts were talking about. The tentative rendering offered here is an attempt to capture the dynamic immediacy that derives from and refers back to the aliveness of experience.

The term *sku*, here rendered as 'gestalt', 'gestalt quality', 'gestalt experience' and, in highly abstract diction, even as 'gestaltism', is indicative of a whole, which must be carefully distinguished from a totality that can be assembled from a number of separate items.[9] A gestalt is an unbroken whole, a complete pattern that cannot be arrived at through an accumulation of parts, but rather imbues the parts with meaning. A word of caution is necessary. The term 'gestalt' may be misleading through the epistemological connotations its use in psychology may arouse. In the Buddhist context gestalt refers to the wholeness of experience where the subject-object split has not yet occurred and the field of experience has not been dissected into isolatable units of interest. To single out features is to break the wholeness of the pattern, therefore, the gestalt experience of Being is not encompassed by a thinking which singles out and objectifies objects of concern and interest.

The triple gestalt experience also shows the connectedness of what might be spoken of as focal settings within the gestalt experience of Being. These gestalt experiences account for the embeddedness of the individual in the multidimensional reality of which he is both a particular instantation and the expression of the whole itself.[10] Within the field of experience these gestalt settings range from the holistic thereness of Being's sheer lucency as the proto-patterning of the contextual horizon of meaning to the presencing of the cultural norms and guiding images that express and serve the individual's aspiration for meaning. Yet though these gestalts are spoken of as if they existed independently, they are interconnected inasmuch as they are all of one fabric—roughly, they are all experience.

Moreover, because of the ubiquitous presence of the experiencer his body image plays a significant role in the formulation of the gestalt or gestalts as embodying perspectives which he can understand and appreciate. In the immediacy of experience, the lived body (*lus*) of the experiencer and the gestalt quality (*sku*) of Being remain interconnected in such a manner that, though distinguishable from each other, they are not objectively reducible one to the other.

Three such process structures or gestalts (*sku gsum*) have figured prominently in Buddhist thought:

1. *chos-sku* (*chos-kyi sku*)

The rendering of this term by 'Being's meaning-rich gestalt', a 'gestalt embodying Being's meaningfulness' rather than merely perpetuating the evasive rendering of this Tibetan term by its Sanskrit equivalent *dharmakāya* attempts to bring out the importance of meaning (*chos*) in experience. Whatever we experience, be this a thing, a person, an event, is always experienced *as meant*. To be precise, the term *chos* primarily refers to a vectorial texture providing the primordial basis for meaning. A lengthy hermeneutical investigation of the term *chos-sku* with extensive references to the rDzogs-chen Tantras has been provided by Klong-chen rab-'byams-pa in several places in his major works. The gist of his assessment is as follows:[11]

> In substance it is an auto-effulgence in terms of (Being's) open-dimensionality/nothingness, radiance, and ceaselessness (of excitation)', while 'in precise terms (it is such that) since the primordial (*ye*) purity of (Being's) expanse having a field-like character (*dbyings*), and (Being's) possibilizing dynamics (*chos-nyid*) as a spontaneous thereness (jointly) constitute a gestalt of sheer lucency (*'od-gsal-ba'i sku*), Being's intensity-

'stuff' *ngo-bo*) or diaphaneity (*ka-dag*) is (what is meant by (Being's) invariant and non-errant meaningfulness (*chos*) and Being's ownmost intensity (*rang-bzhin*) or spontaneous thereness (*lhun-grub*) is (what is meant by Being's) gestalt (*sku*) as a sheer lucency, and this is Being's ultimate self-abidingness.

The embodied experiencer's presence in the experience of Being's gestalt character prompts its reduction to some kind of corporeality (*lus*) that intimates a connectedness of the gestalt with a wider field of which it is a kind of 'crystallization' without, however, being something somewhere:[12]

> Its ownmost body (*rang-lus*) is nowhere to be found as anything because it exceedes all limitations set by conceptual-propositional proliferations.

While basically Being's gestalt character is so rich in meaning that it cannot be exhausted in words, analogies are frequently used to facilitate an appreciation and understanding. The most frequently used analogies are summarized as follows:[13]

> Analogies for it are the following ones: the sun, because (Being's) ec-static intensity (*rig-pa*) is a sheer lucency; the ocean, because it is profound; a lotus flower, because it is not marred by blemishes; a mountain, because it (stands) invariant (and unshakable); the sky, because it is wide-open and has neither a center nor periphery; a lion, because it possesses and has primordially possessed a resoluteness that overcomes everything.

In this connection two 'definitions' from the rDzogs-chen Tantras may be given; the one is from the *Mu-tig phreng-ba*:[14]

> Being's meaning-rich gestalt has done with what is subject to the ravishes of time;
> In its nothingness it is a radiance and in its radiance it is an all-encompassing (force);
> It is not marred by reflexive-representational thinking (as the latter's) organismic input phase has dissipated and
> It is dissociated from whatever is conceptual-propositional.
> Like the sky—in its all-encompassingness (yet) a nothingness;
> Sell-purificatory, dissociated from all analogies.

The other passage is from the *sGra-thal-'gyur-ba*:[15]

> Being's meaning-rich gestalt is dissociated from the conceptual-propositional;
> It has no attributes that might (make one) believe in it as being something in itself.
> Its facticity or nothingness and (its actuality or) radiance are inseparable, (yet allowing for its)
> Separation into a *chos-sku*, *longs-sku*, and *sprul-sku*.

The upshot of these lengthy discussions is that *chos-sku* is a process structure that is virtual and actual at the same time.

2. *longs-sku* (*longs-spyod rdzogs-pa'i sku*)

'The gestalt(ism) of Being's contextualized horizon of meaning' comes as Being's autopresencing in which the experiencer by virtue of being co-constituted with the experiencing process is fully engaged. The emphasis is on the coming-to-presence in actually embodying Being's dynamic possibilities as ways of the experiencer's world-engagement. Thus, Klong-chen rab-'byams-pa speaks of its coming-to presence as follows:[16]

> In substance, one speaks with reference to its coming-to-presence in its autopresencing out of Being's field-like vastness as being born. Actually, since it has nothing about it that might be termed 'birth' it is without death and has overcome the deadliness of death.

The panorama of possibilities presented by this gestalt is a process described in terms of a starting-point, a way, and a climax which is not so much a dead end as a new possibility of unfoldment. The vectorial character of each phase displays a fivefold pattern such that:[17]

> The starting-point of (ground/reason for) its sheer lucency is Being's ec-static intensity (*rig-pa*); the starting-point of its concreteness is (the individual's) genus- and species-specific (psychic) potential (*kun-gzhi*); the starting-point of its going astray is mind/mentation (*sems*); the starting-point of its way is the lamps (*sgron-ma*); the starting-point of its understanding (itself) is the (individual's) appreciative acumen (*shes-rab*).

Similarly, because of the presence of this gestalt as a challenge to work out the possibilities it offers, its 'way' may be conceived of as a moving up to Being as intimated by the traditional five paths of preparation, linking-up, seeing, developing the vision, and 'no-more-learning', or travelled within Being itself such that this 'inner' process circle as a whole acts like a catalyst transforming the 'starting'-point into an 'end-state'. Of the latter aspect of the way Klong-chen rab-'byams-pa says[18]:

> The way of its possibilizing dynamics is Being's field-like expanse (*dbyings*); the way of its ec-static intensity is (one's) appreciative acumen (*shes-rab*); the way of its sheer lucency is two lamps (*sgron-ma*); the way of the barrier-free approach is the simultaneity of its coming-to-presence and dissolution (into the nothingness of Being's) freedom-dissipation (*shar-grol*); the way of the final-leap approach is the field and its excitation (*dbyings-rig*).

and finally[19]:

> The climax of its primordial awareness modes is the emancipatory dynamics in the proto-patterns of world-engagements (*rigs-su grol-ba*); the climax of its light qualities is the extinction of the lighting-up (coming-to-presence) of mistaken identifications (*'khrul-snang nub-pa*); the climax of its understanding (itself) is the dissipation of the conceptual constructs due to errancy (*'khrul-rtog sangs*); the climax of its auto-presencing is its dispatch to its dwelling (or plane) where everything is over and done with (*zad-sar skyol-ba*); the way of its finality is its submerging in Being's field-like expanse (*dbyings-la thim-pa*).

The inherent richness of this gestalt expresses itself in its presenting a panorama of what may be said to be a prepredicative life-world in and of which the experiencer is an integral aspect who through his involvement with it by way of his existential knowing (*ye-shes*) lays the foundation for the emergence of what eventually become socio-cultural specifications or norms. Thus, summing up the lengthy hermeneutical discussion of this gestalt in the *Rig-pa rang-shar*, Klong-chen rab-'byams-pa concisely states:[20]

'In precise terms, Being's possibilities and dynamic qualities [all that makes life worth living] have become available (reached up, *longs*) to their full measure of effectiveness, and (solicit the experiencer's) engagement (*spyod*) in the purity of Being's sheer lucency; life's twofold purpose (of self-realization and other-enrichment) by virtue of its spontaneity finds its (simultaneous) fulfilment (*rdzogs*) and (the transactive structure of the copresence of self and other) is revealed (*pa*) by the primordial awareness modes on their way to their full measure of effectiveness; the coming-to-presence (the lighting-up) of rays of light from the basic and illumining properties (points to) the gestalt character (*sku*). These five facets between themselves define Being's gestalt as a world-spanning horizon of meaningfulness (*longs-spyod rdzogs-pa'i sku*).

3. *sprul-sku* (*sprul-pa' i sku*)

The rendering of this term by 'the gestalt of Being serving as a guiding image' or referring to it simply by the short time 'guiding image'—the literal translation would be 'projective gestalt'—is based on the following considerations. This gestalt derives, as it were, from the two gestalts discussed so far, though not in a causal manner, but rather prompted by their dynamics. Of this gestalt Klong-chen rab-'byams-pa states:[21]

> In substance there issue from the gestalt Being's field-like expanse and its excitation rays of light that have a distinct gestalt character (*zer-gyi sku*) and serve the (spiritual) interest of others (*gzhan-don*).

This serving the spiritual interest of others is done by arousing them to the development of their own inner wealth of possibilities.

As such this gestalt is an integral aspect of Being's triune gestalt character as which the experiencer images Being's dynamics working in and through him. This insight has been beautifully expressed by Klong-chen rab-'byams-pa:[22]

> Because of its openness/nothingness Being assumes the
> character of a meaning-rich gestalt and because of its

radiance the character of contextualized horizon of meaning and

Because of the rays of light (as an integral aspect) the character of a guilding-image. This triad of gestalts is such that none can be added to nor subtracted from the others.

Since (their) dynamic qualities have been holistically present since (Being's) primordial (beingness)

They are not shrouded in the darkness of imperfections and other kinds of reprehensibilities.

(As) before (so) hereafter, not undergoing displacements or changes, (this triune gestalt) remains as one and the same throughout the three aspects of time;

In all Buddhas and sentient beings it remains as one and the same.

This is what is meant by (the whole's) endogenous incentive (to realize) and (the individual's) concern with pellucidity and consummation.

Rephrased in modern terms the last part of this aphorism means that a human being is in co-evolution with the whole. If the whole (or universe) can be said to be mind (*sems*) as a process evolving into ever higher levels of clarity or pellucidity (*byang-chub*), then, through our connectedness with it we share in its evolution, and Aldous Huxley's often quoted dictum that 'each one of us is potentially Mind-at-Large' gains added significance.

The repeated reference to this gestalt's coming-to-presence in agreement with any individual's perceptive acumen not only suggests that there may be as many guiding images as there are living beings, but also a hierarchical organization of its own, rather than being something monolithic. On the lowest social level dominated by organismic mentation concerned with survival and self-expression, much of which is 'behavioral', this guiding image, specified as an 'impure', 'opaque', 'unrefined' projective gestalt (*ma-dag-pa sprul-pa'i sku*), comes, as Klong-chen rab-'byams-pa[23] informs us, in the guise of a hunter or a prostitute. On the 'cultural' level where reflexive and self-reflexive thinking evolves and is active in creating a symbolic model of the individual himself and his environment, it is specified as a projective gestalt that guides the living beings (*'gro-ba 'dul-ba'i sprul-pa'i sku*) and comes in the guise of any one of the six puissants (*thub-pa*) guiding the beings in any one of the six domains of living beings. Thus, for instance, in the human world it is the historical Buddha, while in the world of gods it is Indra who has in the course of time undergone considerable transformations: from a warrior in Vedic times into a lewd womanizer in the Brahmanical period and finally into a lutist. Lastly, in this hierarchy there is the 'projective gestalt expressive of Being's ownmost intensity or actuality in its subactuality of its dynamic qualities' (*rang-bzhin sprul-pa'i sku*). This is the guiding image that 'introduces', as it were, the individual into his spiritual or supramundane life—the first step in self-transcendence in the strict sense of the word.

The above examination of the multiple nuances in which what is summarily referred to by the technical term *sku*, be this singularly or triadically (*sku-gsum*) manifests itself, makes it abundantly clear that Being's gestalt character does not represent a control hierarchy, but, seen from 'below', is a multilevel reality of self-transcendence, while, seen from 'above', is a unitary process of unfolding whose integrated levels the individual lives simultaneously, because he shares in them in an integral manner.

Reference is often made, as in the present text, to still another gestalt of Being:

4. *ngo-bo-nyid-kyi sku*

On the one hand, this term refers to the inseparability of the three previously mentioned gestalts and therefore is not a separate fourth gestalt as suggested by language that because of its linear and itemizing character constantly locks us firmly in a frame—Heidegger's *Gestell* (enframing)—from which it is most difficult to break out. On the other hand, this term points to what I have called "Being's intensity-'stuff'" (*ngo-bo*). That this 'stuff' is not matter in any of the senses in which the term matter is used in the Western context, is indicated by the particle *nyid* in *ngo-bo-nyid*. This decisively Tibetan Subtlety I have tried to convey by speaking of the *ngo-bo-nyid-kyi sku* as 'the gestalt of Being-in-its-beingness'. Just as Being's beingness is not some *thing* (material or mental or what-not) so also its gestalt does not have any anthropomorphic features, as is succinctly stated by Klong-chen rab-'byams-pa:[24]

> Its [Being's] intensity-'stuff', abiding as a gestalt, neither moved nor changed;
> Its 'ownmostness', a dynamic [superluminal] light, rose as [Being's] voice; and
> Its 'resonance' was its spirituality and ec-static intensity.
> Although it abided as a gestalt, it had neither face nor hands;
> Although it abided as light, it had no color;
> Although it abided as an ec-static intensity, it neither sallied forth nor witdrew;
> It [just] was the greatness of [Being's evolutionary] predisposition, on its part an inner brilliance.

There exists, as we would say, an intimate connection between this gestalt and the gestalt embodying Being's meaningfulness (*chos-sku*) such that the latter is the *act* of understanding the former of which it is its 'excitation', variously referred to as 'ec-static intensity' (*rig-pa*) or 'pristine (primordial, originary) awareness (*ye-shes*):[25]

> The deeply felt understanding (*rtogs*) of Being's beingness gestalt (*ngo-bo-nyid-kyi sku*) is the gestalt embodying Being's meaningfulness (*chos-kyi sku*);
> Through an ec-static cognitive intensity in and with respect to the latter there (comes-to-presence) Being's gestalt as a world-spanning horizon of meaning (*longs-spyod rdzogs-pa'i sku*);
> The manifold (of its projections) in its brilliant clarity is Being's guiding images gestalt (*sprul-pa' i sku*);
> Since this is difficult to understand by those who have no rapport (with this process) there is a gestalt experience of mystery (*gsang-ba' i sku*).

From this and other passages it becomes evident that the rDzogs-chen thinkers' overriding concern with Being's gestaltism and wholeness as dynamic notions had long ago anticipated the 'modern' idea of the vacuum (field) as a very active substance such that any particle produced is to be viewed as an excitation of the field, in no way independent of it. In the light of modern (maybe not quite so modern) physics the following passage speaking of 'ground' (*ngo-bo gzhi'i chos-sku*) an the act of 'understanding' (*rtogs-pa'i ye-shes chos-sku*) becomes readily intelligible:[26]

> Between the gestaltism of meaning in the beingness of Being as a dynamic 'ground' (*ngo-bo gzhi'i chos-sku*) and
> The gestaltism of meaning (made explicit through) the pristine awareness in (the act of) understanding (*rtogs-pa'i ye-shes chos-sku*)
> There is no difference in the beingness of Being as a dynamic 'ground'.
> In the beingness of the sun
> There are neither darkness nor shadows nor coldness;
> When (the sun) becomes shrouded in darkness by passing clouds
> This does not mean that the sunlight does not exist.
> Being's beingness neither increases nor decreases:
> Through the difference in understanding and non-understanding
> There are sentient beings and Buddhas who (nonetheless derive from) one and the same (source)—
> Being, the ground (without grounding), remaining unchanged throughout the three aspects of time.

Similar to the *chos-sku* having its field (*dbyings*) of which it is its excitation (*rig-pa*) as indicated in the following passage:[27]

> That which lights up as the external, the vast expanse where meanings are born (*chos-dbyings*), and
> The ec-static intensity (*rig-pa*) as the within, the gestalt in which meaning becomes embodied (*chos-sku*)
> Come about simultaneously
> In the same manner as the open sky and
> The bright sun or moon
> Have risen (into view) at the same time,

the gestalt in which Being's beingness (*ngo-bo-nyid-kyi sku*) becomes expressed, emerges out of the lighting-up of Being's beingness (*ngo-bo-nyid-kyi snang-ba*):[28]

> With the lighting-up (coming-to-presence) of Being's beingness (*ngo-bo-nyid-kyi snang-ba*)
> There has arisen the gestalt of Being's beingness (*ngo-bo-nyid-kyi sku*)—
> (This is) like (the simultaneity of) the sky and the sun.

Lastly, the same idea has been expressed aphoristically in the evocative statement:[29]

> The lighting-up of Being's beingness
> Is like the cloudless sky;
> The gestalt of Being's beingness is like the energy of the sun.

The upshot of this comparative study of the *ngo-bo-nyid-kyi sku* and the *chos-kyi sku* is that the former is ontological, the latter experiential, and that the transition from Being to experience occurs with Being's holomovement (*gzhi-snang*).

NOTES

1. *Theg-mchog* II, p. 32.
2. *Tshig-don*, p. 234.
3. *ibid.*
4. Manfred Eigen and Peter Schuster, *The hypercycle: a principle of natural self-organization.*
5. *Theg-mchog* II, p. 35.
6. *Chos-dbyings*, p. 233.
7. *gNas-lugs*, p. 76.
8. *Zab-yang* II, pp. 207f.
9. On wholeness as distinct from totality see David Michael Levin, *The Opening of Vision*, pp. 454-456.
10. Erich Jantsch, *Design for Evolution*, p. 99, speaking of three modes of inquiry, the rational, the mythological, and the evolutionary, remarks:

    > ..in the evolutionary approach we *are* the stream, source and flow, carrier and carried, the whole stream and yet only part of it—as a water molecule is the river and yet only part of it.
11. *Theg-mchog* II, pp. 121f.
12. *Theg-mchog* II, p. 122.

13. *ibid.*
14. p. 518.
15. p. 129.
16. *Theg-mchog* II, p. 123.
17. *ibid.*, p. 124.
18. *ibid.*
19. *ibid.*
20. *ibid.*, p. 125.
21. *Theg-mchog* II, p. 126.
22. *Chos-dbyings* III, 7, p. 80.
23. *Theg-mchog* II, p. 436.
24. *Zab-yang* I, p. 294.
25. *rDzogs-pa-chen-po lta-ba ye-shes gting-rdzogs-kyi rgyud* (in *rNying-rgyud*, vol. 3, pp. 33-65), p. 54.
26. *rDzogs-pa-chen-po nges-don thams-cad 'dus-pa ye-shes nam-mkha' mnyam-pa'i rgyud* (in *rNying-rgyud*, vol. 8, pp. 124-478), p. 175.
27. *dGongs-pa zang-thal*, vol. 5, p. 118.
28. *rDzogs-pa-chen-po thig-le gsang-ba de-kho-na-nyid nges-pa'i rgyud* (in *rNying-rgyud*, vol. 5, pp. 515-525), p. 516.
29. *Thig-le kun-gsal* (in *rNying-rgyud*, vol. 5, pp. 124-289), p. 125.

Chapter Five

THE EMPOWERMENTS AS PSYCHOLOGICAL STEPPING-STONES

The rendering of the Tibetan term *dbang-(bskur)* by 'empowerment(s)' in preference to the, from a certain perspective, equally appropriate terms 'investiture' and 'inauguration' is prompted by the consideration that the latter two terms emphasize the ceremonial and basically 'outward' aspect of the performance, while 'empowerment' stresses the psychological-experiential and hence 'inner' aspect of the process. According to the generally accepted sequence of four empowerments each subsequent empowerment is both a deepening and intensification of the experience. It is described in terms of a movement from the 'external' (*phyi*) to the 'internal' (*nang*) and from there to the 'arcane' (*gsang*) and the 'super arcane' (*gsang-ba yongs-su rdzogs-pa*) or as a progression from the more concretely formulated and physically represented (*spros-bcas*) to an at first less concretely formulated level (*spros-med*) and from there to levels that defy any concretization, be this in the physical or mental realms (*shin-tu spros-med* and *rab-tu spros-med*)[1]. Although there is an inner logic to this sequence[2] there is no strict linearity involved inasmuch as each empowerment contains and thus prefigures the course of the subsequent ones. Hence, even with respect to the first empowerment there is more to it than meets the eye.

The purpose of the empowerments is to mobilize the individual's inner potential and have it mature into what is best described as that individual's autonomy as an expression and a measure of his relations with his environment. As such autonomy is inextricably intertwined, if not to say identical, with the individual's cognitive capacity in its progressive emancipation from organismic and representational restrictions. Its highest expression would then be what has been termed the ec-static intensity (*rig-pa*) as it becomes first experienced in its pristine awareness modes (*ye-shes*). It is permissible to speak of autonomy as a kind of central control, provided one bears in mind that this control is not absolute or dictatorial but always contextually organizational, be this the sociopolitical or the sociospiritual context. Forming an integral aspect of a socio-cultural dynamics ranging over nine levels—Śrāvakas, Pratyeka-buddhas, and Bodhisattvas as publicly discernible (ostentatious) members of society, the followers of the Kriyā, Caryā, and Yoga disciplines as less publicly discernible members, and the followers of the Mahā, Anu, and Ati (rDzogs-chen) teaching as the least publicly discernible members—each level has evolved its own process of ritualization involving the four phases of a growing interiorization so that, on this basis, one can speak of thirty-six (9 × 4) 'empowerments'.[3] However, whatever the degree of ritualization and its attendant normalization may be, the empowerment works *within* us to the effect that in whichever sociospiritual domain we may find ourselves, we bring out the best on this particular context as a stepping-stone for moving on further. The experiential character of the empowerments can be gleaned from the following passage:[4]

> In substance (its dynamics, *ngo-bo*), empowerment means (the system's) self-existing pristine awareness (*rang-byung-gi ye-shes*) that has not come under the power of something else or other.
>
> Its definition (*nges-tshig*) is that it empowers (inaugurates the experiencer to a level from which he will) hold sway over everything summed up by samsara and nirvāṇa.
>
> An illustration (*dpe*) is the following: once a person has been inaugurated to the (office of a) king, he assumes the power that is his very own (exerts his autonomy, *rang-dbang*) and establishes himself firmly on his throne.

It is from the viewpoint of a lived through experience that the empowerments were likened to rivers whose water is life-giving:[5]

> the river of the empowering force that is nothing else but the beingness of Being;
>
> the river of the empowering force that is (the system's) self-existing resonance;

> the river of the empowering force that is the five pristine awareness modes; and
> the river of the empowering force that is the five gnosemes (transforming themselves into) the dominant figures in the prototypes of conscious life.

In a highly cryptic manner these rivers/empowerments are associated with the development lines, flow patterns, or chreods (*rtsa*) that constitute the dynamic body image. In this sense we might make use of the images suggested by H.C. Waddington and say that these rivers/empowerments water the epigenetic landscape (one's body) along its valleys/chreods traversing the various zones ranging from the affective-organismic—

> Dullness, aversion, passion and
> Arrogance perpetually flow like water—

to the spiritual and ec-static—

> Understanding as four pristine awareness modes.

The emphasis on the experiential character of the empowerments must not make us overlook the fact that no experience exists in abstraction from the embodied experiencer who by virtue of his embodiment finds himself already in a social context, a kind of territorial space he has staked out in his interaction and communication with others. Both interaction and communication stem from an individual's presentation of himself to another individual in such a manner as to evoke corresponding processes. In this mutual self-presentation ritual plays a significant role. Ritual is a kind of social language that serves to symbolize a social order and to reaffirm its moral values. Every ritual makes use of utensils appropriate to the function the ritual serves. One such utensil was a flask (*bum-pa*), filled with water and used to sprinkle the water in it on the head of the person to be inaugurated as king and thereby confirming him in his exalted position. Water has always been used for purificatory purposes and ablutions are specifically mentioned by Tibetan authors to explain their term 'empowerment' (*dbang*) as an equivalent for the Sanskrit term *abhiṣeka* ('sprinkling'). When, in the Buddhist context, Rong-zom Chos-kyi bzang-po points out that this involves the restoration and recognition of the individual's original potential,[6] he seems to have had the following story[7] in mind:

> Previously, there was in India a city by the name of Ser-skya (Kapilavastu). A young prince had gone to see a theatrical performance and roaming about on foot he was not different from any other beggar. A minister spotted him, gave him a bath and restored him to his position of power. Henceforward his attendants were again under his sway. Similarly, when the primordial 'Buddha'-experience had stirred from its post to witness the five colors (of Being in its symmetry transformation from its virtual state into its actual state) it went astray and lived among the mistaken identifications of samsara. There was no emancipation for it among the six kinds of life-forms. But when it was confronted with itself (in its beingness) it was restored to the position of power that is the 'Buddha'-experience. This is the empowerment to (and by) kingship and pristine awareness (*rgyal-thabs ye-shes dbang-bskur*).

The technical term in this passage is understood by Klong-chen rab-'byams-pa[8] as referring to two aspects of the empowerment, the 'outer' one (*rgyal-thabs spyi-lugs*) conferring power over the physical universe, and the 'inner' one (*ye-shes spyi-lugs*) conferring power over the mental-spiritual universe made up of mentation (*sems*) and pristine awareness modes (*ye-shes*).

This distinction is of utmost importance. While for the large mass of those following the ordinary spiritual pursuits the social context and its territoriality is mostly their ordinary sociocultural world with the king and his populace, for the rDzogs-chen thinkers the context is Being's abidingness (*gnas-lugs*). This is operative in us as the ground and starting-point (*gzhi*) of all our endeavors[9] with its endogenous pristine awareness (*ye-shes*) as its central dynamics already 'on the move' (the way, *lam*) to its destination (the goal, *'bras-bu*). The whole process is summarily referred to by the term *dkyil-'khor* or *maṇḍala* ('configurational setting'), to use the more familiar Sanskrit term.[10] As a process, the *dkyil-'khor* or *maṇḍala* exhibits a spiral movement that starts from the whole, referred to as the 'basic configurational setting that is Being's spontaneity' (*gzhi lhun-grub rtsa-ba'i dkyil-'khor*). In its movement it forms a sociohuman reality that is itself a process of uncovering a universe in which the human individual is being disclosed to an understanding of his being. This process of forming a sociohuman reality is Being's activity as its and the individual's re-creation of the world such that an outer reality is mirrored and rebuilt as an inner world—or, as already suggested by Novalis,[11] it might also be the other way round:

> Das Äussre ist ein in ein Geheimnis erhobnes Innre, vielleicht auch umgekehrt
>
> (The outer is but inner raised into a state of mystery, it could also be the other way round).

This formative phase is referred to as the 'activity configurational setting that is a reflection as the way' (*lam gzugs-brnyan thabs-kyi dkyil-'khor*). It is this 'activity' (*thabs*) that negotiates an access to, if not to say, creates its own result (*'bras-bu*) that is formally identical with what the process had started, but is different from the 'mere' thereness of the starting-point by being a clarified level, significantly referred to as the '(system's) ownmost configurational setting that (in its) clarity is (Being's or the individual's destination or goal (*'bras-bu rnam-dag rang-bzhin-gyi dkyil-'khor*).

In the emerging sociohuman setting that is Being's own creation on its way to itself, it presents itself, in human terms, through the image of the teacher to itself in the image of the student, both being linked to each other by the spiritual bond that is Being's resonance with itself and everything else;[12]

> The bond between teacher and student
> Is the unbroken bond of resonance
> With love flowing uninterruptedly between them.

Accordingly, all empowerments are imaged and experienced as occurring within the realm of a *dkyil-'khor* or *maṇḍala* which, as noted previously, as a process-structure is the self-presentation of Being (to itself) by way of a symbolic re-creation of itself (*thabs*) as the experiencer's universe that, in the narrower sense of the word, is the site uniquely singled out by the cognitive principle (the whole's ec-static intensity and/or its 'fanning-out' in pristine awareness modes) to live in. Specifically this site is the experiencer's multilevel live body on its level of presenting 'a precious mystery'. This self-reflexive (self-experiencing) process instantiates itself in a double manner: (1) sense-perceptively—the senses through an iterative feedback process between an inner and outer world leading to a new vision by which we remold our experience of reality and of which we become aware by a change in our emotional attitude—and (2) in practice—the intensification of already ongoing process. Even before the actual empowerment takes place the experiencer (student) must have learned, at least in a rudimentary manner, to see the world→ his domicile → his body with *fresh eyes*, that is, to see things as meanings. For instance, the walls of his mansion are imaged as being made of jewels glistening in five colors, as symbols of five pristine awareness modes shining in their respective inner glow. The cushions on which the objects of sensuous and sensual pleasures (a mirror, a lute, a conch, fruits, and a scarf) rest are seen as symbols of the beauty of one's 'physical' world which one would never feel if one were to suppress one's senses. The same transformative vision applies not only to the 'household utensils', but also to the members of his household. The utensils are the five flasks (positioned at strategic points of orientation) as symbols of the protopatterns of his synergetic conscious/spiritual existence; the five decorative scarves round the neck of the flasks serve as symbols of the complementarity/indivisibility of the male and female aspects of the organizing principle in the protopatterns of this synergetic conscious/spiritual life. The members in this household, on the physical level, should be like one's brothers and sisters as one's energetic and inspiring helpers in one's striving and as good and goddesses.

There are four empowerments, each subsequent one becoming less dependent on concepts and propositional presentations, yet presented and described by concepts. Technically they are known by their code name as

1. 'flask' empowerment (*bum-pa'i dbang*),
2. 'mystery' empowerment (*gsang-ba'i dbang*),
3. 'knowledge-through-appreciation, empowerment (*shes-rab ye-shes-kyi dbang*), and
4. 'word-and-meaning' empowerment (*tshig-don ngo-sprad-kyi dbang*).

1. Five flasks are used in the act of conferring or, rather, confirming the power that is already at work in the individual, but needs some cleansing to 'wash away' the dross that has accumulated and made him blind to its potential. The arrangement of the flasks in the four directions of the compass with its center, reflects the spatiotemporal distribution of the experiencer's various projects-at-hand or regions of concern. Each functions as a zero-point for its milieu of data disclosed by this zero-point and is related to specific dynamic regimes (*'khor-lo*) within the organism, which are organized around and oriented to the experiencer as the center of his total experiential situation. Furthermore, there is, as in the evolution of the *dkyil-'khor* or *maṇḍala*, a kind of spiral movement involved: while in this empowerment process the starting-point is formally identical with the result and while the identity of the starting-point (the system's pristine awareness, *ye-shes*) is maintained throughout the process, the result is yet different in character than it had started with. Lastly, each flask illustrates the interdependence or correspondence of structure and function.

The flask in the center is lifted above the experiencer's head and a drop of water from the flask serves, symbolically, to cleanse the dynamic regime presenting the system's (Being's or the individual's) self-organizing dynamics (*bkod-pa'i 'khor lo*). This gesture is accompanied by the words preceded by their appropriate phoneme or 'first utterance':[13]

> *OṂ*!
> This flask (symbolizing) Being's possibilizing dynamics (*chos-nyid*) in its field-like expanse (*dbyings*)
> Is filled with the natural water of Being's openness/nothingness (that is its) radiance (*stong-gsal*)
> My dear child, being empowered by it
> May you understand (*rtogs*) the abidingness (of Being in this its) field-like expanse.

What the student, addressed by 'my dear child' emphasizing the intimate relationship between teacher and student, has to understand by this cryptic statement is the paradox of there being a presence that yet is nothing and vice versa (as intimated in the Western context in the above quoted aphorism by Novalis):

In the vibrant dimension of (what is Being's) field-like expanse (and) possibilizing dynamics (*chos-nyid*) as (Being's) nothingness (*stong-pa*), there abides its pristine awareness in (its dynamics of a) coming-to-presence in or lighting up (*snang-ba*) as (something) fully determinate (*chos-can*). This (complementarity of the 'how' and the 'this') is what is intended and symbolically illustrated by the flask and the water in it. So, (my dear child,) venture on the certainty that (Being's) pristine awareness in presenting a field-like expanse that is the source of all meanings (*chos-dbyings ye-shes*) abides in you [presenting Being's infiniteness in your finiteness].

The next phase is initiated by lifting the flask in the eastern portion of the spatial arrangement of the five flasks to the heart that stands for the dynamic regime presenting the individual's mental/spiritual dimension (*dran-pa bsdus-pa'i 'khor-lo*):

HŪṂ!
This flask (symbolizing) Being's vitalizing core intensity (*snying-po*) that is not some thing that has been born (and hence will die),
Is filled with the natural substance of (its) incessantness.
My dear child, empowered by it
May you understand (*rtogs*) Being's reality in its not posing any danger (one might be afraid of).

What the student has to understand by this statement is that he is the whole as it unfolds in him and in this unfolding illuminates the phases and aspects of it movement:

In the vibrant dimension of pure experience (*sems-nyid*) that is without birth and (open) like the sky, an ec-static intensity (*rig-pa*) that does never cease, abides in its auto-excitatory presencing, which is Being's initially pure actuality. This [complementarity/indivisibility of the field and its excitation in terms of experience and intensity] is what is meant and illustrated by the flask and the water in it. Recognize (this dynamics as) the mirror-like pristine awareness mode (*me-long lta-bu*'i *ye-shes*).

With this understanding and awareness of Being's wholeness present in the experiencer who, in a certain sense, 'mirrors the whole', the scene is set for working out the details in one's becoming oneself in the ec-static intensity that is the creativity that pervades the immediacy of existence.

Certainly, the world is full of vibrations laid out in a finely woven net of qualities and flavors with which we sensuously and sensually 'communicate'. Here, in establishing a relationship between an inner 'subjective' and outer 'objective' reality, access to a holistic and self-consistent reality is gained. This is intimated by lifting the flask in the southern portion of the spatial arrangement of the five flasks, now including a temporal dimension through its clockwise movement, to the throat standing for the dynamic regime of the individual's linguistic/symbolic dimension (*ro-rnams bsdus-pa'i khor-lo*) and the statement:

> *SVAḤ*!
> This flask (symbolizing) Being's-self-existing pristine awareness ['in action']
> Is filled with the natural substances of the objects of sensuous and sensual pleasures.
> My dear child, empowered by it
> May you come to possess (*thob*) the power of your thoughts becoming spontaneously realized.

This empowerment is a challenge to explore the flavors and the wealth of qualities the world holds, and so it is a venturing into what had always been there but never noticed to be there:

> The (fact) that in Being's self-existing pristine awareness as a function of its ec-static intensity the qualities of whatever one sensuously and sensually desires have been there spontaneously since time before time, is illustrated by the flask and the water in it. So venture on the certainty that the realization of all thoughts by recognizing what (the complementarity/indivisibility in this phase) is all about, lies in Being's self-consistency pristine awareness mode (*mnyam-nyid ye-shes*) (which is to say that whatever comes into existence must be consistent with itself and with everything else).

To the extent that the process initiated and reinforced by each subsequent empowerment approaches its climax it is 'felt' as an extraordinary intensification of well-being that matches the ec-static cognitive intensity in its feeling tone of bliss. The next step is to lift the flask in the western portion of the spatial arrangement of the five flasks to the navel standing for the dynamic regime of the individual's physical/physiological dimension (*skyed-byed 'khor-lo*) which has been set up by the sexual act running its course of excitement, plateau, climax, and resolution, the whole of which has both a physical and spiritual dimension. This is obliquely indicated by the accompanying words:

> *ĀḤ*!
> This flask (symbolizing) Being's impassibility (*chags-bral*) that is not some thing that has been born,
> Is filled with the streaming profusion of bliss supreme (*bde-chen*).
> My dear child, being empowered by this
> May you come to possess (*thob*) the power of a passion that is not subjectively appropriated (*chags-pa 'dzin-med*).

What the student has to understand is that

> The meaning (and substance) of bliss supreme is the impassibility of pure experience that is without birth but has been so since time before time. (Yet its felt quality of bliss supreme) stems from the stream that is full of the elixir that is the purest radiation-dominated aspect (of the fundamental forces moving through the hierarchically organized) dynamic regimes in one's body. This (complementarity/indivisibility of the physical and spiritual) is what is meant and illustrated by the flask and the water in it. So, recognize the fluctuations between the descending (into details) and the ascending (into enriched meaningfulness) as well as the damming up of your psychophysical potential that is (basically) bliss supreme (into an instability phase from which new fluctuations may start) with no dichotomies involved, as Being's specificity-initiating pristine awareness mode (*so-sor rtog-pa'i ye-shes*).

Lastly, the process climaxes in pure creativity extending over all levels and establishing its own dynamic dimension. This is intimated by lifting the flask in the northern portion of the spatial arrangement of the five flasks to all the other four dynamic regimes with the words:

> *HAḤ* !
> This flask (symbolizing) Being's pristine awareness in its insubstantiality (*zang-thal*)
> Is filled with the substances of the five (kinds of) motility (*rlung*) that never stops.
> My dear child, being empowered by it
> My you come to possess (*thob*) the power of Being's superb creativity (*rtsal*) in all its completeness.

What the student has to understand by this final empowerment is that

> What is meant and illustrated by the flask and the water in it is (the complementarity/indivisibility of) the vibrant dimension of the insubstantiality of (Being's) pristine awareness as a function of its ec-static intensity that is an ultimate emancipatory dynamics (active) since time before time, and the five kinds of motility that are the radiation-dominated aspects (of the fundamental forces) shining out of (this insubstantiality dimension) as originary awareness modes. So recognize the superb creativity that has been complete since time before time, of Being's self-existing pristine awareness as a function of its auto-excitatory ec-static intensity that (the moment) it comes into existence by itself dissolves by itself, as the tasks-posed and tasks-accomplished pristine awareness mode (*bya-ba grub-pa'i ye-shes*).

Careful attention to the diction of these quotations will reveal the subtle distinction between understanding (*rtogs*) and possessing (*thob*). The possibilizing dynamics of the whole mirrors itself in us who are now called upon to act out the possibilities we see so that they become our assets in the true sense of the word. Johann Wolfgang von Goethe's insight expressed in his dictum:[14]

Was du ererbt von deinen Vätern
Erwirb es um es zu besitzen
(What you have inherited from your forbears
Acquire it in order to possess it)

captures the above sense of understanding (what is already there) and possessing (by acquiring it). The assets to which we refer as our 'possessions' are not items among other items, they are *ourselves* in our aliveness that is an energizing force (not to be confused with Bergson's entity-like *élan vital*), assuming different guises on each level over which it ranges by being simultaneously that level and its dynamics. Hence, the 'power' (*dbang*) to which our attention is drawn by the 'empowerments' (*dbang-bskur*), is not something we pick up or lay aside, but is ourselves roused to self-realization that is nothing short of being the whole once again. The multilevel dynamics of this 'power' has been succinctly stated by Klong-chen rab-'byams-pa:[15]

> Outwardly, by having acquired and possessing (*thob*) the power [of experiencing and in this process being able to symbolically re-create] the presencing (of what becomes one's outer world, *snang-ba*) the conditions for such (opaque) presencing dissolve into (possibilities of pure and transparent supramundane reals (*zhing-khams*);
>
> Inwardly, by having acquired and possessing the power [of experiencing one's psychophysical constituents as presenting a] phantasmal 'body' (*sgyu-lus*), the material concretization of (what is believed to be) one's physical body dissolves into Being's sheer lucency (*'od-gsal*); and
>
> Arcanely, by having acquired and possessing the power [of experiencing oneself as Being's] vastness and ec-static intensity (*dbyings-rig*), the trend of becoming divided against oneself and slipping into mistaken identifications (*'khrul-rtog*) stops by itself.

As is evident from the many functual nuances in meaning implied by the notion of a 'flask empowerment' this empowerment is aimed at effecting a transition from the narrowly circumscribed, essentially nonimaginative and hence merely discursive way of thinking to a more imaginative one that becomes less and less conceptually restrained and more and more creative in its image-forming activity and emancipatory dynamics. Imagination is indispensible for and intimately linked, if not fused, with an individual's understanding of himself and his world, which occurs on different levels his mind as a dynamic principle evolves and 'perceives' as having a gestalt structure, embodying a meaningfully organized experience.

In a static view, the flask is a container object and the water is a container substance and, by analogy, the individual's body contains a mind (or whatever name we may give to this 'other' entity). But, in a dynamic view, so characteristic of rDzogs-chen thought, this old dualism becomes thoroughly discredited: the cognitive principle (mind/mentation or pristine awareness or ec-static intensity) is 'immanent, not in a solid spatial structure, but in the processes in which the system organizes and renews itself and evolves'.[16] But old metaphors die hard and continue to be used even if context has changed. An interesting example is the explication of the term 'flask empowerment' (*bum-pa'i dbang*) and the phrase 'coming to possess the empowerment' (*dbang-bskur thob/thob-pa*)[17]. Here a parallel is drawn between the flask and the water in it and the gestaltism of Being and its (pervasive) pristine awareness that as Being's possibilizing dynamics turns itselt into its corresponding gestalt:

> Having placed (a flask) on the crown of (the disciple's) head (the teacher says:)
> *HŪM*! This flask (symolizes) the pure vastness (of Being from which) meanings (are born, *chos-dbyings rnam-dag*)
> May you, being empowered with this flask (symbolizing) the pristine awareness (organizing this vastness)
> Into (Being's) meaning-rich gestalt (*chos-sku*) that does not put an end to what lights up and is interpreted (as the phenomenal world, *snang-srid*),
> Come to possess the non-partisan and uncurtailed power (that goes with this experience).

A word by word, that is in Tibetan, a syllable by syllable explication states:[18]

> *bum* means Being's core intensity (*snying-po*) as its very light (*'od*);

pa means Being's ceaseless possibilizing dynamics;
dbang means Being in its being without birth as a (concrete) reality (in us);
bskur means (effecting the) non-duality (of Being and ourselves); and
thob-pa means Being's core intensity (*snying-po*) as its meaning-rich gestalt (*chos-sku*).

The upshot of these cryptic statements is that, from a static viewpoint, the process 'ends' with what it has 'started', but from a dynamic viewpoint, there is neither beginning nor end, but only the dynamics of an unfolding or, as the same text declares:[19]

In Being's core intensity that is Being's superdiaphaneity that has no name (*snying-po ka-dag ming-med*)
There is neither possession nor non-possession;
Non-understanding of it gives rise to duality.

2. The second empowerment, as its name 'mystery empowerment' (*gsang-ba'i dbang*) implies, aims at making the student experience the mystery of the creative forces that shape not only his biological existence but also the whole universe whose integral part he is. In the ritual act of this empowerment[20] the teacher lifts in the direction where the four previously mentioned dynamic regimes in the body are located, a skull (*kapāla*) filled with the 'elixir of immortality' (*bdud-rtsi*). He accompanies these gestures with the enigmatic words:

HŪṂ!
Overflowing bliss supreme, self-existent—(this) *kapāla* (is)
Brimful with the *kun-bzang thig-le*, (mutual) passion rinsed of the pseudoconcrete.
My dear child, (member of the) highest life-form, empowered by it
May you come to possess the power over (these same forces as they) organize themselves (*byang-sems*) in their (breeze-like) movement (*rlung*) in a (coherent web of) chreods (*rtsa*).

To these he adds by way of explanation and injunction the following words:

> Understand the bliss supreme that arises in the course of the downward flow of the creative fluids that are purer than pure (*dvangs-ma*) in both the male and female aspects of Kun-tu bzang-po within the vibrant dimension of (Being's) self-existent pristine awareness (whose feeling tone) since time before time has been rapture, as (Being's) meaning-rich gestalt (*chos-sku*) that does not admit of any duality and that is thoroughly emancipatory (in its dynamics).

The intimate connection between the skull and the elixir of immortality[21] is relatively easy to understand. Once the student has been introduced into the richer world of the imagination and the wealth of flavors it holds, the old world of mere discursiveness with its stale reductions is 'dead'. There is hardly any other appropriate symbol for death than the skull. But this skull is brimful with the elixir of immortality that promises an aliveness whose intensity is bliss supreme as, in the Western context, intimated by Johann Wolfgang von Goethe:[22]

> Ha! welche Wonne fliesst in diesem Blick
> Auf einmal mir durch alle meine Sinnen!
> Ich fühle junges, heil'ges Lebensglück
> Neuglühend mir durch Nerv' und Adern rinnen.
> ... ...
> "Die Geisterwelt ist nicht verschlossen;
> Dein Sinn ist zu, dein Herz ist tot!
> Auf, bade, Schüler, unverdrossen
> Die ird'sche Brust im Morgenrot!"
>
> (Ha! as I gaze what rapture suddenly
> begins to flow through all may senses!
> I feel youth's sacred-vital happiness
> cource with new fire through every vein and fiber.
> ... ...
> "The spirit world is not sealed off—
> *your* mind is closed, *your* heart is dead!
> Go, neophyte, and boldly bathe
> your mortal breast in roseate dawn!")

More difficult to understand is the reference to *kun-bzang thig-le* and the implied sexuality. Broadly speaking, the term *thig-le* refers to what we would call the genetic material and the information that goes with it. In this context, it is one of two aspects that belong to the lucency and luminescence of Being's 'ownmostness' (*rang-bzhin*) whose spontaneous vibrations present the paradox of a simultaneously colorless and rainbow-colored spectrum, the one as yet 'virtual' and the other 'actual' or, to be more precise, in the process of *becoming* actual through its vibrations. This spectrum is 'perceived' with feeling as structuration strands, the 'light chreods' (*'od-rtsa*), which in their coupling are said to be found in the heart region, called the *tsitta* palace. The projective character of the luminescence of Being's ownmostness sets up its own boundary of vibrationary patterns which may be understood as a kind of spatialization. It is referred to as the 'self-informing, self-organizing dynamics of Being's ownmostness as pure light' (*rang-bzhin 'od-kyi thig-le*). This ownmostness as one's felt actuality is suffused by an ec-static intensity that as Being's temporalization of itself issues from, though remaining linked to, Being's diaphaneity (*ka-dag-gi rig-pa*) whose cognitive, if not to say, supercognitive quality endows the luminescence of Being's mere presence with a rare beauty (*brgyan*) exerting an aethetic lure. This phase, if we may say so in spite of the fact that the space- and time-binding is not sequential, is technically referred to as the 'self-organizing dynamics (of Being's luminescence) into the complementarity/inseparability of male Kun-tu bzang-po and female Kun-tu bzang-mo' (*kun-tu bzang-po'i thig-le*)[23]. It is the ec-static intensity that in its cognitive dynamics is intensely 'felt' in the immediacy of experience by the experiencer (*rang-rig*) as the complementarity/inseparability of Being's (the whole's) openness/nothingness (*stong-cha*) and its lighting-up/coming-to-presence (*snang-cha*). The lighting-up as 'activity' (*thabs*) is 'seen' and 'felt' as the male principle or spouse Kun-tu bzang-po and the openness/nothingness as 'appreciation' (*shes-rab*) is 'seen' and 'felt' as the female principle or spouse Kun-tu-bzang-mo.[24] Precisely because of its being spacious like the sky (*nam-mkha'*) and therefore 'making room' (*go 'byed*) for things to appear, this openness/nothingness is the very possibilizing dynamics (*chos-nyid*) of Being, while Being's lighting-up in all its brilliance is its gestalt in which its meaningfulness is 'visibly' summed up (*chos-sku*)[25] and 'adorns (makes beautiful) the possibilizing dynamics that otherwise would literally be nothing'.[26] The following correspondences, as diagrammed in Figure 5 result:

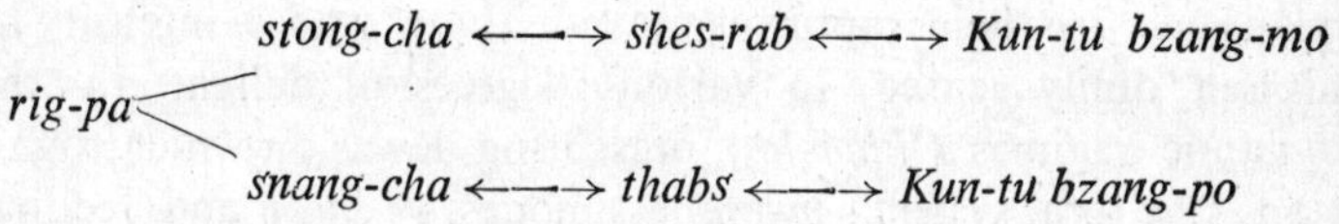

stong-cha ←——→ *shes-rab* ←——→ *Kun-tu bzang-mo*

rig-pa <

snang-cha ←——→ *thabs* ←——→ *Kun-tu bzang-po*

Figure 5

The universal connectedness of the male and the female in its creative dynamics, imaged as the Kun-tu bzang-po and Kun-tu bzang-mo in an intimate embrace, is based on and reflects a mutual passion, antedating, as it were, any materialization that pertains to another phase in the system's dynamics. This passion between Kun-tu bzang-po and Kun-tu bzang-mo is reminiscent of Pierre Teilhard de Chardin's assumption of a psychic (or radial) energy in dialectical battle with physical (or tangential) energy, later on called 'love' between atoms and molecules, except that in rDzogs-chen thought the rigid separation of the psychic and the physical does not hold and that there is no battle (the Westerners predilection for violence), imaginative or otherwise, but a total playful abandonment.

The *kun-bzang thig-le* as an aspect of the *rang-bzhin 'od-kyi thig-le* may be conceived of as the instability phase of the system about to undergo a symmetry break that becomes the 'way' (*lam*) of its self-actualization. From the perspective of its self-organizing dynamics[27] the 'way' comprises two information carriers called 'information carrier in the service of building up one's commonly accepted physical reality' (*kun-rdzob rgyu'i thig-le*) and 'information carrier in the service of maintaining one's spiritual heritage' (*gnas-pa don-dam-gyi thig-le*)[28]. The latter is said to 'reside' in the light chreods (*'od-rtsa*) as an effulgence that by virtue of its motility (*rlung*) evolves into the chreods (*rtsa*) that form a web of interrelated pristine awareness modes fed by 'the sea of bliss supreme' as the ultimate organizing principle.[29]

3. The 'knowledge-through-appreciation' empowerment (*shes-rab ye-shes-kyi dbang*) follows logically from the 'mystery'

empowerment. This empowerment had aimed at making the student 'feelingly' envision and 'envisioningly' feel the dynamics of Being through the forces of life within himself, and which he as a sexually embodied being had, somehow holistically, imaged in the male-female 'polarity' of Kun-tu bzang-po and Kun-tu bzang-mo in their rapturous love-making whose intensity he himself dimly sensed, in various degrees of delight, in the dynamic regimes (*'khor-lo*), presenting levels on which cognitions (the total system's awareness modes, *ye-shes*) and feelings (the total system's delight modes, *dga'-ba*) are inextricably blended into one another, within his lived body as a multi-echelon system. This vision is experienced at a level which lies between the rapture 'felt' by the ec-static intensity of the whole and the everyday-I. To give a 'tangibly' sensuous and sensual form to this vision is the aim of the 'knowledge-through-appreciation' empowerment that addresses itself to a man and a woman who are disclosed each to himself or herself as well as to each other in their embodied sexuality, and is expressed in the coded statement:[30]

> *HŪṂ*!
> (Being's) coming-to-presence and being-interpreted as world (*snang-srid*) is (the reification of its being a supramundane realm (*zhing-khams*) in which bliss supreme reigns supreme and in it
> (Being's) amorously frolicking pristine awareness (*rol-pa'i ye-shes*) triumphs as bliss supreme.
> By engaging in the passionate desire between 'activity' (*thabs*) and 'appreciation' (*shes-rab*) emancipation is won; therefore (you, too,)
> Engage (participate) in (this) ceaseless amorous frolicking! (There lies) bliss supreme.

By way of elucidation that in some respects is a cryptic as the passage it wants to clarify, Klong-chen rab-'byams-pa offers the following:[31]

> You who are fortunate enough (to become so empowered take note that) Being's coming-to-presence and being-interpreted (*snang-srid*) as an environing world (*snod*) and the

organismic life-forms (with their karmic and emotional reactions to it, *bcud*), has in its totality, since time before time, endured in (what is its) eigenstate of deiform energies (*lha'i rang-bzhin*) that presences itself in (the concrete shapes of) men and women. Their bonding in (what is referred to as) 'activity' and 'appreciation', that has existed since time before time, (expresses itself in) the pleasure of their joint amorous frolicking. This means that, since the superthought-intentionality of the Victorious One (*rgyal-ba'i dgongs-pa*, one's own ec-static intensity as bliss supreme) has, since time before time, made its presence felt in four pristine awareness modes (delights), you should not reject them but jointly enjoy them as the very dynamics of (the whole system's) pristine awareness (bliss supreme). Becoming quickly emancipated is then a certainty.

There is first of all, though obliquely intimated by the expression 'since time before time' (*ye-nas*), the symmetry break that marks Being's 'virtual', diaphanous (*ka-dag*) and open (*stong-pa*) state coming-to-presence as its 'actual', radiant (*gsal-ba*) and relatively closed) state, the envelope (*sbubs*) into which it wraps itself, which is Being's own being, its 'ownmostness' (*rang-bzhin*), not someone else's. Because of its dynamics (which it has, figuratively speaking, inherited from its virtual state) it actualizes itself in what amounts to a further symmetry break or bifurcation presenting two new possible regimes (*shes-rab* and *thabs/ye-shes*) or structures (man and woman) that as formulated energies are experienced as gods (*lha*) and goddesses (*lha-mo*). Any such symmetry break implies an increase in complexity that carries with it the challenge to 'get to the source or origin of it'. It is here that the woman plays an important role. In her capacity of expressing and being the expression of Being's openness/nothingness (*stong-pa*), a fecund field-like expanse (*dbyings*) and spaciousness (*nam-mkha'*), and a mystery (*gsang*) that the objectivist/reductionist because of his vulgar and derogatory 'nothing-but' way of thinking equates and identifies with her cunt (*bhaga*)[32], she is able to open up the unformed with its immense wealth of open possibilities or, in cognitive terms, to offer a value-perception or appreciative awareness (*shes-rab*) that, far from being merely passive, is active as an inspiration that in its innovativeness is imaged and to be revered as a 'heroine'.[33] Thus it is the woman who inspires and rouses the man to display his activity (*thabs*) that as the total system's dormant pristine awareness (*ye-shes*) is made to express itself in four intensities of delight (*dga'-ba*) that innervate the four dynamic regimes of psychic energy exchange (*'khor-lo*) and in their self-transcendence dissolve in bliss supreme, the original ec-static intensity, metaphorically referred to as the 'super-thought-intentionality of the Victorious One'. This is what, according to Klong-chen rab-'byams-pa[34] is to be understood by the 'knowledge-through-appreciation' empowerment:

> Thus all that comes-to-presence and is interpreted (*snang-srid*) as an environing world and the organismic life-forms in it (*snod-bcud*) and (judged on the basis of its felt qualities) as samsara and nirvāṇa, comes to existence as the auto-presencing of Being's ec-static intensity. In the union, that does not admit of any duality, of this coming-to-presence as (Being's) ceaseless activity (*thabs*) or the male principle (*yab*) and of the openness/nothingness (of Being) as its non-subjectively-appropriating appreciation (*shes-rab*) as the female principle (*yum*), whatever comes-to-presence comes to existence by itself as a friend of the ec-static intensity such that its pristine awareness (of its ec-static intensity as) bliss supreme that goes beyond the scope of the intellect, in its dynamics of emancipating itself from the (four) restrictive postulates of existence and nonexistence, eternalism and nihilism, (is felt and 'known') as four delights. This is what you should know to be the 'knowledge-through-appreciation' empowerment.

The point to note with respect to this empowerment is that in the concrete human situation, a configurational setting, in which men and women relate to and interact with each other, the woman is both an idea and an 'objective' reality that tends, precisely because of this objective presence, to be turned into a mere sex object.[35] Most important, however, is that through this empowerment the student is not made to simply move from one aspect (the 'appreciative' one) to another aspect (the 'pristine awareness' one), as if the one were 'higher' and the other 'lower', but learns to live both harmoniously, that is, mutually enriching, at the same time. In the *Klong-gsal*, a text that is no longer available except for quotations from it in many sNying-thig works, this is intimated by the statement:

> Despising a woman is tantamount to denigrating Being's spaciousness, and
> Withdrawing yourself from pleasure you court the deepest hell.

4. The 'word-and-meaning' empowerment (*tshig-don ngo-sprad-kyi dbang*), often qualified as 'precious' (*rin-po-che*), is peculiar in many respects. The name itself has a much deeper significance than the literal rendering of it. It is an empowerment (*dbang*) that enables the student to encounter, face to face (*ngo-sprod/ngo-sprad*), the subject that is none other than himself (*don*) through the words (*tshig*) spoken to him by his teacher. In this dialogue between teacher and student a rich array of symbols, illustrative images (*dpe*) are used in allegorical presentation (*brda*) as a genuine means of self-discovery, and put to the student in the form of a question. In the words of Klong-chen rab-'byams-pa:[36]

> It is the empowerment (to understand) that the ec-static intensity (*rig-pa*) (on this level where the last trace of any duality has dissolved by) the (progressive intensification of) the four lighting-up phases (*snang-ba*) in (Being's) sheer lucency (*'od-gsal*) (on its way to recover and display its dynamics) having reached its final destiny (*mthar phyin*), has firmly occupied its rightful place (*btsan-sa-zin-pa*) in (what is Being's) envelope of precious spontaneity thereness (*lhun-grub rin-po-che'i sbubs*) as its own bed.

Allegory (*brda*) as an invitation to think further and to 'arrive at', 'firmly take up one's rightful place' in a comprehending innerstanding (in Being's envelope into which it has wrapped itself as its most precious being in the world it encompasses), had been widely used by early rDzogs-chen thinkers, but by the time of Klong-chen rab-'byams-pa it was no longer employed or even understood.[37] His attempt to revive it seems to have failed, all authors after him, if they discuss the empowerments, deal with them in terms of representational thought and consider this last empowerment as a mere confirmation of what had been going on before and speak of it in vague terms.

In conclusion it should be noted that there is an internal logic to the four empowerments such that each subsequent one continues the process of dismantling the traps built into a human being's cybernetic existence and aids him in 'seeing' the world anew, rather than seeing what little he usually perceives in a merely confirmatory manner, as clearly stated by Klong-chen rab-'byams-pa:[38]

> If a person who is so fortunate as to embark on (these empowerments [as steps in his mental-spiritual growth]) does not, right at the beginning, on the level of 'exteriority', cut off the conceptual-propositional thought patterns, the fictions concerning the phenomenal (the without) and the cognitive operation (the egological within) will not be stopped in their proliferations; if, on the level of (his) 'interiority', he does not gather (them) up into the nonconceptual-nonpropositional (dimension of thought), his psychic potential will not set out on (its) path (of enhanced integration and intensified awareness); if, on the level of (his) 'arcane' dimension, he does not cut off (all that went before) by what is still more nonconceptual-nonpropositional, the 'lamps' will not come up to be the path; and if, on the level of (his) 'unsurpassable' reality, he does not encounter Being's beingness in himself by what is utterly nonconceptual-non-propositional, his visionary path would not be bright.

NOTES

1. *sGra-thal 'gyur-ba* (in: *Ati*, vol. 1, pp. 1-205), p. 88.
2. *Theg-mchog* I, p. 231.
3. *Theg-mchog* I, pp. 207f.
4. *Thig-le kun-gsal* (*loc. cit.*), pp. 228f.
5. The *rDzogs-pa chen-po thig-le snang-ba de-kho-na-nyid nges-pa'i rgyud* (in: *rNying-rgyud*, vol. 5, pp. 515-25), p. 516, from which the following quotation is taken, speaks of the four empowerments as the power in the creativity of Being's ec-static intensity (*rig-pa'i rtsal-dbang*)—a force that, according to the *Mu-tig phreng-ba* (in: *Ati*, vol. 2, pp. 417-537), p. 510, is the whole working through us a rivers.

   The *Thig-le kun-gsal* (*loc. cit.*), p. 224 declares of these rivers/empowerments that they have been there in utter completeness since time before time and that one does not have to look for them.

Lastly, the *lHa-rgyud rin-po-che dbang-gi 'khor-lo* (in: : *rNying-rgyud*, vol. 5, pp. 92-112), p. 110 elaborates on this theme by first naming the four great rivers that were in Indian mythology and cosmology believed to descend from Mount Tise (the Kailas) and then pointing out that they serve as metaphors for four empowerments which, however, are not mentioned by name. Thus:

> These four (rivers) come from Mt. Tise;
> Since they flow incessantly they serve as metaphors for empowerments,

and

> Understanding as four pristine awareness modes
> Is the water of the empowerments because of their incessant flow,

and lastly

> These four great rivers of the empowerments
> Because off their incessant flow act as empowerments.

6. *Rong-'grel*, fols. 23b f.
7. *lHa-rgyud rin-po-che dbang-gi 'khor-lo*, p. 93.
8. *Theg-mchog* I, p. 208.
9. *ibid.*, p. 206.
10. *ibid.*, p. 201.
11. *Fragmente*, no. 1785.
12. *Rig-pa rang-shar* (in: *Ati*, vol. 1, pp. 389-855), p. 424.
13. *Bla-yang* I, pp. 115f.; *Zab-yang* I, pp. 78f.
14. Goethe, *Faust I*, "Night".
15. *Bla-yang* I, p. 380; see also Bla-yang I, p. 486 and II, p. 60.
16. Erich Jantsch, *The Self-organizing Universe*, p. 162.
17. *sNang-srid kha-sbyor bdud-rtsi bcud-thig 'khor-ba thog-mtha' gcod-pai, rgyud* (in: *rNying-rgyud*, vol. 5., pp. 525-601), pp. 569, 570.
18. *ibid.*, p. 570.
19. *ibid.*, p. 570.
20. *Bla-yang* I, p. 118; *Zab-yang* I, p. 83.
21. On the hermeneutical interpretation of *kapāla* and *bdud-rtsi* see my *The Creative Vision, s.v.*
22. Goethe, *Faust I*, "Night".
23. *Theg-mchog* II, p. 79.
24. *ibid.*, I, p. 313. See also *mKha'-yang* III, pp. 148, 151, 196ff.
25. *Theg-mchog* I, p. 313; *dGongs-pa zang-thal*, vol. 2, p. 396, vol. 3, p. 319.
26. *Thig-le kun-gsal* (*loc. cit.*), pp. 143 and 145.
27. This dynamics is variously referred to as *byang-(chub) sems* or *thig-le* or *khams*.
28. *Nyi-zla kha-sbyor* (in: *Ati*, vol. 3, pp. 152-233), p. 192. See also *Theg-mchog* II, pp. 79ff.
29. *mKha'-yang* II, pp. 152, 160, 165. While we as human beings are physiologically normalized due to the *kun-rdzob rgyu'i thig-le*, mentally-spiri-

tually we are able to remain part of the dynamics of the whole due to the *gnas-pa don-dam-gyi thig-le*. We may also but it (jokingly?) this way, while the *kun-rdzob rgyu'i thig-le* points to diminished genetic autonomy, the *gnas-pa don-dam-gyi thig-le* points to enhanced genetic autonomy. After all, we are both the whole and only part of it; the whole is never a part over and above the parts as the whole's ostensible organization.

30. *Bla-yang* I, p. 119; *Zab-yang* I, p. 85.
31. *Bla-yang* I, pp. 119f.
32. *mKha'-yang* II, 265.
33. *ibid.*
34. *Zab-yang* I, pp. 85f.
35. *mKha'-yang* II, pp. 271ff.
36. *Zab-yang* I, p. 86.
37. *Zab-yang* I, p. 89. The earlier wide-spread use of allegory is well attested by the *Rig-pa rang-shar* (*loc. cit.*) chapters 38-42, incorporated in the tenth chapter of the *Theg-mchog* and the apparently completely forgotten *Thig-le gsang-ba'i brda'i rgyud* (in: *rNying-rgyud*, vol. 5, pp. 482-92), going back to the time of Vimalamitra and sNyags Jñānakumāra, a disciple of Padmasambhava.
38. *Theg-mchog* I, p. 231.

CHAPTER SIX

THE 'LIGHTING' AND THE 'LAMPS'

> Pure Light scatters its simplicity as an offering to self-existence, that the individual may take sustainment to itself from its substance.
>
> (Hegel, *The Phenomenology of Mind*, p. 701)

In these words Georg Friedrich Wilhelm Hegel has, without ever comprehending their full significance, summed up what in rDzogs-chen (sNying-thig, also spelled sNying-tig) teaching is presented, in a detailed exposition, as the individual's experience of Being's lighting-up (*snang-ba*) that, as pointed out in a previous chapter, is Being's holomovement (*gzhi-snang*), making its presence felt as the first symmetry break occurring in it as the self-transformation of its pure energy/intensity-'stuff' (*ngo-bo, ka-dag*), into its 'ownmost' intensity (or actuality/spontaneity, *rang-bzhin, lhun-grub*) suffused with Being's resonance-intensity (*thugs-rje*) becoming its ec-static (supraconscious) intensity (*rig-pa*). Two points have to be noted and constantly be borne in mind. The one is, ontologically speaking, the 'fact'—Being having become ('made' *factum*) itself its ownmostness—that because of the constitutive and felt presence of its light, a sheer lucency (*'od-gsal*) or, more precisely, a supraluminal light (*'od*) radiating (*gsal*) throughout its spontaneous thereness, we are luminous beings. The other is, experientially speaking, the 'fact' that, because of the felt presence of this light within us, we in our beholdenness to this light are not only capable, but in duty bound to make visible this light through the medium of our visionary organs to the extent that they are alive, which means, alight and so letting the light shine forth as such. This 'as such' is clearly brought out by Klong-chen rab-'byams-pa[1]:

> The lighting-up of this sheer lucency (*'od-gsal-gyi snang-ba*) is not something material-physical (*gzugs-can*) as commonly claimed; by not having anything to do with the infinitesimal building-blocks, the atoms, (of one's physical world and (their) compact (mental) constructs, the categories of substance and

quality (that are the material with which representational thinking operates), it is not subject to disruption and destruction—ravages perpetrated by the four fundamental forces.

This lighting-up of Being's sheer lucency that in us as the *lumen naturale* makes us luminous beings, is, for want of a better term, an intrapsychic process with distinct somatic repercussions. It occurs in a sequence of four auto-intensificatory phases that have been given the code names

1. *chos-nyid mngon-sum-gyi snang-ba* 'the lighting-up that is (the visionary experience of) the immediacy of Being's possibilizing dynamics';
2. *nyams gong 'phel-gyi snang-ba* 'the lighting-up that is (the sensuously felt) progressive self-intensification of vibrations';
3. *rig-pa tshad-phebs-kyi snang-ba* 'the lighting-up that (is 'felt' as) one's ec-static intensity having reached its scope'; and
4. *chos-nyid zad-pa'i snang-ba* 'the lighting-up that is ('felt' to be) the end of Being's possibilizing dynamics'.

The internal logic of this sequence is, as Klong-chen rab-'byams -pa explains[2], such that

> If one does not see Being's possibilizing dynamics in its immediacy as the starting-point (and foundation of one's being), any predisposition for the remaining three phases (in one's growth) to manifest themselves would be lacking; therefore the lighting-up of Being's possibilizing dynamics in its immediacy occurs first in Being as being both the founding and the founded.[3] Through its having become a 'felt' presence one sees the (intrinsic) meaning of all that which constitutes one's concrete reality and (this seeing) is said (to be such that) one has automatically won Being's self-originated pristine awareness.
>
> If, following this (initiatory phase), one does not feelingly preceive the directness (of the impact), one may (expatiate on this experience) with empty words but will not sense the climaxing (of the process). But by feelingly preceiving the (intrinsic) meaning (of all that is) the vibrations (that constitute one's (psychic life) will intensify.

It is important to consolidate the scope of these vibration intensities. If they are not consolidated one will not come to a sensuous experience (of these vibrations) and one will not come to grips with what is and so one has no chance for becoming (spiritually-existentially) awake. But if the scope of these vibration intensities is consolidated, the lighting-up that constitutes the ultimate limit of (one's) ec-static intensity occurs.

Even if this lighting-up of (one's) ec-static intensity has reached its ultimate limits, there would, if it were not to become something other than what it is so far, be no difference from the (finalistic) claim that the triune gestaltism (for Being) is the last word in this matter ('the goal'); nor would there be any difference from the naive, but commonly held, assumption that the entities of one's 'world' defined in terms of substance and quality are the last word (a metaphorical postulate being the 'thing-in-itself'). (The fact is that) (Being's) lighting-up as well as the vibrations (that go with it) subside in Being (itself), which means that, once the egological belief in Being's lighting-up as (something reducible to) infinitesimal building-blocks and compact constructs has gone under, one lives Being's diaphaneity which is the end of the phenomenal, and this is the lighting-up of the end of Being's possibilizing dynamics.

Closer attention to this sequence reveals that each lighting-up phase is self-referential to itself and self-referential with respect to its (the experiencer's) self-development and self-realization—'self' to be understood as authenticity, not as spurious self-aggrandisement—and thus is a phenomenological-hermeneutical account of what Carl Gustav Jung has called the 'process of individuation'. Each phase in the overall process marks a new psychological discovery.

In the code name of the first lighting-up phase the term 'Being's possibilizing dynamics' (*chos-nyid*) has many connotations all of which are suggestive of the 'principle of complementarity' which states that in describing reality we must resort to complementary concepts that exclude each other and yet depend on each other for their very definition. In rDzogs-chen process-oriented thinking this complementarity reflects a 'symmetry break' in the psychic whole (*rig-pa'i ngo-bo*) so that from the experiencer's point of view the one is 'seen' and 'felt' to have the character of an approximation symmetry transformation or break and the other a displacement symmetry transformation or break. Since the individuation process moves in the direction of wholeness attention to that which reflects the approximation symmetry becomes the experiencer's primary concern. Against this background the term *chos-nyid* was understood as a covering both *chos* and *chos-nyid* such that *chos* points to 'meaning(s) in material concreteness' (all the entities, 'physical' and 'mental' that we believe to make up our reality, ultimately reducible to a numbers game) and *chos-nyid* to the 'meaning-mobilizing potential'.[4] This overall complementarity, characteristic of the whole of one's psychic life, involves further complementarities that roughly deal with the observable-and-the-observed and the appreciable-and-'felt' such that 'outer' happenings and 'inner' experiences interact with each other. Following Klong-chen rab-'byams-pa[5] the complexity of complementarity's nuances and interconnected levels of operation can be diagrammed as in Figure 5:

chos ('frozen' intensities)	*chos-nyid* ('vibrant intensities)
'khor-ba (samsara with its individually assessed pleasures and pains)	*myang-'das* (nirvāṇa as the individual's rest from stress and strain)
snang-ba (the phenomenal)	*stong-pa* (the noumenal)
mi-grol-ba (the 'unfree' because of lacking in a vitalizing charge)	*grol-ba* (the 'free' as the system's vector feeling-tone)
dbyings (Being's 'field'-character)	*rig-pa* (the field's excitation or ec-static intensity)

Figure 5

The last complementarity in this listing is, from the perspective of its visionary experience, one of the 'lamps' that will be discussed below.

The second term, *mngon-sum*, originally taken from the Indian logicians' theory of perception and designating the immediacy of a perceptual experience (sensory, conceptual, introspective, and sympathetic), was in rDzogs-chen (sNying-thing) teaching given a novel interpretation that, while preserving the notion of directness and immediacy (*mngon*), was placed into the context of the whole of the living organism. This was conceived of as presenting a hierarchical organization of four dynamic levels that each in its dynamics constituted a stage in the process of the individual's individuation climaxing in the form of a specific energy-intensity, each such stage comprising three (*gsum*) interactional facets.

The four levels or dimensions of the hierarchical organization are referred to as the 'outer', 'inner', 'arcane', and 'unsurpassed-unsurpassable'. Although the term 'levels' suggests some staticness, in their co-ordination these four form a process decribed in the traditional linearity of a 'starting-point' as the tracking down the very foundation of one's being (*gzhi btsa'-ba*), a 'way' as a clearing (*bsal-ba*) and taking stock of the unfolding dimensionality (*tshad gzung-ba*), and a 'resultant' or 'goal' as a new dynamic regime (*'bras-bu*) the starting-point referring to the 'outer' dimension, the way in its dynamics of a clearing to the 'inner' dimension and in its taking stock of the unfolding dimensions to the 'arcane', and the resultant to the 'unsurpassed-unsurpassable'. Within this fourfold (not to be confused with Heidegger's Fourfold, *das Geviert*) the first two dimension are more or less perceptible 'extensions' or intensive magnitudes in space and time, the last two dimensions are 'intensities' becoming ever more unextended: zero equals infinity.

The three facets of the first ('outer') dimension are referred to by the familiar triad of body (*lus*), speech (*ngag*), and mind (*yid/sems*), but the emphasis is on the seemingly latent crucial energy charge (*gnad*)[6] in them, because it is this energy charge that prevents the organism from totally succumbing to the tyranny of the concrete and links it back to the 'intensity' it lost in becoming 'extensive'. This linking backward occurs through the three crucial energy charges operative in the second ('inner') dimension that, as has been pointed out, is a way of clearing away the 'closure' of one's embodied existence and of allowing Being possibilizing dynamics (*chos-nyid*) to reveal itself in its more 'open' dimension as the experiencer's cognitive domain charged with an energy its own (*yul-gyi gnad*). Similarly, just as the 'unspoken' in speech is the energy charge in language, so the bringing to light (*'char-byed*) what is the experiencer's cognitive domain is the crucial energy charge in the experiencer's senses that quite literally are gateways (*sgo'i gnad*) to experiencing by getting on speaking terms with one's outer and inner realities. Lastly, there is the intensity of one's psychic life as 'movement' (*rlung*) and 'intelligence' one's 'ec-static intensity' *rig-pa*), the one the 'carrier' and the other the 'carried', symbolized as the horse and its rider. Psychic life as a combination of 'movement' and 'intelligence' (*rlung-rig*)[7] is the crucial energy charge of our abidingness as spiritual beings (*gnas-pa'i gnad*).

The third ('arcane') dimension as the second aspect of the way as a taking stock of the unfolding dimensions of Being is 'on the way' of leaving extension behind and merging into intensity. Its three facets are one's becoming familiar with intrapsychic transformative happenings (*goms*) that lead to the phase of one's cognitive capacity having reached the limits of its intensity (*tshad-kyi rim*), the maturation (*smin-pa*) as the phase in which the indications of one's 'nearing the end' (*rtags-kyi rim-pa*) are patently 'felt', and the 'ending' itself (*mthar thug*) as the phase where everything is over (*zad-pa'i rim-pa*). The similarity of the 'arcane' dimension with what in Western psychological literature is described as near-death and death experiences is only too obvious. This 'ending' is, on the one hand. the dissolution of one's everyday world, its 'irrealization' —to borrow a term from Carl Gustav Jung, but, on the other hand, it is the 'gathering—a Heideggerian term—of the whole's energy in some supraluminal light frequency that marks the beginning of a new dynamic regime that can, however paradoxically it may sound, be perceived feelingly and hinted at by symbols that are 'the sensuously perceptible *expression of on inner experience*'.[8]

The new dynamic regime as it forms itself is intimated by the fourth ('unsurpassed/unsurpassable') dimension. It first facet is a lighting-up (*snang-ba*) of Being's intensity as a light of supraluminal frequency (*'od*), the second facet is the maturation (*smin-pa*) of this light into 'information' (*thig-le*)[9] according to which the third facet, the completeness (*rdzogs*) of the new regime is formed and manifested as the regime's triune gestaltism (*sku*). The complexity of what in rDzogs-chen (sNying thing) thought is understood by *mngon-(g)sum* can be diagammed as in Figure 6, where for brevity's sake only the Tibetan terms have been given:

The 'outer':	*lus-kyi gnad*	*ngag-gi gnad*	*yid/sems-kyi gnad*
The 'inner':	*chos-nyid* = *yul-gyi gnad*	*'char-byed* = *sgo'i gnad*	*rlung-rig* = *gnas-pa'i gnad*
The 'arcane':	*goms-pa* = *tshad-kyi rim-pa*	*smin-pa* = *rtags-kyi rim-pa*	*mthar thug* = *zad- pa'i rim-pa*
The 'unsurpassed-unsurpassable':	*snang-ba* = *'od*	*smin-pa* = *thig-le*	*rdzogs-pa* = *sku*

Figure 6

The last term, *snang-ba*, in the code term *chos-nyid mngon-sum-gyi snang-ba* alludes to the light character that marks the first facet in the 'unsurpassed-unsurpassable' dimension and then elaborates on its dynamic 'field' character (*dbyings*) with its 'excitation'/intensity (*rig-pa*), as it climaxes in the 'irrealization' of the body and becomes the 'Buddha'-experience (*sangs-rgyas*), this clumsy and concretistic Western term for what is pure process.

The 'lighting-up (that is felt) as an intensification of vibrations' (*nyams gong 'phel-ba'i snang-ba*) is a continuation of the lighting-up discussed before, but differs from it in that attention becomes focused on the vibrations as they become ever more intensified. These vibrations have a dual aspect: the vibrations in the lighting-up itself (*snang-ba' i nyams*) in assuming different oscillation frequencies and forming distinct patterns having distinct colors, and the vector feeling-tones in this psychic energy (*shes-nyams*), such as bliss (*bde-ba*) lucidity (*gsal-ba*), and nondividedness (*mi-rtog-pa*). The 'intensification' (*gong 'phel-ba*) is particularly geared to the auto-patterning of the psychic energy as symbols that point to a 'beyond' intimated by the *ye* in *ye-shes* a 'pristine pre-primordial awareness'.

This lighting-up phase that is still oriented toward images of symbolic significance paves the way for the process becoming ever more centred in itself, that is, for moving from the coded patterns to the coding process. As the penultimate phase in the gathering of the *lumen naturale* in itself and its getting past or jumping out of the whole regress, it is given the code name 'the lighting-up that (is 'felt' as) one's ec-static intensity having reached its scope'. The 'felt' intensity is described as a 'welling up'[10] that is expressive of the intensity in what has traditionally been called 'insight' (*lhag-mthong*, Skt. *vipaśyanā*, and Pali *vipassanā*) in the epistemologically oriented disciplines, but is here redefined as an 'inner-sight' as one of the five aspects of the ec-static intensity.[11] In itself this welling up is a sequence of information bits carrying patterns of infinite rapport with every aspect of one's world and tending to enter into various combinations.[12]

The last 'lighting-up' phase is 'felt' to be the end not only of all phenomena, meanings in material (physical and psychic) concreteness (*chos*), but also of the possibilizing dynamics (*chos-nyid*) underlying them. The 'end' (*zad-pa*) is not a matter of something stopping or its declining into some kind of utter nihility.[13] Rather, it is a matter of completion (*Vollendung*) that in the exhaustion (*ending*) of all possibilities is a gathering of all energies into their most extreme possibility and the beginning of a new, that is *re*-newed dynamic regime, the 'first level' *dang-po'i sa*)[14] at which, in contemporary language, evolution is poised and in which all creative processes are rooted. Certainly, this first level has nothing to do with the classical idea of a *telos*, the place or locus of some thing's static perfection (*Vollkommenheit*). In brief, the 'end' (*zad-sa*) is the 'beginning' (*dang po'i sa*), together forming a spherical vortex, a spiral that, instead of ending, joins up with itself by moving through its own middle and that has neither beginning nor end.

In conclusion, it cannot be emphasized too strongly that the four 'lighting-up' phases are not to be construed as objective facts, they are phenomenological descriptions of a person's experience of dying as a 'transition' into a new dimension of being more intensively alive.

The metaphor of a 'lamp' plays a prominent role not only because of its relationship to the lighting-up of one's luminous being, but also because its image arouses imaginative reflections that will result in new insights into and a deeper understanding as an 'innerstanding' of what is symbolized by this image. Basically, the metaphorical expression of a lamp points to the dynamic light character (*Lichthaftigkeit*) of the universe so that one can say that whatever presences owes it existence to light, the pulsing of electric and magnetic fields, the one setting up the other and so on and so forth, and the frequency of their vibrations determining the color and, beyond that, the rich world of forms as process structures. However, to speak of 'light' in the rDzogs-chen context, is tantamount to speaking of 'cognition'. If light is the primary 'stuff' (*Urstoff*)—to use a word that with its old-established connotation of something solid easily lends itself to be misunderstood as supporting some materialistic reductionism—of which the universe including ourselves is constituted, then cognition, too, is primary and, in this sense, a pristine (*ursprünglich*) awareness (*ye-shes*) that allows for and makes possible formalizations of experiential patterns. It would be extremely helpful if one could understand 'awareness' in a verbal sense as an 'awaring' inasmuch as this pristine awareness is not only a process (a 'way') of understanding, but also a certain manner of seeing which for all practical purposes has as its starting-point the eye.[15] The eye that 'sees' does not exist apart from its cognitive domain: light and eye codetermine each other and what we call the eye is therefore nothing solid, but a dynamic regime. As such a dynamic regime the eye is termed *spyan*—the eye that 'sees' in contradistinction to *mig*—the eye as an object removed from its living context.

From a dynamic perspective the following equation derives :

light ←——→	pristine awareness ←——→	lamp ←——→	eye
(*'od-gsal*)	(*ye-shes*)	(*sgron-ma*)	(*spyan*)

Because of their identity the various combinations or, more precisely, permutations in which these terms occur, are to be understood in an associative, rather than a sequential, manner. This seems to be intimated by the statement[16]:

> The eye (that sees, *spyan*), a lamp (*sgron-ma*) that never goes out,

In order to understand the intimate relationship between the 'lighting' and the 'lamps' we have to keep in mind that the fundamental forces that form and constitute our concrete being are experienced in terms of luminosities (*'od*) and have in addition to their 'radiation-dominated' (*dvangs-ma*) aspect also a 'matter-dominated' aspect (*snyigs-ma*) and a 'mixed' aspect, which means that these forces as vibration patterns come in various observable frequencies. This is intimated in the following passage[17]:

> The superb lamp (shimmering in) five luminosities (that present the) radiation-dominated aspect (of the fundamental forces, *dvangs-ma 'od-lnga*).

Furthermore, the description of these fundamental forces in terms of solids that are no solids—('earth' that has no firmness, 'water' that has no moisture, 'fire' that has no heat, 'wind' that has no movement, and 'sky/space' that has effulgence but no encompassing ability)[18] suggests that in their copresence with each other and their mutual interpenetration[19] they may interfere constructively. In this case their energy adds up to an extra brightness, metaphorically referred to as 'lamp'. If they interfere destructively the result is the prevailing opacity and darkness of one's material existence with the proviso that our live body constituted of flesh and blood is a mixture of radiation-dominated and matter-dominated forces. Although for descriptive purposes this distinction between radiation and matter is useful, it does not imply an unbridgeable gulf between the cognitive and the bodily, rather it points to degrees of clarity within the system as a whole. The fluidity of the facets in the above equation may be illustrated by two quotations from two different works. The one[20] states:

> The pristine awareness as moisture (*ye-shes rlan*) pervades the body's freshness (*bkrag*) and brilliance (*gzi-mdangs*),

and the other[21] declares:

> The motility (force, *rlung*) that brings about freshness and brilliance
> Pervades the body as a whole and
> Is called the 'pervading motility'
> It brings out the body's luxuriant freshness and brilliance.

The subtly intimated permutation of pristine awareness (*yeshes*) and luminosities (*'od*) as protopatternings of the fundamental forces (*'byung-ba*) is explicitly stated in the following manner[22]:

> Thus, through the stirring of the creative dynamics in the pristine awareness (*ye-shes*) in the vibrant dimension of Being's nothingness five luminosities (*'od*) come into

> existence. Since in them the ec-static intensity of Being's cognitiveness (*rig-pa*) is present there occurs a (subjective) appropriation (*'dzin-pa*) of these five light qualities. This subjective appropriation is termed motility (*rlung*). It is the sallying forth of the creative dynamics in Being's resonance as an inner lucency into an outer (dimension).

The multivalence of what is termed 'lamp' results in their being assessed numerically such that one counted up to nine lamps. However, behind this numbering different approaches to what they presented are discernible.

Ever so often reference has been made to Being's ec-static (cognitive) intensity (*rig-pa*) as its or any other system's self-organization dynamics of material and energetic processes as well as its reaching beyond the particular system through which it is operative. This very intensity as a dynamic principle manifests itself in a concrete system such as a human being in distinct functions with respect to the emerging levels of the system's evolution in the direction of its optimization and heightened 'seeing' ability which ultimately is nothing but that with what the system's evolution has started.[23]

A human being's evolutionary starting-point (*gzhi*) is the spontaneity (*lhun-grub*) of Being's potential—the raw material out of which the whole of our reality and we ourselves as an integral aspect are fashioned—that in this felt presence is already on the way to its actualization, its 'ownmost' being (*rang-bzhin*) as the 'Buddha'-experience (*sangs-rgyas*). The dynamics in the thrust toward optimization is experienced in the ec-static intensity (*rig-pa*) of highest rapture (*bde-ba*) that, quite literally, like a lamp illumines the experiencer's universe. It is a light that is as much 'in us' as it is 'out there'. Accordingly, for descriptive purposes a distinction is made between the 'lamp that is Being' (*gzhi'i sgron-ma*) as the overall self-organizing thrust and its inherent ec-static intensity and the 'lamp that is (one's) flesh that houses Being's dynamics as (one's deeply felt) spirituality' (*tsitta sha'i sgron-ma*). Depending on the emphasis on either facet these two lamps are listed in different orders.[24]

The term *tsitta sha'i sgron-ma* is itself a code name for a complex interplay between different levels of the individual's hierarchical organization. One of these levels, referred to by 'flesh' (*sha*), recognizes the physical (biological) nature of the human individual as an integral aspect of his existence and the further specification of it as one's heart (*snying*) points to what is may be the most important energy exchange center in the live body. The heart is usually conceived of as the organic blood pump that is at the center of the vital circulatory system. But more significant is its metaphorical extension such that one can speak of the heart as being simultaneously a subsystem—the individual's biological and personal center—and a supra-ordinate system that reaches beyond the merely biological and personal, although it remains rooted or 'located' in (*nang*) the subsystem, picturesquely illustrated by a flame (*mar-me*) spreading its light from within a container.[25] This supraordinate system is called *tsitta* which is the Tibetan spelling of the Sanskrit word *citta* ('mind/mentation') that in the sNying-tig context has lost its original granular character and become the infrastructure of what is observed as conscious processes. This *tsitta* is imaged as a 'precious palace' (*rin-po-che'i gzhal-yas*)[26], or as a 'precious envelope' (*rin-po-che'i sbubs*)[27]. The image of an envelope serves to illustrate Being's infinity closing in on itself and wrapping itself, doughnut-like, as it were, around itself, thus constituting the concrete individual's infinite finitude. Imaged as a palace the *tsitta* is octahedronal,[28] intimating its relatedness to the eight perceptual patterns that sum up the structure of consciousness as one of the outstanding characteristics seen against the background of the whole's fivefold morphic resonance domain that are imaged as having a gestalt quality (*sku*) that expresses and is the expression of the system's pristine awareness modes (*ye-shes*), each having its own delicate and calm luster (*'od*).

While this lamp may be said to present a master plan for the emergence of a new way of seeing, the third lamp—'the lamp that presents a chreod that is white in color and silky in texture' (*dkar-'jam rtsa'i sgron-ma*)[29]—simultaneously illumines and is the way along which the system's auto-effulgent pristine awareness is channelled from the 'heart' to the eyes that see. Just as a person cannot 'think' without 'having a heart', so also a person cannot see without the heart.[30] This lamp is pictured and seen from the outside as a white silk thread that is inwardly hollow and hence offers no obstacle to the movement of the pristine awareness.

The fourth lamp which is counted as the first in a different set of lamps that seems to have superseded the probably older sNying-tig tradition, is called 'the distance-capturing and filtering lamp' (*rgyang-zhags chu'i sgron-ma*). Its name is descriptive of the process of becoming consciously aware without, however, being any specific conscious awareness. It still operates in the realm of possibilities. This is evident from its definition[32] :

> *rgyang* (distance) means that on the stallion of the five senses
> The subjective mind as rider sallies forth and
> Enters all the cognitive domains to gather what they have to offer.
> *zhags* (fetter) means that appropriating mentation takes in the 'look' of the domains to be appropriated.
> *chu* (water) means that it separates the radiation-'stuff' from the matter-'stuff' in them.
> Moreover, (this lamp) is equally present in both (eyes);
> In brief, it is the light of which the senses are constituted.

This lamp is constituted by the radiation-dominated 'stuff' in the four fundamental forces that through the combination of the creative dynamics in them bring about the organismic life forms (*bcud*) presenting the 'internal' organization of what presences as mentation (*sems-snang*) in the 'external', environmental (*snod*) organization that presences as objective domains (*yul-snang*). Because of its implicit concretization into 'things', this is considered to be the going astray of mentation into mistaken identification (*sems-kyi 'khrul-pa*).[33] It is precisely because of its having been constituted by the fundamental forces that tend to become ever more matter-dominated, that this lamp participatingly illumines and is the light in these forces and, shaping itself, as it were, into the sensory operations such that, for instance, it illuminingly appropriates forms and shapes (with which vision is concerned) in their quality of presenting a structured nothingness (*stong-(pa'i) gzugs*), while it also perceives ('sees') the dynamics of Being's sheer lucency as it pulses in the light chreods (*'od-rtsa*) and thereby is capable of dissolving the opacity (of the ordinary perception of things) into the translucency of gestalt awareness modes.[34]

Although these four lamps as discussed in this order suggest an evolutionary process, they are still considered to be the complex starting-point of the individual's development into a fully conscious, more precisely, supraconscious being. The idea of a starting-point carries with it the notions of a path and a goal. Accordingly, Klong-chen rab-'byams-pa speaks of the path as the time it takes to reach one's goal[35] and calls this fifth lamp 'the lamp that is time in presenting a phase transition' (*bar-do dus-kyi sgron-ma*). In modern terms, this lamp is a space- and time-binding process. Klong-chen rab-'byams-pa explicates this lamp as the recognition of what Being's holomovement is in itself in its presencing itself in the unitary experience of its gestalt and its pristine awareness mode which points to the rich potential in the beginning of one's life. It is illustrated by the image of meeting someone whom one has known before, which in spite of its familiarity turns out to be a novel experience. A more intimate image for what is the linking backward to the origin is that of the reunion of a child with its mother.[36]

The sixth lamp is called *mthar-thug 'bras-bu'i sgron-ma* which on the basis of its terse explanation[37] may be rendered as 'the lamp that presents the climax of the evolution of consciousness such that in it Being's ec-static intensity has come into full play'.

While, as has been shown, both the *Zab-yang* ann *Bla-yang* give a fairly identical account of the first four lamps, the fifth lamp is not mentioned at all in *Bla-yang*, and the sixth lamp listed as a fifth lamp is given the name *'od-gsal ye-shes-kyi sgron-ma* 'the lamp that is Being's sheer lucency in its dynamics as pristine awareness (modes)' and described as an indepth apprai-sal that derives from the steadiness of Being's sheer lucency in what is the experiencer's existence.[38]

The 'distance-capturing and filtering lamp' that enables the experiencer to have a fresh vision of his reality, is again listed in a set of four lamps, apparently belonging to a different tradition within rDzogs-chen thought that is far from monolithic. This set of four lamps can be broken down into two subsets that are complementary to each other. The first subset may be said to be concerned with 'pure' (*ji-lta-ba*) vision which, however, in this its pure form occurs very rarely because it is almost always intertwined with 'patterned' (*ji-snyed-pa*) vision with which the other subset is concerned. I use the term 'pure' in an attempt to emphasize the point that this vision is not a vision *of* something, but a self-reflexive 'seeing of seeing'. This pure vision is described as follows:[40]

> Just as the orb of the sun fades away
> In the vortex of space, a dynamic nothingness (*nam-mkha' stong-pa'i klong-dkyil-du*),
> So in the clear sky that is nothing (*rnam-dag stong-pa'i nam-mkha'-la*)
> Two kinds of lamps ceaselessly fade away,

and[41]:

> Since in the vortex of space, a dynamic nothingness,
> Two kinds of lamps are ceaselessly (shining),
> Their brilliance without (becoming) fragmented into the objects (of representational thinking)
> Comes-to-presence in its self-emergent and self-risen (dynamics),

and[42] with special mention of the two kinds of lamps:

> In the vortex of space, a dynamic nothingness,
> Two kinds of lamps are ceaselessly (shining),
> Let (Being's) ec-static intensity (operating in you) rest on each:
> The invariance-disclosure-nothingness lamp (*thig-le stong-pa'i sgron-ma*) is (Being's) gestaltism in its indestructibility (*rdo-rje'i sku*) and
> The ec-static intensity-field lamp (*rig-pa dbyings-kyi sgron-ma*) is (Being's self-)spatialization as the (clear) sky that is nothing.
> Like the vowel sign *o*
> (These two lamps engulf) the living beings (by) being pervasive of them,

The multivalent technical term *thig-le*, here renderd 'invariance-disclosure' on the basis of its hermeneutical assessment in original texts,[43] indicates an autostructuring process that in its invariance is virtual and in its disclosure actual at the same time. It is virtual (*gzhi-gnas*) because it is 'pure' intensity (*rig-pa*) and as such operative on a scale that is far superior to ordinary imagination and seems to be constantly active in restructuring one's existence and life to its own design. It is actual because on the physical embodiment level (*lus-gnas*) it contains the structural and functional information necessary for the aliveness of the whole organism. In particular, on what is called the lower-order commonly accepted level of reality (*kun-rdzob*), it contains the gametes, the spermatozoa and the ova (referred to as *pha'i thig-le* 'the father's reproductive fluid' and *ma'i thig-le* 'the mother's reproductive fluid') whose fusion initiates the formation of a living being's physical shape,[44] and on what is called the higher-order level of reality (*don-dam*), the 'ordering principle or intelligence' in the biological raw material—these two levels presenting a coordinated hierarchy, not a stratified or control hierarchy. Lastly, it indicates the self-kindled realization level (*rang-byung 'bras-bu*) on which what has been virtually present has actually come into full play.[45]

Similarly, the technical term *dbyings*, here rendered by 'field', is defined as that which sets itself up as the cognitive domain of its ec-static intensity and as the blueprint of whatever is going to come-to-presence, and it is spoken of as a lamp because it illumines the (unity of) what is coming-to-presence (the welling-up of the field's excitation in becoming a gestalt) and its ec-static cognition. One important consequence of the interrelationship and mutual pervasiveness of the two lamps is that the field lamp restrains the welling-up of the invariance-disclosure lamp within its encompassing dimension and prevents it from losing itself in mistaken identifications[46] and that the welling-up cannot be considered in isolation from its field.

Inasmuch as what is termed gestaltism (*sku*), be this with reference to the whole (Being) or to any of its parts (such as a living being), is the expression and the expressed of a cognitive act, in its subtle nuances variously called 'ec-static intensity' (*rig-pa*) or 'pristine awareness' (*ye-shes*), by attending to the gestalt whose invariance may become the dominant content in the experiencing process, its character of actually being a lamp may be lost to view. Thus, it has been stated:[47]

> The invariance-disclosure-nothingness lamp is associated with a mind that is bestirring itself (in attracting attention);
> Since there is such bestirring, the lamp (character) of what it actually is about is not understood.

The ec-static intensity-field lamp
Is dissociated from a mind that is so bestirring itself and
As (a) pristine awareness roams over its field.

That these two lamps operate on a presubjective level is also succinctly stated:[48]

In the sky, an auto-presencing without becoming attached to something
Two kinds of lamps shine brightly without desiring anything.

The fourth lamp in the set of four lamps is significantly called *shes-rab rang-byung-gi sgron-ma* 'the self-kindled intensely appreciative acumen lamp' and has been detailed as implying the following:[49]

Like a burning lamp with its all-consuming flame (*sreg-byed me-sgron*):
shes (indicates the) understanding of all that is in one swoop (and)
rab (indicates its) peak (character) towering over the whole;
rang (indicates its being) independent of anything else; and
byung (indicates its) irrepressible and copious shining.

Together the above mentioned distance-capturing and filtering lamp and the self-kindled intensely appreciative acumen lamp are concerned with what we have paraphrased as 'patterned vision' (*ji-snyed-pa*). The listing of the four lamps in the sequence as detailed in their overall discussion is not fortuitous; rather it presents a circularity that is characteristic of all life processes. Somehow we start from the whole of which we get a glimpse by the distance-capturing and filtering lamp, to follow it up by turning inward to the very dynamics of one's being in the complementarity of the invariance-disclosure-nothingness lamp and ec-static intensity-field lamp, and finally to see the whole from the perspective of the whole mediated by the self-kindled intensely appreciative acumen lamp and through this mediation to become the whole.

The creative character of all these lamps, deriving directly from their being formulation of the fundamental forces, is tersely stated[50] to be such that the distance-capturing and filtering lamp initiates the awareness of the luminosity (*'od*) of Being's possibilizing dynamics, the invariance-disclosure-nothingness lamp the gestalt quality (*sku*) of the total experience and the ec-static intensity-field lamp its pristine awareness (*ye-shes*), and the self-kindled intensely appreciative acumen lamp the very ec-static intensity (*rig-pa*) that marked the beginning of the evolutionary process. We may say that we have come full circle, but at this level of supraconsciousness there are no longer individual 'lamps', but an intricate and interweaving web of such 'lamps' that point to ever farther-reaching dimensions.

The total of nine lamps, reflecting different trends in rDzogs-chen thought, the specific sNying-tig teaching and the overall rDzogs-chen presentation, can be diagrammed as follows in Figure 7. For brevity's sake their Tibetan names have been retained:

The sNying-tig version

Zab-yang listing:		*Bla-yang* listing:
(starting-point)	1. *gnas-pa gzhi'i sgron-ma*	2. *gzhi'i sgron-ma*
	2. *tsitta sha'i sgron-ma*	1. *tsitta sha'i sgron-ma*
	3. *dkar-'jam rtsa'i sgron ma*	3. *dkar-'jam rtsa'i sgron-ma*
	4. *rgyang-zhags chu'i sgron-ma* (=I in the set of four in the overall rDzogs-chen-version)	4. *rgyang-zhags chu'i sgron-ma*
(path)		
(goal)	5. *bar-do dus-kyi sgron-ma*	
	6. *'bras-bu'i sgron-ma*	5. *'od-gsal ye-shes-kyi sgron-ma*

The overall rDzogs-chen version

I (the same as number 4 in the *Zab-yang* and *Bla-yang* listings)

7. II *dbyings rnam-dag-gi sgron-ma* (*dbyings rnam-par dag-pa'i sgron-ma, rig-pa dbyings-kyi sgron-ma*)
8. III *thig-le stong-pa'i sgron-ma*
9. IV *shes-rab rang-byung-gi sgron-ma*

(It should be noted that this sequence is not absolute.)

Figure 7

Inasmuch as all lamps are formulations of the four fundamental forces that constitute our physical universe as well as ourselves such that the 'without' and the 'within', the quantitative, physical/material (*snod*) and the semiqualitative, the emotional/behavioral (*bcud*), occur in co-evolution with each other, these lamps are biological phenomena expressed linguistically by metaphors.[51]

NOTES

1. *Theg-mchog* II, p. 223.
2. *Theg-mchog* II, pp. 220f.
3. The differentiation between the founding (*rten*) and the founded (*brten*) reflects the recognition of the system's gestalt (*sku*) being a fundamental ground or zero-point (a *Boden* or *Urpunkt*) for the operation of the system's pristine awareness (*ye-shes*) that has singled out this gestalt as the 'embodiment' of its psychic dynamics.
4. *Theg-mchog* II, pp. 220f.; *Tshig-don*, p. 390; *Bla-yang* I, p. 376.
5. *Theg-mchog* II, p. 221f.
6. The technical term *gnad* is difficult to translate; it points to that what makes something 'tick', the cardinal charge in it. Without going into details it may suffice to point out that the idea of *gnad* has nothing to do with any form of vitalism.
7. Klong-chen rab-'byams-pa has drawn an important distinction between *rlung-sems* (*Yid-bzhin*, pp. 681, 683-86) and *rlung-rig* (*Bla-yang* II, p. 90; *Theg-mchog* II, p. 217; *Tshig-don*, p. 377). In either case *rlung*, compared with a horse, is a metaphor for what in psychoanalytical literature is termed 'libido'. It carries its rider, the individual's 'mind' (*sems*) wherever it wants to do, mostly into the opposite direction of where the rider would like to go. By contrast, *rlung-rig* points to the separation of the spiritual (*rig*) from the instinctive (*rlung*).
8. C.G. Jung, *Letters* I, p. 59, quoted in Marie-Louise von Franz, *Projection and Re-collection in Jungian Psychology*, p. 82.
9. *thig-le*. On the many meanings and applications of this technical term see my *Matrix of Mystery*, *s.v.* In its most rudimentary form it may be compared to the DNA molecule as a kind of 'program' of the organism's (the individual's) development.
10. *lu-gu rgyud*, short for *rdo-rje lu-gu rgyud* or *rig-pa rdo-rje lu-gu rgyud*. A detailed description has been given in *Theg-mchog* II, p. 220 (=vol. 2, pp. 164ff. in Dodubche's edition). See also my *Matrix of Mystery*, p. 244 n. 64.
11. The five aspects or, maybe we should say, functional variations of this intensity (*rig-pa*) are briefly mentioned in *Bla-yang* II, p. 114 and *Bi-ma snying-thig* I, pp. 420-22.
12. *'brel-pa*. The ideas of a universal connectedness and of an entering into connection are very old in Buddhism. With the Indo-Tibetan preoccupa-

tion with numbers quite an array of such combinations are given. In the *Chos thams-cad rdzogs-pa chen-po byang-chub-kyi sems-su 'dus-pa'i mdo* (in: *rNying-rgyud*, vol. 1, pp. 320-43), a collection of small texts, on pp. 329-31, ten paired connections are given:

(1) the presencing of the phenomenal and its interpretation (*snang* = *srid*);

(2) the environing world and the organismic beings in it (*snod* = *bcud*);

(3) samsara and nirvana (*'khor-ba* = *mya-ngan-'das*);

(4) cause and effect (*rgyu*=*'bras*);

(5) sense objects and the senses (*yul*=*dbang-po*);

(6) expertise and discernment (*thabs*= *shes-rab*);
(Being's) field and (its) pristine awareness (*dbyings*=*ye-shes*);

(7) higher order reality and conventionally accepted reality (*don-dam*=*kun-rdzob*);

(8) mind and ideas (*sems*= *chos*);

(9) a Buddha and a sentient being (*sangs-rgyas*= *sems-can*); and

(10) (a person's) existentiality and (his) ownmostness (*rgyud*=*rang-bzhin*).

A triadic combination is (Being's) dynamics as starting-point, path, and goal (*Theg-mchog* II, p. 372), from another perspective the excitation of Being's field (*dbyings-rig*), the movement (in it as) pristine awareness modes (*ye-shes-kyi rlung*), and (its presence as) sheer lucency (*'od-gsal*). See *Theg-mchog* II, p. 324; *Tshig-don*, p. 390. A fivefold combination results in the five pristine awareness modes (*ye-shes lnga*). See *Tshig-don*, pp. 393f.

13. *Tshig-don*, p. 398.
14. *Tshig-don*, p. 397.
15. As we now know, seeing is not merely some passive registering of data on a light-sensitive retina, but much more an active shaping (*gestalten*) in which subjective and objective features, one's bodily organism, itself a sense organ over which all other senses are spread out, and one's environment, combine.
16. *Seng-ge rtsal rdzogs* (in: *Ati*, vol. 2, pp. 245-415), p. 258. Other statements to the same effect are:

    The pristine awareness as a lamp (*sgron-ma'i ye-shes*), the superb eye (*spyan*)
    (*ibid.*, p. 362)

    and

    The pristine awareness (as a function of Being's) ec-static intensity (*rig-pa'i ye-shes*) as a lamp (*sgron-ma*)
    (*ibid.*, p. 316)

    and

    The eye (that sees) as a lamp (*sgron-ma'i spyan*).
    (*Tshig-don*, pp. 201-03).

17. *Seng-ge rtsal-rdzogs*, p. 362.
18. *Zab-yang* II, p. 255; *Thig-le kun-gsal*, p. 158.
19. *Mu-tig phreng-ba*, p. 499.

20. *sGra-thal 'gyur-ba*, p. 110.
21. *Thig-le kun-gsal*, p. 261.
22. *mKha'-yang* II, p. 161 and in almost identical terms in *mKha'-snying* II, p. 71.
23. The various stages in this self-organizing process have been symbolically represented, in what seems to have been the sNying-thig teaching proper as presented by Klong-chen rab-'byams-pa in his *Zab-yang* and *Bla-yang* before it was incorporated in the overall rDzogs-chen teaching as presented by Klong-chen rab-'byams-pa in his other writings, specifically the *Theg-mchog* and *Tshig-don*, by five or six lamps.
24. In *Zab-yang* II, pp. 138f., where the *gzhi'i sgron-ma* is mentioned first because in this text the emphasis is on the overall evolutionary process and its unfoldment, and in *Bla-yang* II, pp. 246f., where the *tsitta sha'i sgron-ma* is listed first because here the emphasis is on the individual's experience of the salient feature of what is meant and felt by *sgron-ma*.
25. *Zab-yang* II, p. 138; *mKha'-yang* II, p. 378.
26. *mKha'-snying* I, p. 29; *rin-chen gzhal-yas* in *sGra-thal 'gyur-ba*, pp. 111, 126; *Seng-ge rtsal-rdzogs*, p. 258.
27. *mKha'-yang* II, pp. 267, 328.
28. *mKha'-snying* I, p. 62.
29. *Zab-yang* II, p. 140; *Bla-yang* II, p. 247.
30. See also Stephan Strasser, *Phenomenology of Feeling*, p. 7.
31. Its hollowness and its being a way is expressly stated in the *Thig-le kun-gsal*, p. 251, where its name is accordingly given as *dkar-'jam khog-pa stong-pa'i rtsa* 'the white and silky and hollow chreod', and as *dkar-'jam stong-pa'i rtsa* in the *Rig-pa rang-shar*, p. 609.
32. *Mu-tig phreng-ba*, p. 499.
33. *Theg-mchog* I, p. 75.
34. *Theg-mchog* II, p. 92.
35. *Zab-yang* II, p. 141.
36. *Tshig-don*, p. 350; *gNas-lugs*, p. 110 where the intimacy of their union is emphasized.
37. *Zab-yang* II, p. 142.
38. *Bla-yang* II, p. 247.
39. *Rig-pa rang-shar*, pp. 527, 533, 560, 628; *sGra-thal-'gyur-ba*, pp. 114, 168; *Nyi-zla kha-sbyor*, p. 208; *Bla-yang* I, pp. 299f., 461, 484, II, pp. 246f., *mKha'-yang* II, pp. 215, 391, III, pp. 94, 96.
40. *Rig-pa rang-shar*, p. 536.
41. *ibid.*, pp. 558-9.
42. *ibid.*, p. 490.
43. *Mu-tig phreng-ba*, p. 497; *sGron-ma 'bar-ba*, p. 301.
44. *Theg-mchog* II, p. 80.
45. *Tshig-don*, p. 266.
46. *Theg-mchog* II, p. 21.
47. *Rig-pa rang-shar*, p. 491.
48. *Seng-ge rtsal-rdzogs*, p. 265.
49. *Mu-tig phreng-ba*, p. 498.

50. *Tshig-don*, p. 207; *Theg-mchog* I, pp. 359f.
51. Their biological character is plainly indicated by Khrag-thung Rol-pa'i rdo-rje who in his *gNas-lugs rang-byung-gi rgyud rdo-rje snying-po* (pp. 591ff.) speaks of six lamps and assigns the lamps nos. 2, 3, and 4 in the above figure to the physical/material, and the lamps II, III, and IV to the emotional/behavioral.

Chapter Seven

RTSE-LE RGOD-TSHANS-PA SNA-TSHOGS RANG-GROL'S 'THE SUN'S LIFE-GIVING FORCE'

rTse-le rGod-tshangs-pa sna-tshogs rang-grol, also known as Padma legs-grub and Karma rig-'dzin rnam-par rgyal-ba, was born in the year 1608 in a village on the border of Kong-po and Dwags-po. The year and place of his death are unknown. In his youth he studied with eminent teachers belonging to the bKa'-brgyud (especially the Bhutanese dKar-brgyud) and rNying-ma traditions which he attempted to harmonize. In this attempt he rises far above his contemporaries who for the most part endulged in futile and acrimoniously conducted doctrinal disputes. He is not an innovator and also does not want to be one. He draws heavily on his predecessors and condenses their often extremely lengthy presentations in a lucid manner.

THE SUN'S LIFE-GIVING FORCE OR THE EXPLANATION OF THE INTRINSIC MEANING OF THE INDESTRUCTIBLE LIGHT THAT IS THE SUBLIME AND MOST MYSTERIOUS AND UNSURPASSABLE MESSAGE OF ALL SPIRITUAL PURSUITS

Homage to the primordial Buddha-experience that is one's own mind[1]

Overarching, all-enfolding, from its beginning a primordial process of (darkness) dissipating and (light) expanding, of twofold purity[2]—the gestalt embodying Being's meaningfulness (*chos-sku*);

In its actuality/ownmostness (*rang-bzhin*), spontaneous, ceaseless, auto-luminescent, performing a variety of dances in peaceful and ferocious roles—the gestalt of Being's contextualized horizon of meaning (*longs-spyod-rdzogs*);

A wondrous resonance, wise in fulfilling the expectations of myriads of living beings by its dancing like the moon on

water—the gestalt of Being serving as a guiding image (*sprul-pa'i sku*);
In the true sense, indivisible, Being's beingness/energy-'stuff' gestalt (*ngo-bo-nyid sku*), famed as the guide supreme, splendorous and incomparable—may (this quaternity) take care of me.

What could be greater than this most profound rDzogs-chen that is the
Most supreme elixir extracted from what is the quintessence of the many teachings in the
Various pursuits that take into account the sundry distinct
Capabilities and predispositions of those to be guided, unfathomable by ordinary thought?

Although there may be plenty of steps linking up directly
With the basis of the way, the way itself, and the destination (to which the way leads),
Why would an intelligent person who is capable of linking himself to what is utterly certain
Not take the step to enter into (this process)?

Those of little intelligence chase after what is 'so profound' and what is '(assumed to) be so'
Like deer after the water in a mirage; although they may run after it for hundreds of aeons,
Apart from augmenting their torment they will never find any peace.
You must therefore plumb the depth of the ocean of life's meaning.

Here I shall present an accurate summary of the purpose of
The essence of all essences (*snying-thig*), the crucible of quick and profound instructions,
The supreme path that, in this one's lifetime, can bring to the fore an utter pellucidity and
Appear for living beings in the manner of a dancer in resonance with the whole (of Being).

Furthermore, this rDzogs-chen teaching that has reached the limits of all spiritual pursuits like the finial ornament crowning a royal banner in the center of a vast range of procedures that are the infinitely far-reaching modalities of the benign actions (*'phrin-las*)[3] of the Victorious ones and their sons, involves the following:

(a) an outer (aspect) or 'mentality' (*sems*) section,
(b) an inner (aspect) or 'vortex' (*klong*) section,
(c) an arcane (aspect) or 'information' (*man-ngag*) section, and
(d) a still more arcane (aspect) or unsurpassable (*bla-na-med-pa*) section.

The best among these four sections is the crucible that contains the very quintessence of what is most profound, a fine blend of existential instructions on (Being's) overall purposing laid out in the great class of Tantras belonging to the unsurpassable section. In very concise terms I shall summarize the meaning of the *snying-thig* which is more arcane than anything arcane, by outlining the three phases through which it progressively unfolds:

1. A general explication of how, by way of Being as ground and starting point (*gzhi*), diaphaneous and spontaneous, one may either go astray into samsara or rediscover one's freedom;
2. A detailed explication of how one is going to experience the way (*lam*) through instructions in the barrier-free (*khregs-chod*) and final-leap (*thod-rgal*) approaches;
3. A concluding summary that explicates how to reach the climax (*'bras-bu*) which is (experienced as the inseparability of Being's) gestalt dynamics (*sku*) and its pristine awareness (*ye-shes*).

1

The first (topic, the general explication) comprises

1.1 The ground or Being (*gzhi*) as it is believed, from a biased perspective, to be something (thematically) knowable, and

1.2 The ground or Being as Being's abidingness (*gnas-lugs*) in its diaphaneity.[4]

1.1

This involves the six claims that Being is either (i) spontaneous (*lhun-grub*), or (ii) indeterminate (*ma-nges-pa*), or (iii) determinate (*nges-pa*), or (iv) can be changed into anything whatsoever (*cir yang bsgyur btub*), or (v) is compatible with any state of affairs (*gang-du yang khas blang-du rung-ba*), or (vi) kaleidoscopic (*khra-bo*). Thus, each of these six 'masks' (*rnam-pa*) of Being is said to involve the fallacy of giving a one-sided view of Being. What are the reasons for their fallaciousness?

(i) If Being is claimed to be spontaneous in the sense of being such that defects and virtues have both been there since their very beginning, there is no point in trying to experience it as one's way since it contradicts Being's diaphaneity (*ka-dag*) and, even if one were to do so, there would still exist the defect of freedom being pointless.[5]

(ii) If Being is claimed to be indeterminate such that it could become anything one might intellectually postulate it to become, it follows that any moment freedom could turn into errancy;

(iii) If Being is claimed to be determinate it would never undergo any change, which implies that the grime of unknowing could never be removed;

(iv) If Being is claimed to be changeable into anything whatsoever (at any time), it follows that there can be no stability and that freedom as the (ultimate) effect (of one's striving) would turn again into its (initiating) cause;

(v) If Being is claimed to be compatible with any state of affairs it follows that, since you cannot discover anything substantial about it or anything of a foundation to rest on, you will have to accept the fiction of either eternalism or nihilism.

(vi) If Being is claimed to be kaleidoscopic it follows that its purity could never serve as an emancipatory incentive, because its association with a welter of conceptual bifurcations cannot possibly be Being in its diaphaneity. Therefore, since these six masks of Being, each in its own way, involve the fallacy of not being free from one-sided presuppositions, they are not considered to give an adequate idea of Being and present only partial and biased perspectives of Being's abidingness. So also it is stated in the *sGra-thal-'gyur-ba* (p. 181).

(This abidingness which is settled in itself
Is established as a pseudo-abidingness in seven ways;)[6]
In view of its (manifest) variedness it is (claimed to be) spontaneously there;

In view of its flitting quality it is (claimed to be) indeterminate;
In view of its invariance it is (claimed to) have determinacy;
In its dynamic surging as the phenomenal it is (claimed to be) changeable into anything whatsoever;
Since it comes as all and everything it is (claimed to be) acceptable as anything;
Since it is pure of errancy it is (claimed to be) superdiaphanous;
Since it has different modes of coming-to-presence it is (claimed to be) Kaleidoscopic.
Since the rDzogs-chen appears in the guise
Of different masks such as the above and
Although there are many such masks,
When it comes to Being's settledness in its abidingness
The view of it is not (some) one, nor is it (some duality, rather it is free from (any such imputations),

and in the *Kun-bzang klong-drug* (pp. 169f.) it is stated:

All these (claims) reflect gradations in the intellectual acumen (of those who make them);
In themselves they have been pure since their beginning (in and as Being's superdiaphaneity).

1.2

While all these claims are only beliefs that vary with different intellectual capacities, none of which understands Being in its superdiaphaneity, of what kind is Being that does not involve these fallacies?

As a sheer lucency that is free from the extreme of eternalism in the sense that it cannot be reduced to the categories of substance and quality, and also free from the extreme of nihilism since it constitutes a vast array of capabilities that are spontaneously there, it is an (energy) field of supernothingness (*stong-pa chen-po'i dbyings*) and a pristine awareness of a pure possibilizing dynamics (*chos-nyid rnam-dag-gi ye-shes*) such that neither can be added to nor subtracted from the other. Spoken of as the purposing of the invariant gestalt dynamics embodying Being's meaningfulness that lies beyond the domain of what can be thematized and verbalized, thought about and expressed by language, (or as) the superdiaphaneity of Being's initial abidingness, it is the primordial ground (*thog-ma'i gzhi*)[7]. As to its facticity/energy-'stuff' (*ngo-bo*) it is said to be diaphanous (*ka-dag*); as to its actuality/ownmostness (*rang-bzhin*) it is said to be spontaneous (*lhun-grub*); and as to its rising in the projective glow of creativity, presenting the inseparability of facticity/energy-'stuff' and actuality/ownmostness, it is said to be an all-encompassing resonance (*thugs-rje*). In brief, these three facets are like the different masks of a single reality. In the *rDo-rje-sems-dpa' snying-gi me-long* (p. 358) it is stated:

> Everything pertaining to Being must be known as the triad of facticity, actuality, and resonance,

and in the *Mu-tig phreng-ba* (p. 513) it is stated:

> Its facticity—diaphanous; dissociated from any basis for talking about it;
> Its actuality—spontaneous; complete in its coming-to-presence in whatever form;
> Its resonance—all-encompassing; rising on its own.

This abidingness of a diaphaneity that (in its) field character is a higher order reality, (in its) ec-static intensity (one's) self-originated pristine awareness, (in its) primordiality-(constituted) nothingness (*ye-stong*)[8] the gestalt embodying Being's meaningfulness, and (in its) possibilizing dynamics a sheer lucency, is not found (or given) as something justifying the labelling of it as samsara or nirvana, as happiness or misery, as an existent or non-existent, as being so or not being so, eternalistic or nihilistic, emancipatory or straying (into bondage), intelligent or non-intelligent and so on and also is not defiled by any (of these predications). This meaning-rich gestalt dynamics is always and everywhere present, pervading everything from the highest imaginable reality (Kun-tu bzang-po) down to the smallest louse. All the Sutras and Tantras agree with this statement. Thus the *rGyud bla-ma* (commentary)[9] states:

> This dynamic (field-like) expanse that has no temporal beginning or end
> Is the dwelling of all that is.
> Because of its existence all living beings
> May attain nirvana.

What is thus termed 'one's wholesome predisposition toward meaning, having existed since beginningless time' (*thog-med dus-kyi chos-khams dge-ba*)[10], is the same as what is termed 'Being's abidingness as Mahāmudrā' in the instructional works about the Mahāmudrā.

In this context, many learned people of the gSar-ma (New)[11] tradition have raised various objections against our usage of this term 'superdiaphaneity'. But if we look at what it intends, since it is actually synonymous with such expressions as 'pure from the beginning' (*gdod-ma-nas dag-pa*) or 'primordially pure' (*ye-nas dag-pa*) or 'pure from before any beginning' (*thog-ma-nas dag-pa*)[12] or 'naturally pure' (*rang-bzhin-gyis dag-pa*) and so on, there is no flaw in speaking of 'diaphaneity', because if this is inadmissible, then other similar expressions in the Tantras such as 'one's wholesome predisposition towards meaning, having existed since beginningless time' or 'Being's abidingness as Mahāmudrā' should also become a bone of contention. Therefore no fault attaches to our diction.

At any rate, if this diaphaneity is nothing as such, does this mean that it is an absolute emptiness? The answer is 'No' because, although the pristine awareness of (this) diaphaneity (*ka-dag-gi ye-shes*) in its ec-static intensity and nothingness (*rig-stong*) cannot be framed thematically or verbally, it yet surges forth as the pristine effulgence of the pristine awareness of Being's actuality/ownmostness or spontaneity (*rang-bzhin lhun-grub-kyi ye-shes*), that is both radiant and nothing (*gsal-stong*), and since it has the ceaselessly creative dynamics of rising as the pristine awareness of Being's all-encompassing resonance, it is imbued with the vitalizing energies of (Being's) nothingness, radiance, and ec-static intensity and utterly free from all kinds of limitations. In the *Klong-gsal* it is stated:

> Its facticity, by virtue of being the pristine awareness of (Being's) diaphaneity,
> Is free from all dividing concepts that (pertain to Being's) low-level excitation;
> Its actuality, the pristine awareness of (Being's) spontaneity,
> Abides in the auto-effulgence of its nothingness and radiance;
> Its resonance, an all-encompassing pristine awareness,

> Abides in (Being's) unceasing coming-to-presence that yet remains nothing.

Thus, (from the perspective of its) facticity Being abides as the inseparability of its ec-static intensity and nothingness, (from the perspective of its) actuality it abides as its radiance and nothingness, and (from the perspective of its) resonance it abides as its coming-to-presence and nothingness. This is what we call Being's abidingness as the primordial ground as which its diaphaneity constitutes itself.

I shall now explain how the rationale behind one's going astray derives from the general ground (*spyi-gzhi*) that is Being's diaphaneity. After all that has been said about the abidingness of Being's primordial diaphaneity, it does not seem to make any sense that there could be any going astray and one wonders why the living beings in the three world spheres have come into existence. The answer to this question is that, although there is neither a cause factor nor its modifiers (*rgyu-rkyen*) for this going astray in what is Being's facticity or diaphaneity, this going astray comes incidentally about by the combination of Being's actuality or spontaneity and Beings resonance in its ceaseless operation. This is stated in the *bKra-shis mdzes-ldan chen-po'i rgyud* (pp. 213f.):

> Indeed! Although there is in me no going astray, it is out of my creative dynamics that this going astray comes about. When out of the invariance that is Being (in its virtuality) Being's actuality has arisen in a ceaseless manner, out of the indeterminacy that is Being's resonance a stepped-down version of (the original) ec-static intensity (*ma-rig-pa*) comes about by itself. To give an example, just as there are no clouds in the sky itself, yet clouds form incidentally, so also in Being there is no such thing as stepped-down version of an ec-static intensity, yet such a drop in intensity comes about from what seems to be Being's resonance (with itself as a whole), and in this way the abidingness of Being in its spontaneous thereness has set in.

The primordial beingness of Being in its diaphaneity as an inner dimension exists as an inner radiance like a flame in a jar and it emerges in the manner of its outer shell being broken. Then fanned by the wind of (the system's) self-originated pristine awareness Being's ec-static intensity breaks loose from Being which it pervades (*gzhi thog-nas*) and the eight gates of Being's spontaneity that is a coming-to-presence of its own, open up. This coming-to-presence of (Being's) facticity is a ceaseless auto-luminescence; that of its actuality is a primordial effulgence in the manner of five luminosities; and that of its resonance is a 'making room', similar to what is done by the sky's spaceousness. This is what is called 'Being's holomovement' ('Being having risen in its wholeness as a presence out of Being', *gzhi-las gzhi-snang-du shar-ba*). Which are the eight gates of Being's spontaneity?[13] They are

(i) the gate through which Being sallies forth as if it were Being's resonance (with itself in its wholeness);
(ii) as if it were light frequencies;
(iii) as if it were a gestalt dynamics;
(iv) as if it were a pristine awareness mode (commensurate with this gestalt dynamics);
(v) as if it were a non-duality;
(vi) as if it were the dissipation of all limits;
(vii) as if it were an opacity that is (reserved for) samsara; and
(viii) as if it were a diaphaneity (reserved for) the pristine awareness modes (involved in the experience of nirvana).

These eight gates may be summed up under the last two gateways leading to either the diaphanous or the opaque.

During this (self-manifesting) process whatever comes-to-presence and is interpreted (as this or that) arises (initially) in light frequencies and gestalt qualities and hence is termed 'the superpresencing of the (supramundane) field-character of Being's spontaneity' (*lhun-grub-kyi zhing-snang chen-po*).

Here, (i) out of the creative dynamics of its facticity/energy-'stuff' (*ngo-bo*) there comes-to-presence the (supramundane realm in which is housed) Being's gestalt as a contextualized horizon of meaning (*longs-sku*);

(ii) out of the creative dynamics of its capabilities (*yon-tan*) [that are Being's actuality/ownmostness] there comes-to-presence the (supramundane) realm (in which is housed) Being's gestalt as a guiding image (*rang-bzhin sprul-sku'i zhing*); and

(iii) out of the creative dynamics of its resonance (*thugs-rje*) there comes-to-presence an opacity with its passage into samsara that in its auto-presencing is like a dream.[14]

When in this process of Being becoming its holomovement one recognizes it as an auto-effulgence of Being itself, then in the first moment (of this space- and time-binding) by cutting off this (tremor-like) glinting right in its onset one understands what it is all about. (If it comes to) a second moment the creative dynamics of a pristine awareness that is dissociated from a going astray, grows ever more intense (which means that) Being matures into its (evolutionary) climax such that its auto-presencing submerges in the dynamic expanse of its diaphaneity and dissolves by itself into the freedom that it is itself and (as such) is spoken of as the Teacher Kun-tu bzang-po who has become (Being's) pellucidity and consummation before there ever was either samsara or nirvana, or as the Kun-tu bzang-po emancipatory dynamics since it has dissolved (recovered its freedom) in Being's actuality in which there is no errancy with respect to its coming-to-presence as Being's spontaneity. If, however, one does not recognize this auto-presencing of Being as an auto-presencing, this (failure) becomes the reason for going astray into the status of a mentation-governed (sentient) being (*sems-can*) within the three world spheres. This is what is discussed in the generally accepted Buddhist texts under the name *kun-gzhi* 'closed system potential'. It has many designations according to the functions it performs: as being a cause factor conducive to releasement it is termed 'the closed system potential of what is the primordiality-(constituted) thing-itself as a blending' (*sbyor-ba don-gyi kun-gzhi*); and as a cause factor in one's roaming about in samsara it is termed 'the closed system potential that operates as the sundry programs for conscious life' (*bag-chags sna-tshogs-kyi kun-gzhi*). Thus it has been stated in the texts of the ordinary pursuits:

> This closed system potential is the ground of all and everything
> (thematic and therefore)
> It also is the ground of nirvana.

Here, however, the following statement in the *Thal-gyur* (p. 104) is of relevance:

By not recognizing what it is in itself
It becomes the beginning of samsara.

However, the question might be raised—when by experiencing for oneself this process of Being's holomovement from out of Being so as to become its spontaneity, will there not occur again later on a going astray once this spontaneity has subsided in the reach of Being's diaphaneity and, by dissolving into it, has regained the freedom it (has been and) is? The answer is that there is no chance for it. The Kun-tu bzang-po emancipatory dynamics that is Being itself and the emancipation a yogi feels by experiencing the path leading to it are analogous to a person who has been totally cured of the plague or to a seedless fruit from a berry bush by virtue of the fact that there is no chance for what once was a cause factor to become a cause factor again. All the other beings who do not recognize the holomovement of Being's spontaneity from out of Being's primordial diaphaneity to be an auto-presencing embark on a course of mistaken identifications, as is stated at length in the *sGron-ma snang-byed*[15]:

From Being that thus abides
The cause factor and the seed of the going astray
Is (Being's) radiance aspect; by externalizing itself
This cognitive capacity may (seem to be) luminescent and cognizant;
(As) a stepped-down version of an original ec-static intensity—a coming-to-presence by a momentary outward-directed flickering in (Being's) superdiaphaneity—
It is objectified and taken to be a Self by the intellect which
Becomes mistaken about the difference between Being (as such) and Being (as known),
Pertaining to Being and its holomovement.
Thus the cause factor that is the going astray meets its modifiers that are the objects (of the cognitive domain).

Furthermore, there is the (following) triad of (i) a 'solipsistic ipseity low-level intensity' as the very cause factor (in the ensuing evolution of the (human) system, *rgyu bdag-nyid gcig-pa'i ma-rig-pa*) that is (the system's) experience as such (*sems-nyid kho-rang*), of (ii) a 'systemic low level intensity' (*lhan-cig skyes-pa'i ma-rig-pa*) that is like the cognitive agency that does not recogize itself for what it is, and of (iii) a 'discursive fiction-entailing' drop in the ecstatic intensity (*kun-tu brtags-pa'i ma-rig-pa*) that is (like) the cognitive agency that believes (Being's) auto-presencing to be something other (than Being). However, this triad of different aspects is a single process that constitutes the cause momentum[16] in the going astray.

By not recognizing this triune process of facticity, actuality, and resonance for what it is, the momentum modifier (*rgyu'i rkyen*) is set up; through (Being's) spontaneity in its auto-effulgence of its pristine awareness modes that are nothing and yet radiant, as a halo of light (*'od-khyim*) the objective reference modifier (*dmigs-pa'i rkyen*) is set up; and by not recognizing (what is so set up) as being a sheer lucency that yet is nothing and concretizing it into an objective cognitive domain and an owner of this objective cognitive domain, tne subjectification modifier (*'dzin-pa'i rkyen*) is set up. Thus on the basis of six cause factors and their modifiers there occurs the going astray.[17]

The *Klong-gsal* states:

> In the first place (the going astray) starts from six stepped-down versions of an original ec-static intensity.[18]

Subsequently, from concretizing the coming-to-presence of the creative dynamics of Being's nothingness in five luminosities, there originates an actional motility (*las-kyi-rlung*) and through its power of habitually reifying the intrinsic light frequencies of the pristine awareness modes, the five fundamental forces come concretely into presence so that from the radiation-dominated aspects of the five external fundamental forces the fivefold inner psychophysical make-up (*khams*)[19] with its six object phases in the intentional structure of cognition (*skye-mched*)[20] originate, whereby the whole of the environing world and the organisms in it (*snod-bcud*) gradually evolves and materializes.

The living beings born in the six classes of beings in the three world spheres are enmeshed in the net of the subject-object division that (is the expression of) Being's lowered ec-static intensity, they are tossed around in the vicious circle of enworldedness (*srid-pa'i 'khor-lo*) set up by the twelvefold network of connectedness. As a result of their engaging in evil actions due to their proclivity of going astray into affective vagaries, they are squeezed and oppressed by many kinds of frustration. Although all this occurs through their not recognizing their frustration for what it is, their constant and compulsive efforts only further the cause factor in and sow the seed of wandering about in samsara, time and time again. This is as things go for the living beings in the three world spheres. In the *Thal-'gyur* (p. 109) it is stated:

> From the gathering of piles of aimless actions (tited to) the operational fields of
> One's psychophysical groupings and (one's) psychophysical potential
> Affective vagaries are gathered that in immeasurable ways
> Collect the sundry notions living beings have about their body.
> Out of this manifold variety of connected facets
> All the differences in their incongruous shapes come about,

and in the *Mu-tig phreng-ba'i rgyud* (p. 477) it is stated in greater detail:

> Thus the three world spheres comprising
> The five psychophysical groupings, the five sensory capacities,
> The five limbs, the five entrails,
> The five cognitive domains, the five affective pollutants,
> The five temperaments, the five ego-related deliberations, and the five conceptual bifurcations
> Are the materialization of samsara with its subject-object division.
> This going astray makes its presence felt
> In the manner of a quickly spinning wheel.
> Going round and round, we remain for a long time in this vicious circle.

While it may be true that we have sunk into this swamp of samsara which has been there since time without beginning, does this mean that there is nothing we can do to reverse this trend of going astray and find release? No, that is not the case because, although everything belonging to samsara is impure and opaque as such, in an ultimate sense, it has never moved away from (Being's) vast expanse of nothingness, its possibilizing dynamics. It is only on the generally accepted level (of one's limited awareness) that there is this frolicking of a coming-to-presence that yet is nothing existent as such, just like a dream. In other words, from out of the reach of (Being's) nothingness magic display of a luminous coming-to-presence occurs like clouds in the sky forming themselves, staying there, and dispersing into the dimension out of which they have come, with no possibility of ever to pinpointed as being something concrete and real in an absolute sense.

So, if one is fully alert to this as it is in itself and understands it deeply, freedom will come with little difficulty. In particular, as I have explained previously, each and every being's existentiality is pervaded by Being's primordial abidingness, the pristine super-awareness of its diaphaneity that makes up the higher order reality (of ours). This neither steps out of itself nor changes into something other than itself, it neither diminishes nor increases. Anyone who deeply understands and realizes it is not so much as an atom different from the primordial Kun-tu bzang-po. So also the *Mu-tig phreng-ba* (p. 477) states:

> Thus the manifold of what is coming-to-presence
> Is set up as the duality of an external environing world and the organisms internal to it
> By taking what comes-to-presence to be something what it is not,
> Like seeing a rope as a snake.
> Moreover, if one investigates (what seems to be a snake) one will find it to be a rope,
> And so the environing world and the organisms in it have primordially been (Being's) nothingness.
> The higher order reality has assumed the guise of the generally accepted reality.

The text goes on to say (p. 478):

> The nature of the two realities is that
> The world (as we perceive it) is only real in a generally accepted manner
> But bears no connection with the higher order reality.

Apart from the vast expanse of (Being's) nothingness
Its facticity is the (dissipative) freedom of everything.

Lastly, the *Klong-gsal* states:

The facticity of Being's optimization thrust is present in all living beings
Like oil pervading sesame seeds.
When Being's lowered ec-static intensity dissipates, the body set up by the fundamental forces
Is returned to the reach of (Being's) pristine awareness, leaving no residue.

Thus, if you are endowed with the vital energy to make a living experience of these instructions, you have the chance of recovering the freedom that you are.

2

Having thus given a general presentation of Being's abidingness in its dual dynamics of errancy and emancipation I shall now give a detailed explication of the way as it is (pursued) by either the one for whom all barriers have been removed (*khregs-chod*) or the one who still has to take the final leap (*thod-rgal*). This also has two aspects:

2.1 The explication of the meaning of the barrier-free approach by way of distinguishing between mentation (*sems*) and ec-static intensity (*rig*), and

2.2 The explication of the final-leap approach by way of (elucidating) the framework (of mentation and ec-static intensity), their respective pathways, gates, crucial charges and other related topics.

2.1

All the teachings agree that Being's thrust toward optimization or Being's abidingness as the pristine awareness in (the primordiality-constituted) thing-itself (that we are, *don-gyi ye-shes*)[21], as discussed in the previous section, pervades the whole psychophysical potential of sentient beings and that by taking this as the real basis for making an experience of the way, the climax of (Being's unity in its triune) gestalt dynamics and pristine awareness modes (commensurate with it) is realized. Nonetheless, one must clearly distinguish between mentation (*sems*) and ec-static intensity (*rig-pa*) in view of the fact that it is solely (one's) pristine awareness as a function of (Being's) ec-static intensity that is to be taken as one's frame of reference in the process of experiencing Being's energetic thrust. This is the specific intention of the rDzogs-chen approach which is quite out of the ordinary.

So, in the first place, even in the context of the starting-point, one has to distinguish, as discussed before, between Being's diaphaneity (*ka-dag*) and a closed system potential (*kun-gzhi*). Being's diaphaneity is the 'stuff' that (expresses itself in) Being's meaning-rich gestalt dynamics (*chos-sku*) because it has many specific features such as the following ones: (i) it is not defiled by any aspect of the wide-spread grime pertaining to samsara, (ii) it is the birth-place of the three pristine awareness modes or is that which has these as its defining characteristic; (iii) it is the root for everything that is summed up as nirvana, (iv) it is dissociated from all conceptual-propositional proliferation that deal with the (thing)-quality relationship and in itself is not a (mental or physical) construct, (v) it forms the real basis for all that constitutes the way such as vision, creative imagination, and its enactment in one's life, and (vi) is the astute perception of the infallibility of the relationship between cause and effect concerning the complexity of the capabilities constituting the greatness of the Buddha-experience with its (ten) powers[22], (four) intrepidities[23] and so on, all of them not blurred in any manner.

The closed system potential is the founding stratum for all the programs (tendencies and propensities) leading to samsara because it has many defects such as the following: (i) it stays on in the indeterminate status of its stepped-down version of ec-static intensity, (ii) it acts as both a cause factor and its modifier of all affective pollutants in the wake of the crowd of divisive concepts due to one's inconsiderate actions and their inveterate tendencies, (iii) it serves as the progenitress of samsara by setting up and bringing to maturity all the constructs that make up the triad of one's embodied existence (*lus*), environmental domain (*snang*), and mentation (*sems*).

This very closed system potential can further be distinguished as follows:

(i) With respect to the systemic drop in the ec-static intensity it is termed the closed system potential of what is the primordiality-(constituted) thing-itself (*ye don-gyi kun-gzhi*),

(ii) With respect to its being the agent who projects and re-absorbs all the individual actions pertaining to samsara and nirvana it is termed the closed system potential of what is the primordiality-(constituted) thing-itself as a blending to either states (*sbyor-ba don-gyi kun-gzhi*),

(iii) With respect to its being the root from which grows the principle of connectedness pertaining to samsara through the working of mentation and its operators it is termed the closed system potential that operates as the sundry programs for conscious life (*bag-chags sna-tshogs-pa'i kun-gzhi*), and

(iv) With respect to its being the founding stratum of embodied existences in the three world spheres, be these one's coarse physical body,[24] one's luminous body,[25] or one's body as it is felt to be present when at its energy level that just suffices to detect its presence,[26] it is termed the closed system potential that (expresses itself) in an animate organism (such that its) body is (the expression of a process of embodying levels of mental life that acts as) programs for it (*bag-chags lus-kyi kun-gzhi*).

Thus the closed system potential which is a single unitary process, though classifiable into the above four aspects in view of the specific functions it exhibits, is in all cases characterizable as something begrimed that has to be cleansed. Therefore, (what is referred to as) the primordial rationale behind the emancipatory dynamics (*thog-ma'i grol-gzhi*) and the final emancipatory destination (*mthar-thug-gi grol-sa*) is actually Being's very super-diaphaneity, not the closed system potential. The *Kun-bzang thugs-kyi me-long-gi rgyud* (p. 258) states:

> Anyone who claims that the closed system potential is (the same as Being's) meaning-rich gestalt dynamics[27] is far away from me,

and the *Mu-tig phreng-ba* (p. 580) declares:

> The meaning-rich gestalt dynamics (experience) is such that (in it) one has done with what is impaired;

It is nothing and yet radiant, and in being radiant it is all-encompassing;
It is not vitiated by representational thought and in it organismic thinking has vanished;
It is dissociated from conceptual-propositional limitations;
Like the sky it is all-encompassing and yet nothing;
It is dissociated from everything demonstrable as this or that,

and the *Rig-pa rang-shar* (p. 737) states:

The closed system potential is (something) vitiated by a cognition that conceives of it in sundry ways
Due to the subjectivizing tendency in dichotomic thought.
The closed system potential is the material of Being's stepped-down version of its ec-static intensity.

These and many other passages stress the need to distinguish between Being's diaphaneity, a meaning-rich gestalt with no grime to it, and a closed system potential, the begrimed stepped-down version of Being's ec-static intensity.

While from the discussion of the distinction between Being's diaphaneity and Being's spontaneity one may have an inkling of what it is all about, one must in the same manner distinguish between mentation and ec-static intensity.

Since what is called 'mentation' is an incidental grime that is also termed 'dichotomic thinking' and since 'pristine awareness as a function of Being's ec-static intensity' is, as has been explained above, Being's primordial abidingness or the actual thrust toward Being-in-its-beingness which is one's wholesome predisposition toward meaning that has been there since time without beginning, these two do not have or constitute one and the same domain of cognition. 'Mentation' is what has to be cleansed, 'pristine awareness as a function of ec-static intensity' is what has to be deeply felt and understood. 'Mentation' has to do with what is one's generally accepted reality, 'ec-static intensity' is a higher order reality, Being's possibilizing dynamics. 'Mentation' is that very cognitive capacity that arises automatically as the organismic thinking operating in a subject-object feedback loop in each of the six kinds of living beings, 'ec-static intensity' is the very stuff of the auto-luminescence of (Being's) pristine awareness modes, the inseparability of (Being's) three gestalts and the unity of nothingness and radiance. 'Mentation's' very stuff is

(i) the closed system potential in its move into conscious perception (*kun-gzhi'i rnam-shes*) and what spreads out from it:

(ii) the egological consciousness (*yid-kyi rnam-shes*) with its fiction of an apprehendable object,

(iii) the egological affectively toned consciousness (*nyon-mongs-can-gyi yid*) with its fiction of a subject ascribing to itself the emotional triad of passion, aversion, and an in-between (that is neither),

(iv) the consciousness, representing the coarse dichotomy in connection with the five senses (*sgo lnga*), each having its specific cognitive domain. From this complexity there arise the five poisons of the affective pollutants[28] and from these the twenty proximate pollutants and from these the sixty thousand affective pollutants. Thus, in this proliferation process mentation alone is the cause factor and root of the going astray into and roaming about in samsara with its three world spheres.

(On the other hand), the root of pristine awareness as a function of Being's ec-static intensity is the pristine awareness modes in Being's abidingness with its facets of facticity/energy-'stuff', actuality/ownmostness, and resonance as the very dimension of the three dynamic gestalts of Being as well as the five specific pristine modes: the pristine awareness mode that is the very dimension of Being from which meanings are born (*chos-dbyings*), the mirror-like pristine awareness mode (*me-long*), the pristine awareness mode that is Being's self-consistency (*mnyam-nyid*), the specificity mapping pristine awareness mode (*sor-rtog*), and the task accomplished pristine awareness mode (*bya-grub*). Lastly, it is the pristine awareness mode that is encompassing the whole of its cognitive domain and is of two kinds: a pristine awareness mode that is sensitive to Being's abidingness as it becomes seen in its immediacy (*ji-lta-ba*) and a pristine awareness mode that is sensitive to what is cognizable in it (*ji-snyed-pa*)[29].

In brief, the concrete cause factor or root for the coming to pass of the Buddha-experience in which Being's immaculate reality has become manifest is this very ec-static intensity of Being. Therefore, the infinite ways of differentiating between mentation and ec-static intensity may be gleaned from the Tantras that deal with the profoundness of certitude. Thus, the *Mu-tig phreng-ba* (p. 517) states:

> The distinction between mentation and pristine awareness
> Must be known by the wise,

and this text goes on to say (p. 517):

> Mentation, the closed system potential with its (enworlding) programs
> Is the grime that affects embodied beings.
> Mentation takes subjectively the apprehendable as its object
> And thus is the way of samsara.
> If one is dissociated from this mentation, the Buddha-experience is there
> And the grime that affects all embodied beings is cleansed.
> In its ec-static cognition and illumining lighting-up
> It burns away all dichotomies;
> It is Being's very nothingness and radiance that is without any grime,

and in the *Kun-bzang klong-drug* (pp. 164f.) it is stated:

> Listen, great being! If one does not distinguish between what mentation and pristine awareness are in themselves, (the situation) is similar to the sun shrouded by masses of clouds so that it is no longer able to shine forth. Consequently, the yogis who are wise concerning what mentation is, understand that the objects of the external world have no being of their own. The yogis who are wise concerning what pristine awareness is, hold sway over this pristine awareness as the very function of Being's ec-static intensity.

There are countless statements to this effect, not only in this rDzogs-chen teaching, but also in the many Sutras and Śāstras which unanimously agree on this theme. There are, however, many people who do not understand this because of their biased interpretations of the intended meaning. Thus, the *'Da-ka ye-shes-kyi mdo* advises.

Since the Buddha-experience lies in the deeply felt understanding of (what is) mentation, do not entertain the idea that it must be sought elsewhere.

The meaning of this statement is that since the understanding of the dynamic essence of mentation is the pristine awareness as a function of Being's ec-static intensity, and thus it agrees in intention with what has been discussed here.

In brief, since the dynamic core in what impels one to make a deeply felt experience of (what is referred to as the Buddha-experience) is the pristine awareness as a function of Being's ec-static intensity, and since mentation is a projective glow or the creative dynamics (of this intensity), it is by taking hold of this ec-static intensity that mentation has no longer any power to go astray, just as when the king has ascended his throne and his minister has been put under lock and key, the populace is under his control.[30]

* * *

When it comes to make a deeply felt experience (of this process), one must in order to set out on the Vajrayāna path first pass through the entrance doors of the empowerments (*dbang*) that bring about a person's (spiritual) maturation and the instructions that make him (regain) the freedom (that he has always been). Even among these two, spiritual maturation is of primary importance and (to this effect) one must fully realize the empowerments in all their external, conceptual-propositional aspects,[31] their internal, nonconceptual-nonpropositional aspects,[32] their arcane, strongly nonconceptual-nonpropositional aspects,[33] and their beingness aspect[34] that is utterly nonconceptual-nonpropositional. In this connection, the dividing line between whether one has realized the empowerments or not is one's capacity or incapacity of maturing spiritually or whether the meaning of the empowerments has impressed itself on one's mind or not. Although this distinction is important,[35] nowadays people are only concerned with whether they should or should not ask for the ritual accompanying the empowerments and do not bother at all about whether the meaning of the empowerments has impressed itself on them or not or about what qualifies someone to be a teacher or to be a student and what the empowerments are all about and what the guarding of one's existential commitments involves.[36] Consequently, there is not even a semblance of what are the specific qualities of having realized the empowerments and those who, in their immaturity, pretend to explain and listen to the instructions and to make a felt experience of them, are unable to regain the freedom (that has been theirs) even if it stares into their faces. But in the case of those who deal with these empowerments properly, the student who has really realized what the empowerments mean will, at the beginning of the process that makes him regain the freedom that has been his, be able to make great efforts until the indications (of their impact) and the certitudes that derive from each of the infinite varieties of the ordinary and special preliminary practices (*sngon-'gro*) are fully present. Thereafter, when it comes to the main part (*dngos-gzhi*) of the practice, there is nothing to prevent the concrete reality of (Being's ec-static intensity as one's) self-kindled pristine awareness to be born in one's being. Although there are many aspects of this concrete reality to be experienced, they will here be summarized under the (i) the barrier-free (*khregs-chod*) approach and (ii) the final-leap (*thod-rgal*) approach.

(I)

Concerning the first of these two, the barrier-free approach:

In order to cut away all imputations that derive from doubt (about what it is all about), by recognizing what the meaning of Being's abidingness is in itself (and as it is revealed through direct) vision, one has, first of all, to cut off dichotomic thinking at its root, then to spy out the faults of mentation, and finally, investigate (mentation) in terms of its three aspects of arising, staying on, and passing away. The sequence of the specific guidances in this context is tied to the instruction by the (inner) teacher and (these guidances) are given according to the student's intellectual acumen.

The substance of vision is as follows: since ordinary people in this world[37] never go beyond the subject-object dichotomy with its (affective vagaries of) attachment, aversion, and deludedness, they do not understand what vision is.

The outsiders (that is, the non-Buddhists) or extremists (*mu-*

stegs pa) who rely either on the eternalistic claim of the eternalists (*ther-zug-pa*) or the nihilistic claim of the Carvāka Nihilists (*rgyang-'phen-pa*), entertain three hundred and sixty (reductionist) views about what is perishable, all of which are a perverse understanding of what vision is.

Among the insiders (that is, the Buddhists) there are the Śrāvakas with their (vision of reality) in terms of its frustration, its origination, its cessation, and the path to its cessation, the Pratyekabuddhas with their (vision of reality as constituted by) a twelvefold chain of interconnected facets that can be (intellectually) pursued in either direction;[38] and the Bodhisattvas who, with their claim that what comes-to-presence (*snang-ba*) is the commonly accepted reality while its nothingness/openness (*stong-pa*) is the higher order reality, are the first to really make a sustained experience (of reality) through settled determination and steady pursuance. Nonetheless, these followers of a spiritual pursuit of transcendence (*phar-phyin theg-pa-pa*) have only a partial understanding of what the vision of Being's non-ontological character is.

For the followers of the Kriyātantra, the commonly accepted reality is the deiform energies of the three proto-patterns of existence (*rigs-gsum*)[39] while the higher order reality is its symbol quality (*dag-pa*) that is free from the four judgmental extremes.[40] For the followers of the Upa and Yoga systems, the commonly accepted reality is the coming-to presence of the five[41] or one hundred[42] proto-patterns of existence in deiform energies while the higher order reality is the nothingness of their presence. For the followers of the Mahāyoga, the commonly accepted reality is such that whatever one sees or hears is a dynamic configuration of peaceful and fierce forces while the higher order reality is their remaining free from the three aspects of arising, passing, and (momentary) staying, the non-duality of these (two realities) being the inseparability of true reality. The followers of the Anuyoga claim that pure experience (*sems-nyid*) in its dissociation from conceptual propositional limitations is a dynamic field-like expanse (*dbyings*), its pure radiance with no objectifications intruding is an pristine awareness (*ye-shes*), and their non-duality is bliss supreme (*bde-ba chen-po*).

In brief, all these views that are presented in five or six Mantrayāna pursuits do not understand what vision really is since they extend only as far as the limits any intellectual model sets up.

What, then, is meant by vision here (in the context of rDzogs-chen)? It is an ec-static intensity that can only be experienced in one's self (*rang-rig*)[43], a diaphanous (awareness, *ka-dag*), a pristine awareness that is not some construct (*'dus-ma-byas-pa'i ye-shes*), dissociated from representational thought processes (*bsam-bral*), Being's initial abidingness (*gdod-ma'i gnas-lugs*), a self-originated organizing singularity (*rang-byung thig-le nyag-gcig*), a primordial emancipatory dynamics (*ye-grol*)[44], an ever-widening vortex (*klong-yangs chen-po*). Since as the actuality of this very nothingness of Being it has been through its primordiality a spontaneous thereness and as such has not come into existence as something, and since its (projective) radiance and inner glow (*gsal-mdangs*) never stops (shining) it may well serve as the predisposition for all of samsara and nirvana, yet in its facticity/energy-'stuff' it is not defiled by anything and in whatever guise it may come-to-presence it does not go beyond its nothingness. It does, however, go beyond the limitations set by such qualifications as shape and color, good and bad, existing and non-existing, eternalism and nihilism, and even where such a notion as 'it goes beyond and limitations' is entertained it is neither improved nor vitiated by the models one constructs as a result of one's proclivity to believe in one's intellectual constructs. It is this initial pristine awareness (in us) reflecting Being's primordiality (*ye gdod-ma'i ye-shes*), dissociated from representational thinking and its verbalizations, that is what is meant by vision.

When one experiences and understands it for what it is, once one has becomes free from the fetters of doubt due to dualistic beliefs based on ego-centered thought processes by the profound and wondrous power that issues from the various symbols the (inner teacher) displays before us, as well as by his appropriate gestures and instructions and, in particular, by the vitalizing spark of his that enters us, this is what is called 'a vision that is an understanding as much as this understanding is a vision' (*lta-ba rtogs-pa*). Actually, this understanding does not come as something new from somewhere else as though there were still a difference between what is to be understood and the agent who understands, rather it is this pristine awareness that is (in us) in its own right that recognizes itself for what it is.

Is it enough to solely understand this meaning of vision that is the starting-point of the barrier-free approach? In the case of some gifted persons of a very high intellectual-spiritual acumen, the understanding of the meaning of vision and (the regaining of the) freedom (that has been ours) may come at the same time. But for the rest of people it is not enough to merely have this recognition. For these people, the adventitious programs (their inveterate tendencies) and the plethora of (emotional and intellectual) obscuring factors must fade and dissipate into the dynamic field-like expanse of Being. Thus it is stated in the *Las rnam-par dag-pa'i mdo*:

> The Bodhisattva Nivaraṇaviṣkambhin asked the Exalted One: 'What is this maturation of one's actions all about?' The Exalted One replied: 'In itself it is Being's possibilizing dynamics.' Again:
>
> If that is so, doesn't it stand to reason that all sentient beings would become free without having to make the slightest effort?'
>
> 'No, it does not stand to reason because until you have churned the milk you won't get any butter or, until you have refined the ore you won't get any silver. Similarly, as long as sentient beings don't cultivate creative imagination and strive for realization their (spiritual) darkness won't dissipate and the light will not dawn in them (*sangs mi-rgya*)'.
>
> 'If Being's possibilizing dynamics has been there since time before time, then why search for it by means of creative imagination?'
>
> 'Dichotomic thinking arises incidentally like clouds in the sky and it is through creative imagination that it is dispelled.'
>
> 'But would the fact that dichotomic thought is incidental not imply that once it has gone it could come again?'
>
> 'No, once you have this dissipative-expansive (Buddha-experience) dichotomic thought has been cut off at the root; it is like small-pox which, once properly cured (will not come again).'

Furthermore, ordinary people generally (proceed as follows):

at first they attempt to make the mind that does not yet stay with (a specific social value system) to stay with it (*gnas-par byed-pa*), which is the Śrāvaka's perceptual stance (*nyan-thos-kyi lta-stangs*), then they attempt to have the mind that stays with (such a value system) firmly entrenched in it (*brtan-par byed-pa*), which is the Bodhisattva's perceptual stance (*byang-chub sems-dpa'i lta-stangs*), and lastly they attempt to resolve this impasse of rigidity (*grol-bar byed-pa*), which is (described as a) fiercely angry perceptual stance (*khro-bo'i lta-stangs*). (These stances are expressive of) the body's cardinal charge (*lus-kyi gnad*), speech's cardinal charge (*ngag-gi gnad*) which (reflects the dynamics of the organism's aliveness in terms of breathing taking on colors, shapes, rates of inhalation, exhalation, and retention, and the mind's cardinal charge (*sems-kyi gnad*) which involves an inner calm (*zhi-gnas*) and related features that may or may not have an objective reference. On the basis of these cardinal charges[45] they strive for a concentrated peak experience (*rtse-gcig*) by gradually suppressing the stirring and spreading of dichotomic thinking. The first step (in this procedure) is to become aware of the difference between steadiness and restlessness through a direct feeling of the mind's throbbing; the second step is the consolidation of pure experience through a direct feeling of attainment; the third step is the realization of the certitude that comes with such a state of concentration through a direct feeling of one's familiarity with it; and the fourth step is the realization of the autonomy in one's control over the steadiness aspect (of the mind) through a direct feeling of the rigidity (that derives from steadiness). All this is described in the general treatises as well as in the Mahāmudrā literature such that the direct feeling of (the mind's) steadiness is, in the first instance, like a waterfall rushing over a precipice; in the second instance, like gently flowing river; and in the third instance, like a calm lake. The rDzogs-chen teaching describes the above generally in terms of a 'settling into the dynamic still point of one's natural condition' (*rnal-du dbab-pa*) and an 'entering into one's legitimate dwelling' (*sor-'jug*) and so on. In practice, there are individuals who go about the above step by step or with one stroke. However, the manner of imparting the instructions in the above according to the practicing individual's intellectual acumen that may be of an exceptional, intermediate, or ordinary quality, each of which may again be subdivided in a set of three such qualities, is to be learned from a competent teacher who has deeply felt the above for himself.

Thereafter, with respect to the substance of wider perspective (*lhag-mthong*) steadiness comes as the mind's ornamentation and its spreading comes as its frolicking, and their non-duality becomes the passage into the vibrant dimension of Being's identity with itself and, while the encounter with the beingness of Being in one's being through an investigation of what comes-to-presence as the external world and the encounter with the beingness of Being in one's being through an investigation of the cognitive intensity as one's inner world as well as the encounter with the beingness of Being in one's own being through an investigation of the non-duality (of the without and the within) has been dealt with extensively in the various treatises about spiritual guidance, they can be summarized in terms of (i) an encounter of the beingness of Being in one's being in and through its very beingness (*rang-ngo thog-tu sprod-pa*), (ii) a decisive cognition (effected) with one stroke (*thag-chig thog-tu bcad-pa*), and (iii) a boosting of the resoluteness (one feels) in this emancipatory process of Being (*gdeng-grol thog-tu bca'-ba*). All cardinal charges gather in this triad.

Furthermore, (taking up each topic in detail):

(i) This pure experience (*sems-nyid*) that presents the dynamics of (Being's) nothingness, radiance, and ec-static intensity, each being beyond such qualifying predications as shape and color, is in its auto-luminescence a sparkling, naked, brilliant ec-static intensity. In the general diction of the ordinary texts it is called 'a wider perspective that sees things as the really are as Being's abidingness that is (one's) mind in its natural diaphaneity'. In the more technical language of rDzogs-chen it is called 'the superintelligence intertwining with the Kun-tu bzang-po pristine awareness' (*kun-tu bzang-po ye-shes zang-thal-gyi dgongs-pa*). If one right away recognizes this abidingness of Being's primordial and initial diaphaneity as what it is in its very beingness, this is said to be the encounter of the beingness of Being in one's being in and through its very beingness.

(ii) When one encounters this ec-static intensity in it very beingness, then, when one recognize this ec-static intensity in all its nakedness that is there twinkling and scintillating, regardless of whether it spreads with its brilliance into the cognitive domains of the six sense-specific perceptions or stays on in the vibrant dimension of its auto-luminescence or wearily arises as a good or bad idea or is just there in what it is, not being turned (into an object) by what is an objectively cognizable domain, not being vitiated by what is the subjective grasping (of the objective domain), and untrammeled by (considerations of) what has to be given up and aids such giving up, this not passing beyond the meaning-rich gestalt dynamics with its self-kindled pristine awareness is called the decisive cognition (of Being's beingness in one's being effected) with one stroke.

(iii) When one has won the certitude (that comes with) thus cognizing Being's beingness in one's being with one stroke, (one realizes that) what comes-to-presence as the external as the specific differentiations of the six sense-specific perceptions or what comes-to-presence in whatever guise, labelled the dichotomic operation of the mind and its operators, themselves features of this psychic stirring, has, in the first instance, emerged out of the creativity of Being's possibilizing dynamics, is now present as the frolicking of this very possibilizing dynamics, and finally will dissolve by itself in the vibrant dimension of the possibilizing dynamics and nowhere else, this decisive cognition of the triad of beginning, middle, and end as being characterized by its not being fettered anywhere and by its not having to be released from anything, is what is called the boosting of the resoluteness one feels in this emancipatory process of Being.

To sum up, the vitalizing core intensity of the barrier-free approach (to Being in its beingness) is the preservation of whatever comes-to-presence in its being the nakedness of Being's ec-static intensity that can only individually be experienced, without introducing (notions of) good and evil and acceptance and rejection with respect to (the mind's) steadiness and flittingness once one has relaxed in the 'idling frequency' of the self-settledness of pure experience. If one knows this cardinal charge there is no way for (whatever one does) not to become creative imagination, and when there is no reason to purposively create something by imagination, then there is no need to undergo austerites or to entangle oneself in a net of twisted notions. When this ec-static intensity has taken over by its having been recognized for what it is, there is no chance for ever again going astray into the disruptiveness of ordinary thinking and one will no longer move away from what creative imagination actually is. Unfortunately, the meditation masters that roam about these days, for the most part do not even have an inkling, let alone an experiential understanding of what creative imagination is about. There are many who make a cult of inner calm, shoot off their mouths with all sorts of advise, get completely mixed up in their private notions, get wilder and wilder in their dichotomic thinking, chase after every mental projection and become more and more inflated with a so-called meditation that is but their own ego-centered concoction. Since in my *Phyag-chen zin-'bris*,[46] the deeply felt understanding of those who have found certainty through their trust in the cardinal charges discussed here, it may be looked up there. Such knowledge will be very valuable. Also in the *Khyung-chen mkha'-lding-gi rgyud*[47] it has been stated:[48]

> This letting be that is not something to be meditated upon is (Being's) ec-static intensity (in us),
> Beyond speech and the intellect's (ruminations) it is beyond everything.
> Referentiality (comes as the working of its) very source, so what's the point of making an issue of it?
> By (attempting to) steady it it ceases (to be alive), by (letting it) flit it (returns to) its purity in what is its (rightful) dwelling,

and[49]

> The pristine awareness which has nothing to do with a coming-to-presence and (also) is dissociated from (any) nothingness is such that
> It is the source of itself, it cannot be grasped (as an object), it cannot be investigated, and it cannot be vitiated.
> It cannot be changed by anything into something, (as) an ecstatic intensity that is itself, it is the cardinal charge in Being's emancipatory dynamics.
> (One's) body and mind and the emotional pollutants are its (overt) features.
> Although for ignorant ordinary persons these may seem to be a net (in which they are caught),
> For the yogi who does not set it down (as something) nor

interferes with it, it is Being's ec-static intensity (he feels working in an through himself).
Being a self-emancipatory process that has primordially been going on, it is not something that has to emancipated.
Apart from not interfering with it and letting it be in its rightful dwelling, what more is there to do?

Although (the experience described here) goes beyond what can be expressed in words, if one does not recognize and take hold of Being's ec-static intensity in all its nakedness, then words and letters and all the explanations that make use of them will be of no avail and will not help on in attaining (a state of) pellucidity and consummation in this one life-time. But for those individuals in whom the real teacher's vitalizing spark has come alive so that all the preconceptions that come with their ordinary way of thinking, have been pared away, and who make a living experience of (this ec-static intensity) so that it takes over their whole being, there is no need to differentiate between inner calm and wider perspective, because they know their unity in this ec-static intensity. They also do not have to bother about going into a state of composure and carrying it over into the post-composure state, because for them there is no separation between mentation and creative imagination. They do not have to suppress (the mind's) flitting and to establish its steadiness, because (both have found their) overarching unity in the ever-widening vortex (of pure experience) in which all limitations have dissolved. There is no need for them to eagerly wait for or long for the felt experience and understanding to grow and spread in them, because Being's ec-static intensity (working in and through them) has taken up its legitimate dwelling that is Being's abidingness. They also do not have to look for a goal to be attained and an undertaking of attaining it, because the primordial Buddha-experience has been found in their own mind.

Thus, all the cardinal points pertaining to the barrier-free approach in the rDzogs-chen teaching, the banner standing at the peak of all spiritual pursuits, have been summarized here. Since here there is no chance of taking a wrong turn and of getting lost, whatever comes-to-presence (is understood as) not being beyond the frolicking of Being's possibilizing dynamics. So also dGa'-rab rdo-rje declared:

This ec-static intensity is not there as this or that,
Since it never ceases to be there as anything by virtue of its rising in its auto-effulgence,
The whole of what comes-to-presence and is interpreted (as this or that) arises as the realm of Being in its meaning-rich gestalt dynamics.
This arising displays its emancipatory dynamics throughout its being.

Now, with respect to people of an ordinary intellectual acumen I shall discuss the four phases of absorbing sensations (*nyams rim-bzhi*) as they are presented in the mentality section (*sems-sde*) of the rDzogs-chen teaching and related them to the four tuning-in procedures (*rnal-'byor bzhi*) of the Mahāmudrā teaching.

(i) When the beginner enters a state of composure, in the first phase in his attempt to get a hold on his wildly fluctuating cognitive capacity, he has the sensation of (his mind) brimming over (with images and cascading) like a waterfall. From here on, until he has the sensation of (his mind staying) steady like a (calm) lake since his cognitive capacity stays where it has been made to settle, this whole process is called 'a low-level peak experience' (*rtse-gcig chung-ngu*) by some followers of the Mahāmudrā teaching. Actually, this is a state of inner calm (*zhi-gnas*), but if out of it the ec-static intensity of a wider perspective (*lhag-mthong*) should arise in all its nakedness, then the medium- and high-level peak experiences should come very quickly and, finally, there should also come, among others, experiences of perceptual immediacies whose presentational lucency, however, is prone to break down and which seem to be the creative possibilities (of Being in one's being)[50]. When at the time of these sensations the state of composure becomes the cardinal charge (to 'fire' the experiencer) then, even in the post-composure state, whatever comes-to-presence arises as having no truth value[51] but being like a magic play. But if the state of composure does not become a cardinal charge, the pcst-composure state will just be one's ordinary world again.

To sum up, with reference to all phases in this three-level peak experience the followers of the rDzogs-chen teaching in its mentality-related aspect[52] speak of 'having reached a temporary peak experience (*rtse-gcig thun-thub-pa*) when the awareness of the feeling of steadiness is not exteriorizing itself into an objective domain'. The three intensity phases – low, medium, high (*chung-'bring-che*)—in the unfoldment of this experience are said to describe the stages of 'becoming a little bit familiar with it', becoming more and more familiar with it', and 'being fully familiar with when this sensation is wholly present'.

(ii) Thereafter, when one has really experienced this peak experience, as described above, then the pure experience that is one's very own, even if one does not know how to express in words since it cannot be found as anything concrete, will come as carrying a special sense of certainty with its relished feeling, due to one's dedication and enthusiasm and one's real teacher's vitalizing spark (coming alive in us). The followers of the Mahāmudrā teaching claim this state as a take-over by a conceptualization-free experience (*spros-bral*) in which there is a feeling of pity for those who do not recognize the fact that there is no reason for roaming about in Samsara nor for becoming a Buddha since all living beings are embodiments of Being's meaningfulness (*chos-sku*) and that whatever has arisen presents (Being's) dynamic openness/nothingness.

Something similar to this may already come about in the peak experience, but there it is only an intellectual understanding whereas, here, since one feels and relishes this feeling, it is a low-level conceptualization-free experience (*spros-bral chung-ngu*). If, however, one does not lighten this state up with the ec-static intensity of attentiveness, there is the danger of slipping into a stale state of inner calm, as the followers of the Mahāmudrā teaching maintain. For the followers of the rDzogs-chen teaching no such danger exists since the main feature in this experiential process is the ec-static intensity itself.

Furthermore, since all that has previously come-to-presence and (now) is a presence is a presencing of (Being's) openness/nothingness, growing in strength, the rising of (a feeling of) openness/nothingness that is devoid of the infinite variety of notions such as birth, death, and phase transition,[53] is termed a medium-level conceptualization-free experience (*spros-bral 'bring*). When, even if one feels the coming-to-the fore of (any such) notions (dividing the original unity, *rtog-pa*), they dissipate in the very process of their being inspected (*dran-pa*)[54], since apart from their dissolving (again in the original unity) nothing else (with respect to them) exists, there is (by implication) nothing to relish by meditating on it and, even more so, nothing to be distracted by when not meditating—a state that one encounters, usually, in moments of falling asleep. This sensation is termed a high-level conceptualization-free experience (*spros-bral chen-po*).

Also, if in all these instances of a conceptualization-free experience the (feeling of) openness/nothingness preponderates the danger is that those people who have not been taken hold of by a competent teacher may fall into a 'black hole' where the relationship of cause and effect is just swept away. The followers of the rDzogs-chen teaching speak of all these instances of a conceptualization-free experience in terms of a 'sensation of an unassailable in-depth appraisal' in view of the fact that it cannot be harmed by such (concentration/meditation)—modifying features as depression, elation and so on. Although they do not differentiate between high-level and low-level conceptualization-free experiences they agree in their distinction between becoming familiar with and attaining or not attaining this state as in the case of the peak experience.

(iii) Thereafter, when one makes an experience (of the above) without falling into the power of impediments and shortcomings, slip-ups and pitfalls, what is referred to by the statement that 'what has come-to-presence has submerged in mind/mentation' is called the low-level one-flavoredness (*ro-gcig chung-ngu*). Here, what is, externally, the stuff of the apprehendable objects and, internally, the stuff of the apprehending subject dissipate into what is their legitimate dwelling,[55] which means how, through a proper understanding of (Being's) openness/nothingness, the (universal) connectedness of the infinite varieties of the triad of causal momentum, the modifiers of this momentum, and the resultant of (their interaction in constituting) the external and internal worlds (of the experiencer) comes about without encountering any obstruction. After this phase there comes the autonomy in controlling mind/mentation, which means that apart from mere inspection still prevailing since the flavors of what has come-to-presence have been throughly tasted, there may again under certain circumstances, through a preponderance of the stepped-down version of (Being's) ec-static intensity (operating in the individual as) the as-yet-indeterminate closed system potential, occur a straying (into lower levels of existing), but when the (felt awareness of the) principle of universal connectedness grows ever more brilliant, this is claimed to be the medium-level of one-flavoredness (*ro-gcig 'bring-po*). Here, too, there are subtle differences (in interpretation). The followers of the Mahāmudrā teaching declare that when the last trace of inspection dissipates, without one's having to look for the feeling or sensation of opennness/nothingness, this is the one-flavoredness experience, but if one still hankers after (a sensation of) openness/nothingness this is the conceptualization-free experience. Whatever the case may be there is still (a differentiation between) what is a state of composure and what is a post-composure state. The followers of the rDzogs-chen teaching declare that what is termed 'the sensation of Being's self-consistency' (*mnyam-pa-nyid-kyi nyams*)[56] is the composure state in which samsara and nirvana have the same flavor (and which as such) is like the sky and that the post-composure state is the attainment of an assurance that is utterly free from fear due to the thorough understanding of the eight worldly concerns[57] as being like a magic play. While there are some who declare that at the time of the high-level one-flavoredness experience (*ro-gcig chen-po*) the composure state and post-composure states fuse, there actually has never existed an absolute separation between these two states, any such separation is merely a designation we make for general purposes.

Anyhow, without there emerging an actual intellectual activity in terms of an objective situation and the owner of (this) objective situation apart from there persisting a subtle trace of it, left over from former habituation, one relaxes in this high-level one-flavoredness experience when one has thoroughly understood the encompassing nature of creative imagination and the far-reaching principle of universal connectedness.

(iv) While up to this phase, in view of the span of one's life, it is only after one has travelled the remainder of the path in the transitional phase (between death and rebirth) the Buddha-experience may unfold, the emergence of the graded process that goes beyond may come about for those who bring their creativity into full play, but such persons are very rare nowadays. However, if someone makes a concerted effort to gain the experience

(I shall detail), his present cognitive capacity, that has lost its edginess, arises as the inseparability of the composure state and post-composure state and, when what keeps inspection going has vanished, there is the low-level no-more-meditation experience (*sgom-med chung-ngu*); when even the last trace of mind's flitting between what comes-to-presence as the outer world and the grasping of it as (the experiencer's) inner world has regained its (original) diaphaneity in what is its legitimate dwelling, this fusion with (Being's) sheer lucency, like a child becoming re-united with its mother, is the medium level no-more-meditation experience (*sgom-med 'bring-po*); and when this process has reached its destination such that there is no objective domain coming-to-presence as an external world and when the intellect tied to inspection processes has been left behind since the belief in an ego or self as the (experiencer's) inner world has completely vanished, so that the (experiencer's) mind/mentation dissolves in the Buddha-experience, this is the high-level no-more-meditation experience (*sgom-med chen-po*). The followers of the rDzogs-chen teaching call this 'the sensation of Being's spontaneous thereness, an in-depth appraisal in which linear and irreversible time has been transcended'. At this 'time' the climax is such that (the experiencer) has done with intellection and done with the figures of the intellect.

To sum up, the four phases of absorbing sensations as presented in the mentality-related rDzogs-chen teaching as well as the four tuning-in procedures of the *Lhan-cig-kyes-sbyor*[58] teaching of the Mahāmudrā followers have been declared by the mystics of the past to be pretty much the same. Taken in themselves there is nothing definitive in their felt experiences and their understanding. Nonetheless, I shall write about how this comes about according to how such adepts as Yongs-'dzin Blo-gros rgyal-mtshan (born 1332) and others have taught it.

On the whole, there are many different kinds of instructions in both the Mahāmudrā and rDzogs-chen teachings. And, while in the end, the meaning of that which both approaches are driving at may not be altogether different, there are, if we look at their specific features, notable distinctions to be made in terms of whether it is claimed or not that what comes-to-presence is mind/mentation[59], of whether dichotomic thought processes and Being's meaning-rich gestalt dynamics are one and the same or not,[60] and of whether inspection is meditation or not.

The followers of the Mahāmudrā teaching, for instance, claim that the rDzogs-chen people make all sorts of blunders by falling into (what they call) the 'ultimate stuff' (*gshis*), while those in the higher reaches of rDzogs-chen say that up to the moment of the Mahāmudrā experience, the followers of this teaching are defiled by an intellectualistic perspective. Although people make such specific and sectarian claims as these, when an individual who is capable of tuning-in to Being and who, by studying under a competent teacher, comes to deeply understand Being's abidingness in its utter self-completeness and to see the whole of experienced reality to be but the frolicking of Being's possibilizing dynamics, he will not introduce any such separation. So, although it may be claimed by others that the followers of the rDzogs-chen teaching slip into some 'ultimate stuff', the very dynamics of this stuff is just what the ordinary spiritual pursuits call Being's optimization thrust (*bde-gshegs snying-po*) and what even the Mahāmudrā adherents themselves call 'Being as the starting-point Mahāmudrā (*gzhi phyag-rgya chen-po*)[61] or 'Being's abidingness as Mahāmudrā' (*gnas-lugs phyag-rgya chen-po*). All agree in recognizing the felt experience of the way and the logic in the stages in meditation to be the means to bring (the experience of Being) into the open. Therefore the flaw of which the followers of the rDzogs-chen teaching are accused does not stick to them.

Similarly, although it is said that the followers of the Mahāmudrā teaching have a merely intellectualistic perspective, this is just the contention of those inferior individuals who only go into practice.[62] But since those who deeply understand the meaning of Mahāmudrā, realize that seeing the very face of pure experiences, stripped of all intellectual thematizations, in all its nakedness, does not depend on a purely analytical and intellectualistic understanding, the flaw of which they are accused does not stick to them, either.

Furthermore, although both make specific claims regarding dichotomic thinking and Being's meaning-rich gestalt dynamics, they ultimately arrive at the same realization. Since the followers of the Mahāmudrā teaching do not claim that dichotomic thinking that reflects the subject's own mistaken identifications is

Being's meaning-rich gestalt dynamics and since the followers of the rDzogs-chen teaching do not reject a thinking that is 'fired' by its crucial charge, their views are similar in substance.

So also in the case of what comes-to-presence and mind/mentation there is agreement on all key points such that, since where in matters of the higher order reality these are beyond the limitations set by true and false and where on the part of the mere creative dynamics of the ec-static intensity on the commonly accepted (lower order) reality these may come as anything, none of them can be found as some concrete stuff and as to the coming-to-presence there is no point in denying or affirming it.

Even on the issue of whether inspection is meditation or not, there are some stupid people so utterly entangled (in their mental contortions) that they claim that taking one's mind prisoner is (what) the followers of the Mahāmudrā teaching (understand by) meditation, but this is only their own flaw. (The fact is that) all the great and capable persons in the bKa'-brgyud tradition make the inspection of (Being's) auto-luminescence (*rang-gsal-gyi dran-pa*) the process of meditation and since this is precisely what the followers of the rDzogs-chen teaching (refer to as) the auto-excitatory ec-static intensity of (Being's) superdiaphaneity (*ka-dag rang-rig*), they merely use different names for what is not different in substance. Neither the followers of the Mahāmudrā teaching nor the followers of the Dzogs-chen teaching would make the intellect with its over-evaluation of inspection the process of meditation.

In brief, then, according to the rDzogs-chen teaching (Being's) facticity/energy-'stuff' (*ngo-bo*) is a superdiaphaneity (*ka-dag*), its actuality/ownmostness (*rang-bzhin*) is a spontaneous thereness (*lhun-grub*), and its resonance (with itself as a whole, *thugs-rje*) is all-encompassing (*kun-khyab*) which together constitute a triune pristine awareness, and according to the Mahāmudrā teaching this (triune beingness of Being) is spoken of in terms of (Being's) substantiality (*gshis*) being (something) unborn (*skye-ba med-pa*), its effulgence (*gdangs*) being a ceaseless operation (*'gag-pa med-pa*), and its creative dynamics (*rtsal*) being its coming-to-the-fore as anything whatsoever (*cir yang 'char-ba*). Thus their claims are alike in that they are different descriptions of a single reality.

Also, with respect to the four phases of the absorbing sensations discussed above, there is a great variety as to whether these experiences will come or not in the sequence they have been discussed in view of the fact that the individual may be one who learns 'step-by-step', 'all at once', or 'in leaps and bounds', and through his endeavors, be they strong or weak, can combine or not combine them with his duties in life. Therefore, one must not, in one's enormous infatuation with and addiction to any single one, take this one to be the last word in this matter. Regardless of whether or not the virtues in the indication that the path is followed are born in one's being, if one has the trust that makes one see one's teacher as the Buddha and one engages in this creative imagination or meditation dilligently, putting all one's heart into it without slackening for a moment, the virtues of feeling and understanding (what it is all about) cannot but be born in one's being.

Although once one knows that this pure experience is the very meaning-rich gestalt of Being (as which Being becomes intelligible to us) and that in the vibrant dimension of its deeply felt understanding there is nothing to be creatively imagined by artificial means with their vested interest, the method of preserving the experiencing of this auto-excitatory ec-static intensity, uncontrived and settled in itself, without relapsing into the roaming about in the world of one's ordinary mistaken identifications, is stated in similar words in all Sutras, Tantras, and Existential Instructions.

The *mTshan-mo bzang-po'i mdo* states:

Do not run after what is past,
Do not set your hopes on what is yet to come,
But look at what is as it is
Here and now.
Without losing it or going astray from it
The wise make the most of it.

The *Yi-ge med-pa* (p. 223) declares:

When the triune creativity in seeing has been mastered what comes-to-presence is the vortex of Being's meaning-rich gestalt;
When there is no distraction by (the divisive notion of) there

being something to be done and someone doing it, Being's possibilizing dynamics becomes the place of bliss;
When one recognize what one encounters to be one's friend, this letting be becomes a single vibrant dimension;
When one is this stream that carries one, what else is there to do?

Furthermore, Śavaripa has stated:

Do not find fault with anything,
Without becoming distracted by anything go about your experiencing (what matters),
Do not hanker after the indication (of success) by the warmth (you may feel).

Paṇ-chen Śakyaśri expressed it in these words:

If you let whatever comes-to-presence be in its legitimate dwelling, there (is present) a spontaneous thereness that is dissociated from any doing something.
If you recognize whatever has arisen for what it is, (Being's) ec-static intensity dissolves in its own place.
If you have cut off the mind's flitting at its root, the divisiveness of ordinary thinking dissipates in (Being's) vast expanse (from which it has started).
If you bridge the time-shifts by your inspection, composure and post-composure states assume a single flavor.

mChims nam-mkha' grags-pa said:

Although you may talk about meditating, there is not so much as an atom of something to meditate on,
Although you may engage in non-meditation, there is no moment to become distracted.
In the seeing of reality there is neither something to meditate on nor someone to meditate.
(When) in entertaining the divisive notions of the intellect there is no moment to become distracted and
(When) non-meditation is without distraction, this tuning-in is meditation.

mKhas-grub g. Yag-sde paṇ-chen declared:

> If you meditate, it is intellection; if your are distracted, you go astray.
> When the intellect has transcended itself, the going astray is the pristine awareness.

Lastly, gNubs-ban yon-tan rgya-mtsho stated:

> Since mind/mentation and Being's possibilizing dynamics are nothing whatsoever,
> When meditating on it one does not meditate on anything.
> Since the notions in whatever specific guise they may crop up
> Are Being's possibilizing dynamics.
> One does not have to meditate on this expanse in which meanings are born in terms of it being something else.
> It cannot be stopped by attempting to improve it by resorting to aids (facilitating the removal of what should be removed).
> Thus, not to become distracted from it throughout the three aspects of time
> Is (the experience of) Being's meaning-rich gestalt.

To sum up, although there are countless statements to this effect in the Sutras and Tantras and the collected writings of the gifted sages of India and Tibet, I shall not continue for fear of using too many words.

* * *

(II)

Having thus briefly given a summary acccunt of how to experience Being's ec-static intensity and openness/nothingness (*rig-stong*) in the barrier-free approach (*khregs-chod*), I shall now briefly explain the meaning of what is intended by Being's lighting-up and openness/nothingness (*snang-stong*) in the final-leap approach (*thod-rgal*) which in its difference from all other approaches is the most wonderful one. Since this is not explained except in the highest levels of the rDzogs-chen teaching itself, not even in the Tantras belonging to the mentality section and the vortex section and also not in the existential information texts, the other spiritual pursuits have not even heard its name. Hence, later scholars for the most part could not get it into their heads and have tried to repudiate it on various grounds. Be this as it may, those superior and highly gifted persons who are worthy vessels (for receiving this teaching) cannot be changed into (followers of) a wrong path. Since even among the great majority of people there are only a few rare individuals who have the requisites to set out on this supreme path, there does not seem to be any point in simply rejecting it (for this reason).

Therefore, I shall summarily explain

A. How this reality concretely resides in one's own being, and

B. How the procedure of bringing it to the fore through a felt experience together with the indication of its presence and the measure of its effectiveness comes about.

(A)

What is the concrete nature of what so often has been said that in the psychophysical potential of (any) sentient being it resides as the thrust toward (the system's) optimization or as Being's possibilizing dynamics as an all-encompassing self-originated pristine awareness?

It is the present ec-static intensity, flawless, radiant and (yet) nothing (in its openness), naked and alert.

Where is it based?

It is based in one's live body as the configuration of the Victorious Ones[63] that has been spontaneously there from its very beginning.

How is it there?

Generally speaking, although from the viewpoint of its facticity/energy-'stuff' (*ngo-bo*) it does not reside in a (conceptual) framework of (it being) something that is born, passes away, and is (momentarily) there nor in the confines of existence or non-existence, eternalism or nihilism, coming or going, and from the viewpoint of its observable qualities (*rnam-pa*) it is there in unison with the triad of one's present body, speech, and mind, in general, as a pristine awareness as a function of the ec-static intensity, it pervades the whole of one's physical being, and, in particular, it resides in the *tsitta*, the palace of a lamp (consisting of the body's) tissue (*sha'i sgron-ma*)[64].

How does it actually reside there?

It resides there like a flame in a container. Moreover, its facticity/energy-'stuff' resides there as a (virtual) meaning-rich gestalt that is dissociated from conceptual-propositional limitations; its actuality/ownmostness is the gestaltism of a social horizon of meanings as a configuration of pristine awareness modes in five hues of light; and its resonance resides there as the ceaseless frolicking of the creative dynamics in the ec-static intensity that is the cognitive activity of six lamps.[65] So also it is stated in the *Klong-gsal*:

> In the live body of all sentient beings
> The (energy) chreods and (their) gates in the *tsitta* and *dung-khang*
> Are the residence of the ec-static intensity,[66]

and

> In the residence of one's precious live body
> (Being's) facticity/energy-'stuff' that is nothing and (yet) radiant resides there as a gestalt;
> Its actuality/ownmostness that is searing in its radiance (resides) there as the light of a singularity; and
> Its resonance that is a lighting-up and (yet) nothing resides there as lamps.

Being's very facticity/energy-'stuff' (also referred to as) a pristine awareness as the function of Being's ec-static intensity, a superdiaphaneity, (the inseparability of Being's) openness/nothingness and its radiance, a gestalt embodying Being's meaningfulness, (through a symmetry transformation becomes its) actuality/ownmostness, (the inseparability of its outward-directed) brilliance and inner glowing, and as such is spontaneously there as a configuration of calm deiform energies that present the five proto-patterns of existence (*rigs*) which constitute the gestaltism of a contextualized horizon of meanings. From its effulgence (there comes the felt quality of) bliss supreme with a configuration of 'blood-drinking' fierce deiform energies (residing) in the *dung-khang* palace. In brief, all the amassment of calm and fierce formulated energies (as concrete expressions of) one hundred proto-patterns of existence, or forty-two 'Buddha'-images,[67] of five gestalts (embodying Being's meaningfulness and dynamics)[68], or of a single proto-pattern of existence[69] and so on, are just the pristine awareness as a function of Being's ec-static intensity operating in one's self. Since this has been Being's spontaneous thereness since its very beginning, (it so happens) that, in the context of the present, its manifests itself in those sentient beings who have gone astray into what is the stepped-down version of ec-static intensity, as their psychophysical constituents, the five fundamental forces, the psychophysical potential (of theirs), the (dichotomic) operational fields, and the eight perceptual patterns, while for those (who attempt to) experience (the underlying dynamics) it comes-to-presence as organizing principles and information packages (*thig-le*) that pertain to both the higher order and lower order levels of reality[70], as lamps (*sgron-ma*), as presencings of hues of light (*'od-snang*), as gestalts (embodying meaning) and as a series of impulses (of Being's dynamics, *lu-gu rgyud*). In the context of the phase transition state all that arises is precisely the universal connectedness of the above, and in the context of finality when the climax, the overt presence of the latent potential, has been reached, the (feeling of oneself as a) meaning-embodying gestalt in a supramundane realm is nowhere else and nothing else (than Being's dynamics), precisely because it has taken it shape from the power in this process.

Concerning the specific details of how this dynamics resides in us, there are many different accounts in the individual Tantras and instructional works. Thus, the Sutras that deal with what is really meant[71] as well as the (texts belonging to) the 'mentality' (*sems*), 'vortex' (*klong*), and 'information' (*man-ngag*) sections in the rDzogs-chen teaching merely declare that the optimization thrust, the indivisibility of mentation and ec-static intensity, resides in the psychophysical potential of the living beings like oil in sesame seed. The instructional works dealing with the actual experiencing speak of it with having only the barrier-free approach in mind. Those works belonging to the arcane cycle of the rDzogs-chen teaching state that all the deiform energies, residing in one's heart, have bodily shapes, faces, and hands and, like in the (practice of the) developing phase,[72] are there quite concretely, and even with respect to the actual experience (of what is taught in the) instructional works, they speak of specific imaginative techniques that have as their reference the shapes and colors of the four lamps.

(B)

It is here in the unsurpassable sNying-tig teaching, more arcane than anything arcane, that what is (Being's precence in us) in its being what-it-is, is discussed in terms of its symbols (*brda*), thing-itself (*don*), and the indication for its dynamic presence (*rtags*)[73]. Thus, as discussed above in the context of it abiding in us, its facticity/energy-'stuff', being in accord with the intention in the barrier-free approach (to Being's) diaphaneity due to its being there as a meaning-rich gestalt, is (us as) the thing-itself; its actuality/ownmostness, being in accord with the configuration in the live body as discussed in the arcane cycle (of the rDzogs-chen teaching) due to its being there as luminosities, is its symbols; its resonance/ec-static intensity, being in accord with the sNying-tig teaching emphasing the immediacy (of experience) due to its being there as lamps, is the indication for its dynamic presence—the seeing of (Being's) vast expanse in its ec-static intensity (*dbyings-rig*). Thus, if one does not understand what symbols, thing-itself, and the indication for its dynamic presence actually mean, in the case of stupid and infatuated people it only makes their heads spin and in the case of the logicians it only serves as a reason to argue against it with words used in ordinary parlance. Under these circumstances it is all the more important to understand the intention of the sNying-tig.

So, then, along which path does this pristine awareness move?

Generally speaking, with respect to one's body as an energy structure (*rdo-rje'i lus*)[74] there are (in it) many pathways or chreods (*rtsa*)[75], one hundred million in all, if one were to count them. From among these seventy-two thousand have to do with the (circulation) of blood, twenty-one thousand six hundred have to do with the (organism's) motor-activity (motility, *rlung*)[76], thirty-two with the dynamics of the organizing principle (*byang-chub sems*)[77], thirty-seven with what is summed up as the (environing) cognitive domain (*yul*), and one hundred and fifty-seven with what it summed up as the five hierarchically organized dynamic regimes of human life (*'khor-lo*)[78] together with three primary pathways.

In the present context the path (along which the pristine awareness moves) is the (so-called) *ro-ma*, *rkyang-ma*, and *kun-'dar-ma* chreods, but in particular, it is the light chreod (*'od-rtsa*) called *ka-ti shel-gyi sbu-gu-can*. Although (the whole system's)' pristine awareness as a function of (its) ec-static intensity pervades everything, it abides, in particular, as the support base for the information package necessary for the production of (an organism) on the commonly accepted level of reality (*kun-rdzob rgyu'i thig-le*) and the information package necessary for the (working of the) pristine awareness modes on the higher level of reality (*don-dam ye-shes-kyi thig-le*).

Although according to the individual's capacity in making an experience of them, they have been spoken of in many different ways such as that they are there as if they were a gestalt, or as if they were a gnosemic nucleus, or if they were a singularity, or if they were some light frequency, these statements must not be considered as in any way contradictory or incongruous. Rather, one should remind oneself of what has been said previously, namely, the facticity/energy-'stuff' of Being's ec-static intensity cannot be established as anything whatsoever, nonetheless it may manifest in any guise whatsoever.

Of the three primary chreods, the one to the right (of the central chreod), called *ro-ma*, initiates an pristine awareness of sheer bliss, the one to the left, called, *rkyang-ma*, is connected with the coming-to-the-fore of the lighting-up of radiance, and the central one, called *kun-'dar-ma*, serves to provide the momentum or the basis of a conceptually undivided openness/nothingness. Although even in those instances where one attempts to experience (what life is about) by making the information package necessary for the production (of an organism) on the commonly accepted level of reality one's path, it is necessary to get to the bottom of the dynamics in the three (primary) chreods and the five hierarchically organized dynamic regimes of human life, here the instruction is concerned with making the information package necessary for (the working of) the pristine awareness modes on the higher order level of reality the way.

Thus, from the tip of the heart, referred to as the *tsitta* palace of the lamp (consisting of the body's) tissue, the *ka-ti shel-gyi sbug-can* chreod that is like a thread of white silk and in which there is neither blood nor lymph, branches off into two points such that from within the central region it runs into the network of chreods in the throat, and from the *dung-khang* palace in the head region it extends downward, inserting itself in the pupils of the two eyes and as such is called the 'lamp of the white and soft chreods' (*dkar-'jam rtsa'i sgron-ma*)[80]. Since this is the path along which pristine awareness will come forth in all its immediacy, it is also called the 'mysterious way of rDo-rje sems-dpa' (*rdo-rje sems-dpa'i gsang-lam*)[81]. This is also the quintessence of what is meant when it is said about a yogi who is tuned in to the sNying-tig teaching with its insistence on immediacy of experience, that at the moment of death Being's ec-static intensity in him, becoming projected into a new regime, proceeds along the eyes. So also the *Klong-gsal* states:

> In particular, the chreod, connected with the heart,
> As a silken thread (branching out) like the horns on a buffalo's head
> Enter the eyes as the controlling power (of seeing).
> This is the brilliant way of Being's possibilizing dynamics;
> With nothing left of words that go with subjective discursiveness,
> The gate through which perceptual immediacy arises is the eyes;
> The other gates are not like this.

After the sun of the pristine awareness that is a function of Being's ec-static intensity has risen along the path of the light chreod (*'od-rtsa*) the 'distance-capturing filtering lamp' (*rgyang-zhags chu'i sgron-ma*) shines through its gate that is the eyes, as (the illumination) of the immediacy of an auto-presencing of (what is the perception of) gestalts in a supramundane realm. This lamp is in itself differentiated in three aspects.

(1) a distance-capturing filtering lamp in which the fundamental forces have gathered and, thereby, serves as the basis for what is the sensory organ termed 'eye';

(2) a distance-capturing filtering lamp in which the controlling force is concentrated and, thus, is the cognitive capacity in

the eye capable of apprehending what presences as color-shape; and

(3) a distance-capturing filtering lamp the pristine awareness is concentrated and, thus, effects the seeing of Being's sheer lucency as it shines at the tip of the light chreod that is a radiation-dominated chreod.

It is through the combined power of these three lamps that the lighting-up of Being's possibilizing dynamics in all its immediacy is seen. So also it is stated in the *sGron-ma 'bar-ba'i rgyud* (p. 290):

By ceaselessly making things appear
At the gate of the eyes (to the extent that they present) the radiation-dominated function in this sense organ,
It resides there as the 'lotus eye'.

Similarly, the *sGra-thal-'gyur* (p. 113) states:

The very gate through which pristine awareness comes to the fore
Is the concentration of all that is the elixir of the live body, radiation-dominated,
It surges forth through the gate that is called *cakṣu(ḥ)*;
From here pristine awareness concretely originates.

It is on the basis of these three inner lamps that by feeling oneself into their underlying dynamics by means of (pertinent) instruction that the three outer lamps come to the fore. Through familiarizing oneself with them, the 'lamp (that presents the) time (it takes to make the) transition from one phase (in one's existence) to another (*bar-do dus-kyi sgron-ma*) as well as the 'lamp (that presents the) climax (of the process by which the system's potential) has come into full play' (*mthar-thug 'bras-bu'i sgron-ma*) come about automatically, particularly since the 'lamp (that is) Being (to the extent that it) abides as the starting-point' (*gnas-pa gzhi'i sgron-ma*) is ever-present and all-encompassing.

Thus these nine lamps form the basis of making an existential experience according to the rDzogs-chen teaching. They may be summed up into six or four lamps.

Having thus dealt with the first three lamps I shall now discuss the three following lamps together with the manner in which one goes about making a concrete experience of them. Any student who is a worthy vessel to fully hold the nectar that flows from the mouth of the teacher supreme, who sees to it that he is not defiled by the slightest infraction of his commitments, will have to go to the solitude of mountains, islands, and dense forests and there, in a place pleasing to the mind, whilst being moderate in appropriate clothing and food, dismiss all one's preoccupations with body, speech, and mind and make a clear distinction between samsara and nirvana. Then, as time permits, one will have to assume posturings (expressive of) the gestalt of Being's meaningfulness, similar to a lion, of the gestaltism of Being's contextualized horizon of meanings, similar to an elephant, and of the gestalt of the guiding-images (through which Being is manifestly operating), similar to a visionary. These have to be adopted in accordance with one's own disposition and one's surrounding and the personal instructions from one's teacher.

The basis (for the existential experience of the beingness of one's being) are the three immobilities (*mi-'gul-ba*) of one's body, one's eyes, and one's mentation. They are

1. Rolling one's eyes up, lowering them, and looking askance are the three crucial charges in the underlying dynamics of the 'gates' (*sgo'i gnad*) of seeing, which displays (specific) stances of perception;
2. The projection of 'immaculate field-excitation lamp' into the sky, a domain clear (like a polished) mirror, is the crucial charge in the underlying dynamics of the objective cognitive domain (*yul-gyi gnad*); and
3. Once one's breathing has been cleared so that it goes on gently and calmly, the composure of one's cognitive intensity, undivided by concepts, in the vibrant dimension of Being's diaphaneity, dissociated from distraction and errancy, is the crucial charge in the underlying dynamics of the motility-intensity complexity (*rlung-rig-gignad*).

These three crucial charges have to be experienced in and through the gyration of Being's possibilizing dynamics. So it is stated in the *sGra-thal-'gyur* (p. 90):

These crucial charges in the immediacy (of experience) pertain to body, speech, and mind;
The crucial charge in each of them will be pointed out explicitly:
By 'body' Being's triune gestalt dynamics is meant
Never must one go beyond its continuous streaming.
By 'speech' one is to point out (its relation to) learning, retention, and transmitting.
By 'mind' its projection into Being's vast expanse is understood.
One must never become separated from the instruction in these three crucial charges.
Furthermore, one has to rely on the crucial charge in (what is) the gates, the objective domain, and the motility-intensity complexity:
The gates is the seeing of Being's triune gestalt dynamics with one's (very) eyes;
Objective domain is the dissociation from (whatever) obsures it; and
The onset of pristine awareness through the calming of the motility-intensity complexity.

These crucial charges have to be studied deeply according to the guidance manuals and experienced according to their oral transmissions.

In the center of the 'immaculate field-excitation lamp' (*dbyings rnam-par dag-pa'i sgron-ma*) that is deep blue in color and enormous in scope, many shapes of no precise determination, such as the vowel sign (*na-ro*) of a sheer light in five hues, or vertically placed posts,[82] corbels[83] and others. Within this lamp there is (installed) the 'singularity-nothingness lamp' (*thig-le stong-pa'i sgron-ma*) which, at first, is of a reddish-yellow color or like the eyes of the fierce deiform energies and later enolves like the tail of a peacock and having a five-colored halo. From the very start of its operation, each singularity remains connected with the next, the first leading into the second and the second into the third, and when one finally has become fully familiar with it, there is an incredible multiplicity on an enormously large scale. (Simultaneously) the inner glow of Being's ec-static intensity, a continual series of impulses (*lu-gu rgyud*)[84] comes-to-presence in a quivering and twitching, coming and going manner similar to pearls becoming scattered and running everywhere. Sometimes all these impulses are ornamented with countless minor impulses (or light packages, *thig-phran*). In brief, they are the coming-to-presence of the proto-patterns of thought in accordance with each individual's psychophysical potential and giftedness.[85]

The *sGron-ma 'bar-ba'i rgyud* (p. 309) states:

Although in the diaphanous perceptual pattern (through which) the eye (operates)
(Being's field-excitation), like the rays of light from a light-giving flaring (lamp),
Is present in an invariant and all-encompassing manner,
It yet abides as a deep-blue auto-effulgence.
Since its coming-to-presence making (things) to come to the fore never ceases
It lights up as the observable qualities in (what constitutes) the external (cognitive) domain,

and (p. 310):

In itself this field-(excitation) is a halo
That in its invariance and primordial supereffulgence
Has abided in all Buddhas and sentient beings,
[Without ever having been created by anyone],
In its primordial non-duality and consistency (with itself and everything else),

and (p. 300):

The singularity-nothingness lamp—
He who, in the mutual trust (that pervades) the whole of reality,
Knows it (in what it is),
Will enjoy this singularity in (his experience of himself as a) gestalt,

and, lastly, the *Seng-ge rtsal-rdzogs* (p. 317) declares:

'Field' (*dbyings*) means the lamp of Being's vast expanse and

'Excitation' (*rig*) means (its) radiance in a continual series of impulses.
'Field' means an aura of light and
'Excitation' means the coming-to-presence of five gestalts.
The 'field' and its 'excitation' with its three pristine awareness modes
Abides in such a manner that none can be added to nor subtracted from the other.

The 'self-originated intensely appreciative acumen lamp' (*shes-rab rang-byung-gi sgron-ma*) is the agency that makes (one) see and understand the auto-presencing of Being's pristine awareness modes and is the very pristine awareness that is a function of Being's ec-static intensity (as it is experienced in one's self) and (thus) the rationale behind the thinking in the barrier-free approach (*khregs-chod*) to the beingness in one's being.

Now, the general run of the Buddhist teaching is to lump mentation (*sems*) and ec-static intensity (*rig*) together, here, however, as has been stated before, already at the very beginning (of the practice) one has to differentiate between (Being's) diaphaneity (*ka-dag*) and a closed system potential (*kun-gzhi*) and, at this point, where one deals with the path, one has again to distinguish between mentation and ec-static intensity for the simple reason that one has to make this ec-static intensity the foundation of the lived through experience of the path.

Thus, the founding stratum or the residence of mentation is the lungs that treasure breathing; its path is the gullet through which the white (inhalation stuff) and the black (exhalation stuff) pass; its gate are the mouth and nose; its function is the whole gamut of the cause-effect relationship that makes up samsara; its essence is the stepped-down version of ec-static intensity, (one's) cognitive capacity in its going astray; its synonyms include 'mentation' (*sems*), 'subjectivity' (*yid*), 'perception' (*rnam-shes*), 'self-perpetuating inveterate tendencies (*bag-chags*), 'intellect' (*blo*), 'divisiveness crystallizing into concepts' (*rtog*), and '(subliminal) flickering' (*'gyu*). Since the aid of this subliminal flickering, figuratively spoken of as the 'horse' (on which it rides) is the (organism's) motor-activity that involves it in headlong actions (*las-kyi rlung*), it is for this reason that one must not concentrate on this motor-activity or mentation or the information package necessary for the production of an organism, all of which pertain to the commonly accepted (lower order of) reality.

The residence, path, and gate of the ec-static intensity have already been discussed before, here, its facticity (or dynamic essence) is the intense energy in the Buddha-experience or Being's triune gestalt dynamics with its three pristine awareness modes and two kinds of sensitivity;[86] its function is to make one reach the summit of all experiences summed up in (what is referred to as) nirvana or to lead one to spiritual maturity and to the freedom (one has been all along); its synonyms are countless and include such designations as 'diaphaneity' (*ka-dag*), 'that which is beyond the intellect' (*blo-'das*), 'auto-excitation' (*rang-rig*), 'a gestalt embodying Being's meaningfulness' (*chos-sku*), 'the one and only information packet' (*thig-le nyag-gcig*), 'self-transcendence through appreciative discrimination' (*shes-rab phar-phyin*), 'the ultimate imprinting' (Mahāmudrā), 'super-completeness' (rDzogs-chen), 'a primordial awareness that pertains to the higher order level of reality' (*don-dam-pa'i ye-shes*). It is this that in the context of the final-leap approach (*thod-rgal*) here is called the 'self-originated intensely appreciative acumen lamp'.

In brief, since all the other lamps that have been discussed are the projective of this lamp and have their basis in it and since this one encompasses all the rest, it the crucial charge in one's travelling or not travelling the reliable path. So also the *sGron-ma 'bar-ba* (p. 293) states:

> Since it abides as that which makes known (what goes on in
> All the other lamps,
> It abides in such a manner that by it
> There is no fragmentation in the whole,

and (p. 294):

> He who knows that the visible and invisible
> Have no eigenstate,
> (This knowledge) is an indication of its (activity),

and, elsewhere, (in the *sGra-thal-'gyur*, p. 128) it is stated:

Since the flickering of the cognitive capacity is (Being's) nothingness (that has assumed the guise of an) objective domain,
The cognitive capacity that sees (this domain) is (not so much) different from Being's ec-static intensity;
It is this latter one that in its very operation dissolves (into its very freedom) and
In the knowledge of its singleness the whole is made to dissolve.

Not only does this lamp make its presence felt in the final-leap approach, it also is the cardinal charge in six perceptual patterns, manifestations of (a person's) going astray due to his ingrained tendencies (programs), and on this lamp alone it depends whether a person will recover or not the freedom (he has been). Therefore, since the foremost of all lamps and even encompassing them is this self-originated intensely appreciative acumen lamp, one has to strive assiduously for (the experience of) its effulgence, a continual series of impulses. According to the *Nor-bu phra-bkod-kyi rgyud* (p. 71):

> If you want to look at the spirituality of all the Buddhas, then look at the gestalt the continual series of impulses (assumes); if you want to understand the superthought of all the Buddhas, then do not become separated from the continual series of impulses; if you want to know the whole of reality, be it in condensed or expanded way, look at the thereness of the continual series of impulses; if you want to have vision, its development by creative imagination, and its enacting in life all together, do not become distracted from the continual series of impulses. Indeed, lordship over the gestalt dynamics of all perfect Buddhas boils down to the continual series of impulses.

Thus, in one's efforts to experience the barrier-free approach and the final leap as forming a unity, one must, throughout the night, plunge into the ocean of and remain tuned-in (to your natural condition) and, furthermore, during the day, not become fettered by denying or affirming that comes with one's obsession of taking whatever appears before one's six perceptual patterns to be real, but rather seal them with the cardinal charges in the four (perspectives of Being's) self-emancipatory letting-be, while in the late evening, without letting the inner errancy of the dreaming process slip into an aimless murkiness, one has to convert it into the sheer lucency (of Being) as if the knowable were poured into a pitcher. (Lastly), in the mornings and evenings, one must pull out the peg of one's utter obsession with and clinging to the distractive trivialities of everyday life such as food and clothing.

Rather, in all circumstances the decisive awareness of the vibrant dimension of (Being's) 'field' and its 'excitation' as the energy in this lived through experience, has to be supported by

(i) vision (*lta-ba*) as a letting-be (that is as firm as) a mountain (*ri-bo cog-gzhag*), in its neither stepping out of itself nor changing into something other than itself;

(ii) creative imagination (*sgom-pa*) as a letting-be that in its going beyond the intellect (attempting to subjectively) appropriate the inseparability of (Being's) coming-to-presence and its nothingness (is as vast and deep as) the ocean (*rgya-mtsho cog-gzhag*);

(iii) an existential instruction (*man-ngag*) as a letting-be of ec-static intensity (*rig-pa cog-gzhag*) that is the peeling off of the bark of inveterate tendencies with their proclivity of going astray (into the lower order reality) by virtue of the effulgence of ec-static intensity, the continual series of impulses (*lu-gu rgyud*), has been taken captive; and

(iv) a lived through experience (*nyams-len*) as a letting-be of (Being's) coming-to-presence (*snang-ba cog-gzhag*) that is a non-swerving from the immediacy of a pristine awareness that is not fettered by feelings of some (pseudo-)bliss, some (pseudo-) lucency, and some (pseudo-)nondivideness by concepts without coming under the sway of the murkiness of depression and the wildness of elation.

Therefore, in view of the necessity of striving for these four letting-be aspects, the root of what really matters, as discussed in treatises dealing with this topic and in the existential instructions, must be known to be found in this very experience of the inseparability of Being's field and its excitation.

I shall now explicate the spreading of four lighting-up phases (*snang-ba bzhi*) as they occur in a sequence of indications and measures of effectiveness (*rtags-tshad*) together with their pegs of certitude that are the measures of their emancipatory dynamics (*grol-tshad*) in those yogis who endeavor to bring about a synthesis of the above experiences. The ordinary indications and measures of effectiveness in the barrier-free approach have been shown to tally with the requisites in the Mahāmudrā and rDzogs-chen teachings discussed above. Here, the sequence of the four lighting-up aspects in the final leap approach as presented in the instructions that deal with their specificities, will be discussed in a summary fashion such that the coming to the fore of each of the four lighting-up phases as well as their indications and measures of effectiveness are explained together.

If one has not, first of all, brought into the open the indications (for the experience to occur) by way of the general and specific preliminary practices, which begin a clear distinction between samsara and nirvana, then, when it comes to the actual experience, the thought processes (involved) and the indications and measures of effectiveness will not come about in harmony with each other. Specifically, by not properly understanding the underlying dynamics in the barrier-free approach, here (in the final leap approach), too, (this underlying dynamics) will not become the path (along which the experience moves), hence it is of utmost importance that, right at the beginning, one gets a firm grip on the flawless basis for these (lighting-up) experiences. Once one has experienced (what has been said) in the proper manner there comes

(i) first a visionary experience that derives from the (mutual) encounter of the lighting-up of Being's field-character (*dbyings*) presenting a luminous halo (*'od-khyim*), of the lighting-up of a lamp (*sgron-ma*) being the (information) singularity (*thig-le*), and of the lighting-up of the ec-static intensity in its gestalt dynamics (*sku'i rig-pa*) being the continual series of impulses (*lu-gu-rgyud*). This visionary experience is called 'the lighting-up that is (the visionary experience of) the immediacy of Being's possibilizing dynamics' (*chos-nyid mngon-sum-gyi snang-ba*). When this visionary experience is at first feeble or infrequent, it is spoken of as 'having caught it by the nose' (*sna zin-pa*); when it is properly seen and recognized it is spoken of as 'reaching the very bottom of it' (*gtan-la phebs-pa*); and when finally there is no difficulty in looking and looking (at this visionary presence) it is spoken of as 'the creativity in it having come into full play' (*rtsal-rdzogs*). It should be noted that the different descriptive terms used to circumscribe the various phases in this visionary experience also apply to each of the subsequent phases of the lighting-up process.

The indications of (one's) reaching the very bottom of Being's possibilizing dynamics in the immediacy (of its) experience become at the three gates (through which an individual interacts with the environing world):

(i) one's body is like a tortoise that[87] has been placed in a metal basin. It does not engage in any extraneous activities and has no desire to go beyond the posturing (*bzhugs-stangs*) of (Being's) gestalt triad. When one's 'body' has been matured (into a 'gestalt') by the 'vase'-empowerment with its conceptual-propositional limitation, (this state of maturity) is, in the rDzogs-chen teaching, said to be the indication of one's having got rid of the craving for doing something;

(ii) one's speech is like that of a mute person. This having got rid of the pouring forth of mere talk and verbiage that goes astray into the ordinary and vulgar is effected by the 'mystery'-empowerment; and

(iii) one's mind is like a bird caught in a cage. The moment it attempts to take off into dichotomic thinking it is caught hold of by the ec-static intensity and has become powerless to go into its mistaken identifications.

While these are specific indications, the ordinary ones are as follows: a trust in and devotion to one's teacher whom one sees as the Buddha in the concrete is born (in one's self) in a genuine manner; kindness and compassion comes effortlessly and one is certain about the relationship between cause and effect; the coarse affective pollutants are suppressed and one's cognitions move in a flexible manner; and since (genuine) bliss, (genuine) lucency, and (genuine) undividedness by concepts rise trough their own power, one's intellect does not get involved in the trivial and distractive activities of this world. In brief, while these indications are said to be pretty much the same as the indications of the way as circumscribed by the three intensity levels of the peak experience (*rtse-gcig gsum*) in the Mahāmudrā teaching, the measure of their effectiveness is that, if an individual reaching the very bottom of Being's possibilizing dynamics in the immediacy of its experience, is not defiled by transgressions with respect to his commitments, the gates leading into evil existences are for ever closed.[88]

Then, when one experiences (this dynamics) in a still more steady manner than before, there comes

(ii) 'the lighting-up that is (the sensuously felt) progressive self-intensification of vibrations' (*nyams gong 'phel-gyi snang-ba*). This has two aspects: vibrations in the lighting-up (*snang-nyams*) and vibrations in the cognitive capacity (*shes-nyams*). Of these the relishing of the mind's-radiation dominated 'stuff' with its fragile qualities of bliss, lucency, and non-dividedness by concepts and so on, are vibrations in the cognitive capacity; since they change and revert (again to the state before their change), increase and decrease (in intensity) they are not to be taken as standards. Here, in this context, one has to take the vibrations in the lighting-up as standards. The lighting-up of the field-(character of Being), coming as a display of (colorless, yet tinted) light (*'od*) that, compared with the previous light, grows ever more in intensity and assumes the shapes of a five-colored searingly brilliant blanket of light, a vertical post, corbels, a spars, a chessboard, and a yurt, or of a tent, a domed building, a thousand-petaled lotus; or it may assume the form of such emblems as a wheel, a scepter, and a jewel as well as countless other shapes such as the seven royal treasures[89] or the eight auspicious symbols[90] and so on. In particular, each of these distinct variations are the effulgence of the five pristine awareness modes such that the mirror-like originary awareness mode presents a vertical post; the self-consistency pristine awareness mode corbels, the specificity-mapping pristine awareness mode butt-ends;[91] the tasks-posed and tasks-accomplished pristine awareness mode a yurt; and the Being's meaning-rich field pristine awareness mode a house of light having the size of a district. Or, the lighting-up of the field-(character of Being) comes-to-presence in thought processes that cannot be exhausted by words such as the mirror-like pristine awareness being like one's eyes watering because of glare; the consistency pristine awareness being like lace and half-lace curtains; the specificity-mapping pristine awareness being like a bouquet of flowers; the tasks-posed and tasks-accomplished pristine awareness mode being like and array of weapons; and the meaning-rich field pristine awareness mode being like a maṇḍala or a fortress.

When this lighting-up of the field-(like character of Being, *dbyings*), is at first, as large as one square cubit and the (information) singularity (*thig-le*) in it, also not larger than a globule, one speaks of it as 'having taken (this lighting-up) by the nose', and when, finally, (the field) grows in size such as to engulf a whole province or the valley in which one lives, and the singularity in it becomes as large as a metal basin or a rattan shield, one speaks of it as 'reaching the very bottom' and as its 'creativity having come into full play'.

At this time the indications are that

(i) the body is said to feel like a person stricken by a disease. Such a person is disinterested in giving himself airs or feeling ashamed or being a dandy;

(ii) speech is like that of a madman. His talk with respect to the world's craving for its mistaken identifications does not fall into the normal pattern; and

(iii) the mind is like that of person having been heavily drugged and has become insensitive. Since all the ordinary dichotomies have submerged and dissolved in the vortex of ec-static intensity, (this mind) has become dissociated from the subjectivism of organismic thinking with its errancy mode that pertains to the commonly accepted (lower order) reality, and does not pass beyond (Being's) vibrant dimension in its nothingness, radiance, and diaphaneity.

At this time the ordinary indications are as follows: since the (mind's) going astray into the belief in the concrete existence (of what it encounters) has ended, the tendencies that give rise to such notions as enemy and friend, attachment and aversion have thoroughly dissipated and it has become free from the concern with trifling matters, sweet dishes and nice clothing, happiness and sadness, the graceful and the horrid, rejection and acceptance, negation and affirmations and so on. All these indications (reflect the) effectiveness of the thoroughly conceptualization-free pristine-awareness-through-appreciative-discrimination empowerment and, since at this time one has generally got rid of the fetters of the belief in the concrete existence of things, the ec-static intensity has been said to be like a bird about to fly, but it is more like a bee circling around where there is honey.

In brief, although many people relate these experiences to the conceptualization-free state (*spros-bral*) of the Mahāmudrā teaching, they seem by virtue of the power of the final-leap approach being an especially quick path, in general, to be similar to the one-flavor (*ro-gcig*) state. It has been stated that by merely 'having taken (this lighting-up experience) by the nose' samsara and nirvana have split and that hereafter one will not re-enter the womb of the six forms of existence, but becomes released in one's natural spiritual realm. 'Reaching the very bottom (of this experience)' and 'its creativity having come into full play' mean that after the union with (Being's) sheer lucency in the transition phase (from one dynamic regime into another) the measure of the effectiveness (of this experience) is such that with the lighting-up of (Being's) holomovement as an open possibility, but not later, one cannot but become free (and dissolve) in either presencing.

Thereafter comes

(iii) 'the lighting-up that (is 'felt' as) one's ec-static intensity having reached the its scope' (*rig-pa tshad-phebs-kyi snang-ba*). The lighting-up of the field-(character of Being) encompasses the whole expanse of the sky, while the lighting-up of the (information) singularity in it, about the size of a scabbard or a large kettle drum, comes in an arrangement of five or nine or more clusters and there is no fixed rule as to whether these come alone or in a series. In each of these singularities there is a lotus flower with four or more petals (on which), at first, the (male) gestalts of the calm (deiform) energies without their (female) consorts or a single gestalt without ornaments appear and, thereafter, clusters of five (on which) the male and female gestalts have joined in intimate embrace. Finally, the gestalt is as vast in scale as the lighting-up itself. Furthermore, at this time, in every single pore of one's body one sees hundreds and thousands of Buddha-realms, if not to say, countless such realms. Although the material phenomena of the external world, earth, stones, and rocks may or may not continue being present, in each blade of grass, in each leaf on trees, and in each atom there appear immeasurable structured patterns of Buddha-realms.

In brief, while the (underlying) thought pattern of this (lighting-up) phase goes far beyond the domain of what can be expressed in words, the (information) singularity assumes a 'waiting' gesture (*sdod-pa*) without trembling and quivering. Furthermore, since from this time onward all that is later on going to come-to-presence in the phase transition has been decided, strands of rays of light from one's heart will touch the gestalts on the clusters. In the space above one's head orbits of light, (in colors) like a peacock's tail, appear hierarchically organized in countless levels and in the upper space (of this total space) there are the configurations of the fierce (deiform) energies, in the center space right in front (of one's self) there is the configuration of the calm (deiform) energies (that make up the) gestaltism of (Being's) contextural horizon of meaning, and in the lower space (of this total space) there are the realms of one's naturally spiritual concerns. In brief, at this time, the polyvalent lighting-up of (Being's) holomovement is coming-to-presence in its thoroughgoing completeness.

At that time the indications are that

(i) the body is like an elephant that has the ability to extract itself in a moment out of the swamp into which it has sunk. Since the materiality of the external and internal world has dissolved in the diphanaeity that is its legitimate dwelling, rocks and mountains, manors and houses turn intangible and insubstantial;

(ii) speech is like the melodious sounds by a young siren, enrapturing the mind of anyone who hears them; similarly whatever a yogi says bears on life's meaning and his words are declarations of truth. He is able to convey countless messages bearing on life's meaning suited to the different intellectual capacity of each and every living being at one and the same time; and

(iii) the mind is like a person, who having been cured of the plague, no longer worries about getting it again. Once the rope that ties one to samsara and nirvana has been cut, one need no longer be afraid of relapsing into samsara and, since the creativity in one's ordinary capabilities, (actually) unlimited, has come into full play, one can rise into the air or drop through the earth, and without in any way being restrained by the fundamental forces one has gained autonomy in displaying different transformations of patterns in mind-body structures. This is (so, because) the effectiveness in the utterly conceptualization-free words-and-meaning empowerment has reached its limits and, to put it briefly, since (Being's) gestalt triad in its completeness (acts) as (one's) way (to wholeness), and since the goal (one is to reach) is (already) prefigured in essence,[92] and since (one's) materiality has dissolved in the light (that is Being), the overt manifestation of Being's pellucidity and consummation in this one's body is the measure of its effectiveness.

Although these experiences have been related to the low and medium levels of the no-more-meditation (*sgom-med*) phase (in the Mahāmudrā teaching), they actually correspond to what is the culmination of the high level no-more-meditation phase; while (here the experiencer) has done with the obscuring acts by body, contextural setting, and mind, it is only after he has got rid of the last trace of the obscuration that is (the welter of) representational constructs, that the immense creativity in the qualities of (what constitutes the triad of) sensitivity, love, and capability is full present, hence beyond (this level) there is no place to go.

After this (lighting-up phase, however,) there comes what is referred to as

(iv) 'the lighting-up that is ('felt' to be) the end of Being's possibilizing dynamics' (*chos-nyid zad-pa'i snang-ba*). This is also spoken of as 'the subsiding of what has come-to-presence as the external (*phyi'i snang-ba*) in the expanse of Being as an interiority (*nang-dbyings*)' or as 'the Buddha-experience as a passing beyond frustration by virtue of Being's gestalt dynamics in discrete formulations (*gzugs-sku*) gathering in the gestalt dynamics of pure meaningfulness (*chos-sku*)' or as 'the goal that has no longer anything to do with the intellect and its constructs (*blo-zad chos-zad*) because one has become dissociated from the thematic vestiges of one's always having to do something'. In brief, the intended meaning of this phase is that Being's spontaneity (*lhun-grub*, as Being's actuality) has submerged in the diaphaneity of Being (*ka-dag*, as Being's virtuality).

At this time the indications are as follows:

(i) the body, dissociated from its materiality, is said to be (feel) like a bird that has flown free from its cage;

(ii) speech is said to be like an echo: on the part of those who have to be guided there is an understanding of the various ways of gaining access to life's meaning, while on one's part there is nothing to be talked about and no one doing the talking; and

(iii) mind is like a person who, struck in the heart by an arrow, instantly dies. Since one has done with (one's) body, feelings, sensory apparatus, and the welter of divisive notions, one cannot but fuse with the Buddha-experience (in which) Being's possibilizing dynamics has dissipated in the vast expanse (of the beingness of Being). Because this is beyond the cognitive domain of the ordinary indications and measures of effectiveness, it is ineffable. So also the *sGra-thal-'gyur* (p. 91) states:

> With the lighting-up of Being (in the) immediacy of its possibilizing dynamics
> One goes beyond the ego-based verbiage of discursive thinking;
> With the lighting-up of vibrations (in this process) that grow and spread into higher and higher regimes
> One makes the coming-to-presence of mistaken identifications subside;
> With the lighting-up that constitutes Being's ec-static intensity having reached the limits of its scope
> One passes beyond the coming-to-presence of the path that is the understanding of Being's gestalt triad;
> With the lighting-up (in which the experiencer) has done with Being's possibilizing dynamics
> One cuts off the stream of samsara that is the triad of (en-worlded) spheres.

In these instances of experiencing the above four lighting-up phases one takes the three immobilities (*mi-'gul-ba gsum*) as one's starting-point. In the wake of their experience the (specific) pristine modes in the four lighting-up phases (grow into the level of) the vibrations growing and spreading into higher and higher regimes. In this very process there come, in addition, three 'waiting' gestures (*sdod-pa gsum*). Which are they?

(i) externally, since the coming-to-presence (*snang-ba*) is waiting, under the impact of its modifiers, (this coming-to-presence) manifests as supranatural realms;

(ii) internally, since the phantasmal body (*sgyu-lus*) is waiting, (the experiencer) becomes dissociated from the mistaken identifications due to distractions; and

(iii) arcanely, since (the unity of) motility and ec-static intensity (*rlung-rig*) is waiting, (the experiencer) does not pass beyond

Being's vortex that is the inseparability of Being's field-(like) character and its (excitation in) pristine awareness modes.

At the time of (the lighting-up in which) Being's ec-static intensity has reached the limits of its scope there come three 'obtainments' (*thob-pa gsum*):

(i) through the obtainment of autonomy concerning (the unity of) motility and mentation (*rlung-sems*) a body-mind structure that thoroughly weakens the forces of materiality comes about and, furthermore, the creativity in the qualities whose (direct) indications are the feeling of warmth while travelling the paths and scaling the spiritual levels, is in full play;

(ii) through the obtainment of autonomy concerning one's taking birth (*skye-ba*) one lives on for the benefit of living beings as long as the world exists in the gestalt of an idea (*sku-gzugs*) that in its presencing which yet is nothing is like the reflection of the moon in water and that is called 'the superb transformation gestalt' in its being visible to others after one's own body has dissolved in pure light. Examples are the many spiritual masters like Padmasambhava and Vimalamitra.[93]

(iii) through the obtainment of autonomy concerning one's continuance (*'jug-pa*) one makes the stream of benignant actions (in which) the inseparable unity of (its) gestaltism and pristine awareness (expresses itself) flow on uninterruptedly once one has seen that there is no longer any necessity to maintain the connectness of one's concrete existence with those who have to be guided and (so) has passed into the diaphaneity that is Being's meaning-rich expanse in which there is nothing of one's old psychophysical constituent, and (taken along) with oneself three thousand or more living beings who through their previous resolutions are suited to complete their unfinished tasks.

Furthermore, in those individuals who have experienced these four lighting-up phases the measure of their effectiveness becomes manifest in the manner they dream and the indications of which it has been said that they come about in one's body and speech, are the same that have been discussed in the context of the lighting-up of Being in the immediacy of its possibilizing dynamics in terms of one's body being like a tortoise that has been placed in a metal basin and so on. The indications are as follows:

(i) for highly capable and diligent persons the measure of their emancipatory effectiveness (*grol-ba'i tshad*) during their present life-span is that their dreams sink into Being's vast expanse; since thereby the process of going astray has been cut off they have become the continuity of Being's sheer light throughout the cycle of day and night;

(ii) for people with medium capabilities the measure of their emancipatory effectiveness is found in the phase transition. The dream process does not go astray because the dreamer has full knowledge of the fact that he is dreaming; and

(iii) for people with low capabilities (the measure of their emancipatory effectiveness) lies in their relaxing in the realms of their natural spiritual domains and as being candidates for gaining the Buddha-experience within five hundred years, they have only pleasant dreams.

Within the ordinary spiritual pursuits, these dreams are said to be indications that one has reached the level of a Bodhisattva, as discussed in such works as the *Suvarṇaprabhāśottamasūtra*, the *Daśabhūmikaśūtra* and other works. They have special dreams on a continual basis such as climbing a golden mountain, sitting on the sun and moon, or emitting rays of light from their bodies that burn away the misery of the beings in the six forms of existence.

In those yogis in whom these four lighting-up phase have found their fullest expression, the four assurances (*gdeng-ba*) about the measure of the emancipatory effectiveness arise on their own:

(i) they have the assurance of being fearless because they are no longer terrified or afraid of any tangible or intangible dangers, or of having to suffer in the hot and cold hells;

(ii) they have the assurance that they need no longer dread being (re-)born as one of the six kinds of living beings or wandering about in samsara with its three levels of existential domains. These are the two lower-level assurances;

(iii) they also have the assurance of no longer having to yearn for the qualities in the Buddha-experience and the relishing of the bliss in the Buddha-realms; and

(iv) they have the assurance that there is no need for wishful anticipations of attaining the goal of nirvana. These are said to be the two higher-level assurances.

The obtainment of these four (assurances) comes about on the basis of having come to the conclusion that all that is Being's ec-static intensity (in one's self) transcending the intellect. When one's true existential reality has come to the fore, the five paths as discussed in the ordinary spiritual pursuits, and the ten spiritual levels of the outer, cause-oriented pursuit, and the sixteen spiritual levels that light up in the inner, goal-sustained pursuits, have been travelled and completed of their own. Among these the five paths have been discussed as follows in the *Thig-le kun-gsal* (p. 242):

> The means for understanding the one way that cannot be travelled (in the ordinary sense of the word)
> Is explained, in ordinary parlance, in terms of five outstanding ways:
> (i) When one stays close to worthy persons and
> Shows one's fullest respect to the teacher
> This is called the Way of Preparation.
> (ii) When the teacher elucidates the meaning of the injunctions and
> When one integrates the two approaches[94] in one's mind
> This is called the Way of Linkage.[95]
> (iii) When one in this life obtains an utter certitude
> By way of four direct encounters[96]
> This is said to be the Way of Seeing.
> (iv) Both the creative imagination in which there is no imaging[97] and
> The creative imagination in which there is imaging[98]
> Are said to be non-addable and non-separable,
> This I call the Way of creative imagination.
> (v) When the design process of the Buddha-experience has come into full play in (what is) the foundation of bliss supreme,[99]
> Without abiding (statically)
> This is shown to be the Way of No-more-learning.
> Therefore, samsara, nirvana, and the three-fold path and
> All that comes-to-presence
> Arises from (one's) mind and presences before (one's) mind.
> There is nothing else that is not (mind).

The meaning of the ten spiritual levels is that a person who sees reality (in its true light), quickly scales all the spiritual levels. Moreover, once he has infused his whole being with (the experience of) his encounter with what the barrier-free and the final leap approaches are about, there arises in him a feeling of supreme joy. This is the first spiritual level—'the joyful one'.

The recognition (of this experience) to be an auto-presencing of Being is the second spiritual level—'the flawless one'.

Familiarizing oneself with (this awareness) step by step is the third spiritual level—'the one unlocking light'.

Seeing ever more clearly Being's possibilizing dynamics in all its immediacy, the lighting-up of Being's field-(like) character and its ec-static intensity,[100] is the fourth spiritual level—'the one emitting light'.

The return of all the pollutants to their natural purity through the power (in this level) is the fifth spiritual level—'the one difficult to practice'.

Seeing how (Being's) gestalt dynamics emerges out of (Being's information) singularity[101] is the sixth spiritual level—'the one (in which Being) has come into the open'.

Turning one's back on samsara is the seventh spiritual level—'the one that goes far'.

The non-recurring of dichotomic thinking is the eighth spiritual level—'the non-shaking one'.

When the panorama of (Being's) lighting-up has become a presence in utter completeness and one has won control over (Being's) pristine awareness (in one's self) and (one's) mind-body working, this is the ninth spiritual level—'the one of proper thinking'.

When the lighting-up of (Being's) pristine awareness has gripped one's cognitive capacity and one thereby understands the inner working of all that is and has control over clouds of supramundane realms (with their) oceans (of pristine awareness modes), one has reached the tenth spiritual level[102]—'the cloud of life's meaning'.

While these ten spiritual levels are identical in name with those pertaining to the concern with Being's pellucidity and consummation in the cause-oriented spiritual pursuit, they are far superior to them in meaning. Those who are about to enter and live on the spiritual level of a person bent on experiencing Being's pellucidity and consummation have to undergo all kinds of difficulties[103] in realizing the path of the two requisites such as the ten transcending functions and so on and yet, even in the (changed) mind-body pattern of theirs and the supramundane realms that evolve from these practices, they still hold on to the difference between an objective (cognitive) domain and mind/mentation. Here, however, through the profound expertise of the quick path no difficulties are involved. Through the recognition and decisive awareness that the coming-to-presence, in all its vastness, of Being's dynamic qualities in gestalts and supramundane realms is the (working of that) sole singularity which is Being's ec-static intensity in its auto-excitation in one's self, even if headlong actions and affective pollutants together with the grime of one's mental constructs are still present, one need no longer cling to the (purely intellectual) distinction between that which has to be eliminated and that which aids its elimination, since through the cardinal dynamics of their clearing up by themselves the path that is so revealed is an especially superior one.

Even with respect to the sixteen intrapsychic levels[104] one does not have to attend to the path on which the affective pollutants become transmuted (in the course of) the four joys[105] gradually becoming rarefied, as this is insisted on in the lower Mantrayāna. Here, their dissolution in the 'dynamic' essence of the four aspects of (Being's) sheer lucency is as follows:

(ia) The (at first diffuse) spreading (*mched-pa*) of the lighting-up of Being's possibilizing dynamics in the immediacy (of its perception) is (a function of) the eye;

(ib) the (more centered) spreading (*nye-bar mched-pa*) of this lighting-up is (a function of) the eye's eyeness;

(ic) the (approximate) securing (*thob-pa*) is the seeing of a continual series of impulses; and

(id) the (exact) securing (*nye-bar thob-pa*) is one's familiarity with it.

(iia) The (at first diffuse) spreading of the lighting-up of vibrations that grow and spread into higher and higher regimes is a sheer light;

(iib) the (more centered) spreading is a singularity;

(iic) the (approximate) securing is the colors of the pristine awareness modes; and

(iid) the (exact) securing is the coming-to-presence of the field-(character) of Being as a manifold.

(iiia) The (at first diffuse) spreading of the lighting-up in which Being's ec-static intensity has reached the limits of its scope, is a single gestalt experience;

(iiib) the (more centered) spreading is the union of the male and female;

(iiic) the (approximate) securing is a radiant cluster; and

(iiid) the (exact) securing is the coming-to-presence of Being's precious spontaneous thereness in a configuration that is thoroughly complete.

(iva) The (at first diffuse) spreading of the lighting-up in which Being's possibilizing dynamics is over and done with is the end of the belief in (Being's) gestalt character;

(ivb) the (centered) spreading is a diaphanous nothingness;

(ivc) the (approximate) securing is the ineffable thing-itself; and

(ivd) the (exact) securing is the very reality of Being's possibilizing dynamic, that cannot be looked at nor located anywhere as anything, having come into full play.

Thus, these facets that have been referred to as the sixteen levels of Being's lighting-up, are specific to the extraordinary rDzogs-chen teaching.

When at the time at which the ten spiritual levels in the cause-oriented spiritual pursuit have come into full play, the last trace of the grime of one's not recognizing the intellectual obscurations still remaining as sedimented propensities in one's closed system potential (*kun-gzhi*) to be Being's undividedness, has dissolved into its (original) purity by itself (*rang-dag*), then, it is said, the Buddhas in the ten directions empower one by their brilliant rays of light so that one grows into the full Buddha-experience.

In the Mantrayāna, however, one unites with (one's) female consort who is (Being's) cognate pristine awareness in the highest realm (*'og-min*) and (with her help) one travels the two inner (most) spiritual levels, the 'light everywhere' as the eleventh, and the 'undefiled lotus' as the twelfth. It is said that on the thirteenth level, 'the scepter-holding one', the climax of the Buddha-experience is made to be overt. Here (in the rDzogs-chen teaching) the causal momentum and its modifiers in the gaining of the Buddha-experience on the higher order level (in the whole), without the fully developed creativity in Being's lighting-up in which its ec-static intensity has reached the limits of its scope and the auto-manifesting of the supramundane realm that is the real highest realm (*don-gyi 'og-min*) breaking apart and becoming biased. These and other aspects that show its superiority I shall not discuss here for fear of using too many words. If one wants to learn more about them one should look into the treatises of and commentaries on the seventeen (rDzogs-chen) Tantras and the precious explications in the Seven Treasures.[106]

In the above I have outlined how a person of highest intellectual acumen and capabilities will, in his very lifetime, regain the freedom that he has been, how a person of medium intellectual acumen and capabilities will do so in his phase transition, and how a person of low intellectual acumen and capabilities will do so by relaxing the realm of his natural spiritual (disposition). To these may be added a still lower person who may do so in a subsequent life provided that he sees the entrance to it and devotes himself to (its realization) without getting on the wrong track. A more detailed treatment of these aspects is found in the different guidance texts and in my summary account, the *Bar-do spyi 'i don*.[107]

An individual who now gives up all the trivial pursuits of this life and makes a wholehearted attempt to experience the barrier-free and final leap approaches, and who does not abandon his existential commitments, cannot but regain the freedom that he has been through the power of the profound gist of this guidance. But those who do not strive for having these experiences, but go in for listening and 'meditating' a little bit, become so puffed up with their arrogance that they just rumble on like thunder, shooting off their mouths with empty verbiage, and remain untainted (unclothed) by even so much as the fragrance of what life's meaning may hold for them. Such persons will never find release from evil forms of existence in samsara, even if they repeat their pious prayers for 'freedom' and 'attainment' a hundred thousand times. I do not think there is any point in wasting many words on them.[108]

Having so far only briefly dealt with the gradations in vision (*lta*) and its cultivation by creative imagination (*sgom*), the spiritual levels and paths as well as their indications (in one's being) and the measures of their effectiveness, I shall now, in accordance with the general tenor of the teaching, discuss the various forms of their sociocultural enactment (*spyod-pa*) to the extent that they help one to make the path a lived through experience, as well as the ambivalence in them as furthering or blocking one's reaping their benefits. Nonetheless, if the meaning of effortlessness in the rDzogs-chen teaching is not clear, it may be difficult to realize its import. Be this as it may be, if one puts all the forms their sociocultural enactments in a nutshell, one can extract from the twenty-one forms discussed in the *Nyi-zla kha-sbyor-gyi rgyud*[109] and other works, seven most important ones. Which are they?

(i) The beginner behaves like a bee, taking his pick from among the many openings through which he may delve into the teaching, and defines their scope by listening to, thinking about, and practising what it has to say; or,

(ii) he behaves like a bird that has settled on its nest, doing away with his preconceptions and misconceptions about the instructions and taking care not to fall into the traps of doubt or other impediments;

(iii) then, once the time has come to actually experience (one's growth process), he behaves like a wounded deer, resorting to mountainous areas where there are no people so as to stay clear of the world's commotion;

(iv) what serves as a helper in this case is to behave like a mute, looking after himself and not engaging in talk about what is good and evil; or,

(v) he behaves like a madman, having left behind the passion for affirming or negating with respect to (one's) friends or enemies, love, hatred, and indifference; or,

(vi) he behaves like a dog or a pig, feeling content with anything he gets and befriending anyone and anything without making a distinction between what is clean or filthy in such matters as food, dress, or living conditions; or,

(vii) he behaves like a lion, king of beasts: not being afraid of the world, he cuts right through the various fetters of hope and fear, and as long as he has not reached his goal, he will not fall into the power of extraneous conditions but will strive to make a lived through experience (of the path), even if it means withstanding temperatures so hot or so cold that his flesh and bones wither away.

Having thus summed up the many forms of sociocultural enactments (of one's vision) in seven (important) ones, they ultimately boil down to the following. Until one, finally, after having first entered this pursuit, has done with the intellect's working (*blo-zad*), one must take as one's basis the ordinary practices of love, compassion, and the concern for pellucidity and consummation. Enthusiastic devotion, visionary experiences, and existential commitments must penetrate right to your bones. Disgust (with the world), wanting nothing, and diligence must be tied to your ego. A yogi or yogini who has the strength to lift himself or herself up, in utmost concentration, into the unity of the barrier-free and final leap approaches, that are the very dynamics in the experiencing, will part with samsara, firmly step into the lineage of 'achievers' (*sgrub-brgyud*), secure the key to the instructions, and distinguish between the different kinds of experiencing. For such fortunate persons destined to become a Buddha, since all that pertains to samsara and nirvana has dissolved in Being's vortex, the ec-static intensity that is in one's self, diaphanous and primordially complete, whatever comes-to-presence and is interpreted (as world, *snang-srid*) appears as one's teacher and surges as an ocean of revitalization; since the domain of what comes-to-presence (as the phenomenal) turns into supramundane realms the mine of impediments in the form of evil conditions has been emptied; since one's pseudo-physical concreteness (*gzugs-phung*) has dissolved in a gestalt of pure light (*'od-sku*), the conditions for illness and death have been eradicated; since pure experience has dissolved in Being's diaphaneity the welter of lies about vision, creative imagination, sociocultural enactments, and goal achievements has evanesced. Once one has realized Being's gestalt triad to be within one's self there should be no difficulty for the quick coming of the time where and when the foundation for the dualistic perspective of Buddhahood being something to be obtained and someone obtaining it, is gone for good.

But if one looks at the varied behavior of the great 'meditation masters' who are afflicted by the poison of their attachment to a degenerate world of strife, who are hardened by their ego-centered pride, who are inflated with the demon of the eight worldly concerns, who are unable to apply themselves to inner experiences for even so long as a day, and who hope that out of their total surrender to the distractions offered by sleep, food, and clothes realizations and their indications will just spring up like mushrooms, (it is no wonder that) even the awareness of the spiritual levels, the paths, their felt understanding and the dynamic qualities in them gets rarer and rarer, just like the rain at the end of the harvest season, in spite of one's hope for the better. Knowledgeable person have seen this state of affairs or, as has already been stated in the *sDong-po bkod-pa'i mdo*:

> Just as many living beings,
> Even if they be given food and drink,
> Will die by starving themselves,
> Those who do not cultivate life's meaning are like these,

and

> Just as Being's possibilizing dynamics will not be seen
> Unless one thoroughly cultivates it,
> So also, even if one sees and hears the water,
> But does not drink it, how will one's thirst be quenched?

Accordingly, the most important thing is to actually experience (what has been discussed) and, although among other things, it is imperative to distinguish between what removes one's impediments and what makes us slip and fall, I have this distinction between mistakes, slip-ups, and pitfalls in the case of the approach to Being's abidingness by way of the barrier-free method, outlined in my *Phyag-chen zin-bris*[110] and it may be learned from there. If one does not properly understand the cardinal dynamics and the meaning of the barrier-free, one is not suited to venture into the final leap approach and, even if one does so, (such an attempt) remains meaningless. Since a person who has been carried right into the cardinal dynamics of the barrier-free approach, passes beyond the domain of obstacles, defects, slip-ups and pitfalls (that beset the) final leap approach; hence there is no need to talk about them and I shall not point them out here so much more so as they have been discussed at length in the relevant treatises (similar to the) the instructions about (which) medicines will remove the impairments of one's eyes.

(3)

In conclusion I shall discuss the method of the realization of the goal, the (unity of Being's) gestalt dynamics and its pristine awareness in its ultimacy. Once one has fully familiarized oneself with the experiential process (as detailed above), the coarse, subtle, and thinnest layers of the grime of one's cognate drop in ec-static intensity that is only incidental, gradually disappears. To the extent that this grime dissipates (*sangs*), the unfoldment (*rgya-bar 'gyur*) of the sensitivity in the pristine awareness as a function of (Being's) ec-static intensity (within one's self) grows more and more intense (in ever higher regimes), which is (the manner in which) Being's possibilizing dynamics (works). To give an example: when a person having become blind due to a cataract is examined by a physician who with the appropriate medicine removes the sight-obscuring matter so that he can open his eyes again, he at first will see only the coarser aspects of the external objects, because the sight-obscuring matter has only been partially removed. But to the extent that this sight-obscuring matter is removed completely, he will eventually come to see everything as it is. Now, in this case, the eye has always been there as the eye, (in its ability to see again) it is not something new that has come from elsewhere in the external world. In the same manner, one's psychic potential as the thrust toward optimization has from all beginning been the pristine awareness of Being's diaphaneity, but shrouded by some incidental grime it has become like a blind man. Through the medicine-like instruction administered by the physician-like teacher, Being's gestalt dynamics and its pristine awareness as they exist in one's self are made to shine like the eye. To this coming into the open of one's existential value one gives the name 'attainment of the goal' as a description of a process; it is not that the triune gestalt dynamics and its pristine awareness have come as something new from elsewhere. On the contrary, the incidental grime that had previously accumulated has been cleared away and one must now take the necessary steps to ensure that it will not accumulate again. This one can understand from passages in the *Las rnam-par dag-pa'i mdo* that I have quoted above. When the freedom (that one is) reasserts itself, a person of highest intellectual acumen will in his lifetime dissolve in Being's field-(like) character in which there is no longer any trace of the (individual's) psychophysical constituents. On this point, the Mahāmudrā and rDzogs-chen teachings, are in agreement. Moreover, in the *Rin-chen spungs-pa'i rgyud* (p. 81) it is stated:

> By understanding that this is one's mind,
> By not introducing a (conceptual) division into (what lights up and what) does not light up,
> All that lights up regains its purity and
> In the insubstantiality of all and everything
> It becomes the internal logic of (Being's) nothingness and radiance.
> The four fundamental forces (named) earth, water, fire, wind,
> Without their individual powers coming to-presence,
> Dissipate in the sky like mist.
> The various obsessions with (one's) mistaken identifications,
> In whichever manner one has thought about them, without coming into existence (as something)
> Together with their aspect of a subject-object dichotomy cease by themselves and
> Are over and done with in their not coming-to-presence as anything (anywhere).
> In the experience and relishing of this illumining process by one's self
> All embodied beings go the same way.

For those who follow the final-leap approach (the situation in the case of a person of highest intellectual acumen is as follows): once the whole material panorama of the mistaken identifications as an external world has ceased to be and he, thereby, quite concretely, has a special autonomy over the (imaginative creation of) supramundane realms (as the objective reference of his) pristine awareness, he, by having acquired the (additional aspects of) autonomy concerning his taking birth and his continuance, works for the welfare of the living beings filling (in numbers) the sky to its farthest limits, by means of his superb transformation gestalt that is like a phantasmal display or the moon's reflection in water.

A person of medium intellectual acumen will regain the freedom (he has been) in any of the phase transitions and, through its indications such as relics, gnosemic language, earthquakes, rainbows, rain of flowers and others, instils confidence in those to be guided.

A person of low intellectual acumen will be born from a lotus in the supramundane realm of his natural spiritual domain and, having received the empowerments and predictions (concerning his future life or lives), he will travel the remainder of the paths to Buddhahood.

But whatever the case may be, when all the obscurations by one's incidental headlong actions and affective pollutants, one's inveterate tendencies and intellectual fog have cleared by themselves, and when one no longer stays in the vast range of the deep-structured confines of the intellect and its (self-perpetuating) tendencies, the confines of dichotomic thinking are eliminated for good. To the (resultant) continuing in the ever-turning wheel (*rtag-pa rgyun-gyi 'khor-lo*) in the vibrant dimension of Being that as such is a nothingness and radiance and bliss supreme in which Being's field-(like) character and its pristine awareness are such that they cannot be separated from nor added to each other, the name 'the gestalt of Buddhahood in all its meaningfulness' (*sangs-rgyas chos-kyi sku*) is given. With regard to whether or not this gestalt appears as having a face and hands and so on, many different treatises catering to every bias concerning the various presentations in the Sutras and Tantras, have spread and become the source of various controversies. In my humble understanding the abidingness of Being in its meaning-rich gestalt cannot be understood by arguing over whether it can be reduced or not reduced to a single denominator or whether it exists or does not exist simply because Being's meaning-rich gestalt is not an object that can be representationally thought or talked about and does not abide in the limits set by eternalism and nihilism. Even if one were to try for hundreds of aeons to prove or deny its existence intellectually by means of subjectivistic constructs, one would never see the face of this meaning-rich gestalt in its nakedness. Rather, when the abidingness of Being's diaphaneity has come into the open in its very beingness, then, I think, this realization of the meaning-rich gestalt by itself, without having to make it the basis of arguments, is all that matters.

By the auto-manifestation of a spontaneously present contextualized gestalt having all the major and minor marks, in (the form of a) configuration displaying the five pristine awareness modes, out of the inner auto-luminescence of the meaning-rich gestalt, it effortlessly performs the functions of the Bodhisattvas of the ten spiritual levels, who have a hold on Being's ec-static intensity. Although through the potency in the ceaseless coming-to-presence of the creativity in the unity of the two gestalt qualities as well as through the fruit that has matured from the seed of raising one's mind to higher levels and one's devotion during the time of the path, inconceivably (many) gestalts of guiding images of compassion wherever (there is a need for) guidance come-to-presence in countless and immeasurable settings that correspond to the lifeworld of those who are to be guided in whatever walk of life they may be found, there is, to be exact, no longer active a mind eager to preserve the difference between self and other, dichotomic fictions of the intellect (obsessed with its claim of there being) something to be done and someone doing something. Rather, through the power of (the combination of) dedication and compassion, like the wish-fulfilling gem or the wish-granting tree, (this complexity) works at fulfilling the hopes and desires of the living beings, and this is the nature of the dynamic qualities and the benignant activities of the Buddhas. Thus the three gestalts or, according to others, the four or five gestalts or the ninefold division of the three gestalts, actually, can be summed up in two gestalts: the one, assuming a contextualized shape, the other remaining the (pure) meaning-rich gestalt, and even these two, in an ultimate sense, have the single flavor of the meaning-rich gestalt. This can be illustrated by the examples of a mirror and the image reflected in it, or the sky and the rainbow in it. Or, if it comes to the thing-itself, the fact that Being's gestalt and pristine awareness, reflected-on meaning (*chos-can*) and meaning-itself (*chos-nyid*), radiance and nothingness, have in the manner of Being's facticity and its lighting-up as well as in the manner of Being's field-(like) character and its pristine awareness modes continued as (being) the supersingularity in its self-consistency, completeness, and spontaneity (*mnyam-rdzogs lhun-grub*), throughout the four aspects of time without ever stepping out of itself or changing into something other than itself, is what is referred to as the 'inseparability of Being's gestalt and its pristine awareness'. Since this has been expanded in considerable detail in all the great texts, I have merely given a brief summary of it here.

This vast mystery that is the message of the Victorious Ones, or
The ultimate elixir that is the core intensity of Being's core intensity
What else could there be apart from this marvelous rDzogs-chen teaching
Which one would not (be able to) fathom even in billions of trichiliads.

Although the bodiless Lord (of love) casting his powerful spell,
As well as Śiva, Umā, Viṣṇu and many other (gods)
Have tried their hardest to prevent it, countless adepts have attained a body transmuted into light
And by arriving on the scene filled India and Tibet.

But nowadays as the sun of the teaching is setting behind the (Western) mountain,
Although people may study thousands of dried up word in the propositions set forth in the treatises,
Their clogged minds, like a lamp without fuel, cannot learn a thing.
Where do these people inflated by their learning look?

Even those people who have boarded the ship of the older teaching
Since they do not hoist the sail of emancipation
And do not change their course with the strong urge to steer away from worldly desires
How will they ever uphold the yonder lineage of the ec-statics?

When the demon of egotism has possessed them completely
They may loudly chant their mantras and thumb their rosaries for hundreds of years, going
'Hūṃ, Hūṃ, Phaṭ, Phaṭ, bSrung, bSrung, bZlog, bZlog',
But only cut themselves off from any hope of subduing the demon within.

If one does not know the emancipatory dynamics of (Being's) vortex in the letting-be of what it is
In the magic working of its ec-static intensity in supramundane realms through its triad of gestalts,

Then, will one's attempt to tune in, by the spectacle of optical illusions as the visible manifestations of the mind's working,
Not be like (those of) a little boy chasing after a bird?

The barrier-free person soars straight up into the naked ecstatic intensity of Being's diaphaneity,
The final leap person transmutes (the world) into supramundane realms without becoming addicted to the brilliance in (their) lighting-up;
Without expecting or desiring the indications of the warmth being felt in the four lighting-up phases,
He occupies the Kun-bzang throne when he can experience them.

Although a stupid person like me
Is unable to completely explain all these topics,
I have been strongly urged to compose this (essay)
By the yogi Tshul-khrims bzang-po.

If there is anything wrong or misleading in (this essay), either in word or meaning,
I confess to the teacher supreme that I did not know better and beg him to forgive me.
All the good and wholesome that is put in plain sight by the good and wholesome in higher thought
I dedicate to the living beings who are as vast in numbers as the sky.
Through the vitalizing power of (Being's) marvelous resonance working through the Buddhas and their sons by way of (Being's) purposing (*dgongs*), through symbols and gestures (*brda*), and in the transmission by word of mouth (*snyan-brgyud*), as well as
Through the power of (Being's) primordial spontaneity with its five pristine awareness modes pertaining to the triad of gestalts (operating in the) psychic potential of the living beings,
May this lamp of the rDzogs-chen teaching, the most profound elixir, dispel the cognate darkness of the living beings,
And may they experience the splendor of (Being's) self-consistency, completeness, and pellucidity and consummation in the vortex of (Being's) meaning-rich field-(like) character with its three facets of (a) pristine awareness.

COLOPHON

This essay concisely sums up the meaning of the *gSang-ba bla-na-med-pa 'od-gsal rdo-rje snying-po*. I have been urged again and again to compose this essay by the venerable Tshul-khrims bzang-po over many years and months, but because I did not feel up to it with what little I had studied, thought about and imaginatively cultivated, and also was lacking in the wealth of experience and understanding that this particular subject matter required, I did not dare to delve into it and kept putting it off. The urging persisted more strongly than ever, however, and I could not simply ignore it any longer. So, with the thought that it might be of some help to a few stupid beginners who are unable to look up the vast corpus of Tantras and Existential instructions, I, sNa-tshogs rang-grol, have written this work, relying heavily on the writings of the learned Klong-chen-pa and Yongs-'dzin nam-mkhar spyod-pa,[111] while staying at bDe-gshegs in the southern region of the snowy gNas-chen-dpal mountains, during the third month of summer when the various alpine flowers were out in full bloom. May this essay inspire all living beings to gain a deeply felt understanding of Being's abidingness just as it has been for all time.

NOTES

1. This short invocation has been given in Sanskrit, that is, in the usual misspelling of Sanskrit words to make them look 'more' Sanskrit. Correctly spelled this invocation would run

   namas svavidyādibuddhāya.

   That this phrase is a mechanical concoction with no knowledge of Sanskrit involved, is borne out by the fact that the author uses *svavidyā* (which he spells as *svavidhā*) instead of the usual *svasaṃvitti.* The interesting point, however, is that this term has been given two different interpretations by the editors or copyists of rTse-le sNa-tshogs rang-grol's work. The printed text paraphrases *svavidyā* by *rang-sems* 'one's own mind', the handwritten copy renders the Sanskrit word by *rang-rig* which in rDzogs-chen thinking indicates the auto-excitation, an ec-static cognitive intensity, of the system as a whole and is quite distinct from the Yogācāra interpretation of this term as 'introspection'.

   The term *gdod-ma'i sangs-rgyas* (Sanskrit *ādibuddha*), here quite inadequately rendered by 'primordial Buddha-experience' as a concession to the Western primitivism of conceiving of the descriptive term *buddha* (a past participle of the verb *budh* 'to wake up') as a *thing*-person (The Buddha, with capital letters to make sure that there is such a thing), is not some Absolute. As Klong-chen rab-'byams-pa (*Theg-mchog* II, p. 294) clearly states, what is so designated evolves in the course of Being's symmetry transformation. On this topic see my *Matrix of Mystery*.
2. *dag-pa gnyis-ldan.* This expression is used in connection with either *chos-sku* 'the gestalt which embodies Being's meaningfulness' or *ngo-bo-nyid-kyi sku* 'Being's beingness gestalt'. The one 'purity' describes the beingness or 'static' aspect of the gestalt, the other 'purity' its 'dynamic' autocatalytic aspect.
3. *'phrin-las.* A lengthy hermeneutical interpretation on the basis of the *Rig-pa rang-shar*, p. 652, has been given by Klong-chen rab-'byams-pa in *Theg-mchog* II, pp. 137ff. Concisely stated, the activity indicated by this term is based on knowledge, the pristine awareness modes (*ye-shes*) of the whole. In popular terms, it is a Buddha's (*sangs-rgyas*) activity (*mdzad-pa*) which differs considerably from that of an ordinary person (*sems-can*) who just blunders through life (*las*).
4. Though much indebted to Klong-chen rab-'byams-pa, rTse-le sNa-tshogs rang-grol differs from him in this decisive point. For Klong-chen rab-'byams-pa Being's abidingness (*gnas-lugs*) is the indivisibility (or complementarity, *dbyer-med*) of Being's superdiaphaneity (*ka-dag*) and spontaneous thereness (*lhun-grub*). See his detailed presentation of this point in *Theg-mchog* I, pp. 281ff. Even if he singles out the *ka-dag* for discussion he understands it in a dynamic sense that prevents its absolutization into something static. Klong-chen rab-'byams-pa's thinking reflects the principle of complementarity in which opposites include each other, though not in a stale, dialectic synthesis. By contrast, rTse-le sNa-tshogs rang-grol attempts to separate what cannot be separated and to elevate

what has been so separated into some absolute that remains purely speculative.

5. In this refutation rTse-le sNa-tshogs rang-grol attempts to condense Klong-chen rab-'byams-pa's detailed refutation (*Theg-mchog* I, pp. 276f.). The main thrust is the repudiation of a static view, rigidly geared to the dichotomy of representational thinking. If samsara and nirvana (Klong-chen rab-'byams-pa's terms for rTse-le sNa-tshogs rang-grol's 'defects' and 'virtues') are given facts nothing can be done about them by the experiencer who implicitly is redundant; samsara would be a static and eternal entity from which anyone tied to or immersed in it could never become emancipated. So also nirvana would be a *fait accompli* and any striving for it would be pointless. Furthermore, the assumption that samsara and nirvana exist simultaneously invalidates the sequence from cause to effect; if the cause, defined as samsara, is present then the effect or goal, defined as nirvana, cannot be present since on the basis of this classificatory assessment the one excludes the other. If, in order to maintain simultaneity, it is assumed that they are one and the same in the manner of an equation, then samsara would have to be nirvana and nirvana be samsara and any differentiation between these two states would be impossible. On the basis of a static world view any striving becomes utterly pointless: what already is so for ever and to attempt to change or refine it is as futile as wiping and polishing a piece of black coal in order to make it shine white, as picturesquely stated in the *Klong-drug-pa* (in *Ati*, vol. 2, pp. 111-214), p. 172.
6. These two lines have been omitted for obvious reasons. See also note 5.
7. On the precise meaning of the term *thog-ma* and its synonyms see below note 12.
8. *ye-stong*. This compound, sometimes expanded into *ye-nas stong-pa*, is of particular importance in rDzogs-chen thought according to which *ye* is conceived of as a noun (see for instance its genetive case *ye'i* in *Tshig-don*, p. 235 and its instrumental case *yes* in *Theg-mchog* II, p. 36) which does not denote a specifiable temporal onset, but refers to the possibilizing source. Also, it should be noted that *stong-(pa)*, usually conceived of as an adjective, is more properly to be understood as an adverb, in Whitehead's diction a vector feeling-tone that has *no* meaning apart from the process it so describes. Our language, too deeply steeped in Aristotelian categories is unable to render decisive rDzogs-chen terms adequately. An approximation is the best one can hope for.
9. On this verse and the problems connected with it see E.H. Johnston's edition of the *Uttaratantra*, p. 72 n. 7.
10. This term is used by Klong-chen in *Bla-yang* I 309. It seems to have had its origin in the sNying-thig teaching, as may be gleaned from *mKha'-yang* III, p. 197.
11. This distinction between the 'new tradition' (*gsar-ma*) and the 'old tradition' (*rnying-ma*) is a purely Tibetan phenomenon and reflects a change in the intellectual, politically influenced, atmosphere. The so-called 'new tradition' takes as its starting point the works by Atiśa (982-1054) and his contemporary Rin-chen bzang-po (958-1055), active

as a translator and reviser of texts already translated into Tibetan, who had little interest in hermeneutical studies that were continued by the 'old tradition' and who for this reason rejected quite a number of texts by claiming them to be 'spurious'. This trend climaxed with Bu-ston Rin-chen grub-pa (1290-1364), the compiler of the standard Tibetan Tripitaka, who excluded the rNying-ma Tantras, with very few exceptions, from his compilation under pressure by his patron who financed the project and who thoroughly disliked the rNying-ma-pas. This dislike became almost an obsession with the dGe-lugs-pas.

12. The Tibetan language has several words for what we would describe in terms of a 'beginning', an 'origin', or a 'primordiality' all of which have been 'associated, throughout Western history, with causally determined processes and their temporal beginnings' (Schrag, 1980). By contrast, the Tibetan terms *ye* and *thog-ma* point to what is already operative before there is a beginning or origin, while *gdod-ma* is used when the holomovement (*gzhi-snang*) sets in. It is with this holomovement—with the exception of the pyrotechnics involved it may be compared with the Big Bang with which the universe is generally believed to have begun, although questions have been raised concerning what 'caused' or, more cautiously, prompted the Big Bang—that samsara and nirvana as options for the individual's engagement in pursuing a course of errancy and bondage (*'khrul-pa*) or a course of understanding and emanicipation (*grol-ba*) present themselves for the first time. Although a distinction can be made between a 'beginning' (*gdod-ma*) and what preceded it (*ye*), similar to the distinction between the actual and the virtual, there is no sharp separation between them; hence we also find the combination *ye gdod-ma*. See, for instance, *mkha'-yang* II, p. 125.

13. These ideas seem to have first been mentioned in the ***Rin-chen spungs-pa*** (p. 90) which speaks of 'eight giving-rise-to operations' (*'char-byed brgyad*), and in the *Nyi-zla kha-sbyor* (p. 224) which speaks of 'eight having-arisen modes' (*shar-lugs brgyad*). The account given in this text presents these modes in their cosmic dimension:

    Because of its thereness as if it were some resonance samsara and nirvana are (as yet) an unbroken whole;

    Because of its thereness as if it were light frequencies everything that is going to come-to-presence is an inner lucency;

    Because of its thereness as if it were some gestalt the cognitive capacity does not lose itself in extraneous (features);

    Because of its thereness as if it were a pristine awareness everything that is coming-to-presence is of an insubstantial-dissipative nature;

    Because of its thereness as if it were (something) non-dual one's cognitive capacity abides in its focusedness.

    Because of its thereness as if it were (something) free from (any) perimeters it does not abide in any of the confines (set by the intellect);

    Because of its thereness as an 'impure' gate the emergence of (an) interpreted world never stops; and

Because of its thereness as a 'pure' pristine awareness gate Being's possibilizing dynamics (expresses itself in) the connectedness of a mother with her child.

In *Bla-yang* I, p. 386 and II, pp. 8f. as well as in *mKha'-yang* II, p. 162, Klong-chen rab-'byas-pa speaks of 'six modes of an emerging' (*'char-lugs* (*thsul*) *drug*) and 'two gates' (*sgo gnyis*) and emphasizes the experiential character of what so emerges:

Because of its thereness as if it were (some) light frequencies the world (one's experienced universe) is permeated by the lighting-up (of it) in five (distinct) hues;

Because of its thereness as if it were (some) gestalt (these) gestalts in their divine shapes are countless;

Because of its thereness as if it were a pristine awareness the supramundane realms of the 'Buddhas' are in their purity an auto-presencing;

Because of its thereness as if it were (something) non-dual (the experiencer) abides in an in-depth appraisal that is not divided by concepts;

Because of its thereness as if it were (something) free from any perimeters, Being's possibilizing dynamics is felt and understood to be an utter insubstantiality; and

Because of its thereness as if it were (some) resonance there arises a natural compassion for sentient beings.

Lastly, in *Theg-mchog* I, pp. 303f. Klong-chen rab-'byams-pa discusses the internal logic of this complex process—complex, because these six modes through which Being's spontaneous thereness is active, do not constitute a sequential series, but occur simultaneously.

The beautiful simile of a mother's connectedness with her child—Being's sheer lucency giving rise to the brilliance of an pristine awareness and eventually receiving it back—is frequently met in rDzogs-chen texts. See, for instance *gNas-lugs*, p. 110; *Zab-yang* II, p. 125.

14. This account is taken over, almost *verbatim*, from Klong-chen rab-'byams-pa's *Tshig-don*, p. 181.
15. This text is included in Klong-chen rab-'byams-pa's *Bi-ma snying-thig*, vol. 2, pp. 1-159. The quotation is on pp. 45f.
16. *rgyu*. Although the rendering of this term by 'cause' or 'causal factor' is correct in the framework of representational thinking, in rDzogs-chen thought this term corresponds more the idea of a 'causal momentum' that persists. A concise statement concerning the triune character of the causal momentum is given in *sGra-thal-'gyur-ba*, p. 142:

The causal momentum in the going astray is Being's (the whole's) lowered intensity;

This lowered intensity is threefold,

and elaborated in *mKha'-snying* I, p. 348:

The triune causal momentum is the lowered intensity of Being in its (original) triad of facticity, actuality, and resonance (*ngo-no*←→*rang-bzhin*←→*thugs-rje*, *q.v.*).

Kun-tu bzang-po, without having done the slightest good, by being intensely cognizant of this triad, is (the evolution of the) Buddha-experience; the living beings in the three world spheres, without having done the slightest evil, by failing to be so cognizant of this triad, roam about in samsara. They do so because they are unaware of (the fact that) Being's facticity is 'nothing' (*stong-pa*), its actuality is radiant (*gsal-ba*), and its resonance is (the paradox of) there being a presence that yet is nothing (*snang-stong*).

On the evolving low-level intensity, characteristic of us sentient beings as a progressive deviation (*'khrul-pa*) from an ec-static intensity (*rig-pa*), the whole's facticity/nothingness becomes the 'ipseity-congruence low-level intensity' (*bdag-nyid gcig-pa'i ma-rig-pa*), setting the scene for the evolution of an individualistic system in which everything is as yet congruous with everything else and in which the evolving universe cannot be distinguished from how the individual acts upon it. In the wake of what looks like a symmetry break and a further drop in the original intensity the whole's actuality/radiance becomes the 'systemic-cognate low-level intensity' (*lhan-cig skyes-pa'i ma-rig-pa*)—'systemic', because it determines what follows from the first symmetry break (the 'ec-static intensity' having become a 'low-level intensity'), and 'cognate', because it has still not severed itself from the original low-level intensity of the ipseity-congruence level and 'its' world may still be fluid. In a further drop in the original ec-static intensity that inexorably follows from the first (and second) drop, the whole's resonance/intensity becomes the 'discursive fiction-entailing low-level intensity' (*kun-tu brtags-pa'i ma-rig-pa*) through which the experiencer is trapped in a welter of broken symmetries.

17. *rkyen*. Usually four modifiers are listed—the fourth being the simultaneous operation of the three mentioned. rTse-le sNna-tshogs rang-grol seems to combine in his presentation both the explicit statement concerning a triad of modifiers in *mKha'-snying* I, p. 348 and the wording of Klong-chen rab-'byams-pa's *Bla-yang* I, p. 456.

18. *ma-rig-pa drug*. Mentioned first in the *Rig-pa rang-shar*, p. 676, they are:

1. The lowered ec-static intensity that is one's mind as the root (of one's becoming enworlded and having to roam about in samsara, *rtsa-ba sems-kyi ma-rig-pa*);

2. The lowered ec-static intensity that becomes engrossed with an objective domain into which it goes astray (*'khrul-pa yul-gyi ma-rig-pa*);

3. The lowered ec-static intensity that starts from itself as its ground becoming the rationale behind the going astray (*'khrul-gzhi gzhi'i ma-rig-pa*);

4. The lowered ec-static intensity that is the subject pole in the (mind's) bifurcation (*'dzin-pa rtog-pa'i ma-rig-pa*);

5. The lowered ec-static intensity that is pursuing its way that is but its own fiction (*bcos-pa lam-gyi ma-rig-pa*); and

6. The lowered ec-static intensity, that is the deludedness of the non-recognition of Being's sheer lucency being an auto-presencing (*ma-shes rmongs-pa'i ma-rig-pa*).

A detailed explanation of what each of these six aspects do in orchestrating the complexity of an individual's psychic make-up on the level of his samsaric existence, is given by Klong-chen rab-'byams-pa in *Theg-mchog* I, pp. 321f.

19. For their outer-inner correspondences see my *The Creative Vision*, p. 42 Figure 4.
20. rTse-le sNa-tshogs rang-grol here refers to the object phase in the intentional structure of any cognitive process, leaving out the act phase. The object phase are the traditional five sense objects, such as color-shape, sound, smell, taste, and touch, and the sixth object phase that is one's ideas and notions.
21. The phrase *don-gyi ye-shes* seems to be an abbreviation for the more exact expression *ye-don-gyi ye-shes* and is synonymous with *ye-don-gyi sangs-rgyas*. This latter term is used in *gNas-lugs*, p. 76.
22. *stobs bcu*. They continue an idea that goes back to the early phase of Buddhism. Their final version is first found in Vasubandhu's *Abhidharmakośa* VIII 28c and detailed in his *Bhāṣya* on this *kārikā*. Concisely stated they are the powers in the awareness of (i) what is possible or not, (ii) what the results of one's actions will be, (iii) what concentrations, (iv) emancipations, (v) in-depth appraisals, and (vi) attainments imply, (vii) where different ways of life styles will lead, (viii) one's previous situations, (ix) the cycle of birth and death, and (x) the certitude that whatever tended to prevent a person from growing is over and done with.
23. *mi-'jigs-pa bzhi*. They have been referred to in Vasubandhu's *Abhidharmakośa* VII 32 und discussed in his *Bhāṣya*. They emphasize the experientially felt qualities of the powers listed in the previous note. Specifically, the first two 'intrepidities' are, more positively stated, the assurances that come with powers 1 and 2, while again, in terms of fearlessness, they are those that come with powers 2 and 7.
24. In the printed text a gloss has been added to indicate that this body pertains to the world of predominantly sensual desires known by its Indian name of Kāmadhātu (*'dod-khams*).
25. According to the glcss in the printed text this body belongs to the world of sensuously felt, aesthetic forms, the Rūpadhātu (*gzugs-khams*).
26. According to the gloss this body belongs to the world in which psychic life with its images has been suspended, the Ārūpyadhātu (*gzugs-med khams*). All three levels (*'dod-khams, gzugs-khams, gzugs-med khams*) are manifestations of the drop in Being's ec-static intensity (*ma-rig-pa*, that pervasive level where one does not know any better).
27. It should be noted that rTse-le sNa-tshogs rang-grol uses *ka-dag* 'Being's superdiaphaneity', which he imperceptibly absolutizes because he is no longer a pure process-oriented thinker as was Klong-chen rab-'byams-pa whom he otherwise holds in high esteem, as *chos-sku* which 'embodies', as it were, Being's superdiaphaneity, but is not statically identical with it.
28. For details see my *From Reductionism to Creativity*, pp. 116-18, 223-27.
29. In his *Yid-bzhin mdzod*, p. 689, Klong-chen rab-'byams-pa explains the *ji-lta-ba* as the fusion of the *chos-dbyings* and *mnyam-nyid* pristine

awareness modes, and the *ji-snyed-pa* as the fusion of the *me-long*, *bya-grub*, and *sor-rtog* pristine awareness modes. The *ji-lta-ba* belongs to the *chos-sku*, and the *ji-snyed-pa* to the *gzugs-sku*. See also my *From Reductionism to Creativity*, p. 260.

30. *rgyal-po blon-po dmangs*. This illustration of Being's autonomy in terms of a political organization is first recorded in the *Dur-khrod phung-po 'bar-ba'i rgyud* (in: *rNying-rgyud*, vol. 4, pp. 586-603), associated with Vimalamitra, a key figure in early rDzogs-chen thought. In this text (pp. 589f.) the king is Being's (the human system's) ec-static cognitive intensity (*rig-pa*), the minister is mentation (*sems*) presented in an unfavorable light, and the populace are the senses (*sgo lnga*) who either toil in their respective domains under the direction of a corrupt minister or, when this kind of minister has been locked up, engage in acts of worship. A lengthier account is found in the *Thig-le kun-gsal* (in: *rNying-rgyud*, vol. 5, pp. 124-289), pp. 154f., a text said to have been handed down from dGa'-rab rdo-rje who heads the transmission list, to 'Jam-dpal bshes-gnyen (Manjusrimitra), and in the *Thig-le gsang-ba'i brda'i rgyud* (*ibid.*, pp. 482-92), p. 489. This text is associated with Vimalamitra. Klong-chen rab-'byams-pa uses the image of the king, having ascended his throne, the minister, having been locked up, and the populace, having been brought to submission, to illustrate the meaning and practice of an attitude of *Gelassenheit*. This Heideggerian term comes closest to what in Klong-chen rab-'byams-pa's terminology is *rig-pa cog-gzhag*—the letting-be that is Being's ec-static intensity for whose autonomy the king is well-chosen image. Inasmuch as the king, Being's ec-static intensity, is the whole and as such 'thinks in terms of the whole', as contrasted with the limited interests of an ego-centered outlook, Klong-chen rab-'byams-pa replaces the more general term *sems* by the specific term *yid*. See *Tshig-don*, p. 336, *Theg-mchog* II, pp. 191f., *Bla-yang* I, pp. 441f., and elsewhere in his many writings.
31. By way of a gloss the printed text explains this descriptive term as pointing to the so-called 'flask empowerment' (*bum-dbang*).
32. Here, too, a gloss explicates this term as pointing to the 'mystery empowerment' (*gsang-dbang*).
33. A gloss states that this term describes the 'knowledge-through-appreciation empowerment' (*shes-rab ye-shes*).
34. There is no gloss to the fourth empowerment. rTse-le sNa-tshogs rang-grol uses neither the rNying-ma (rDzogs-chen) nor Mahāmudrā terminology, but the one used in *Guhyasamājatantra* XVIII 113, which is highly esteemed by the gSar-ma (in this case, the dGe-lugs-pa) tradition.
35. By way of a gloss the printed text offers the following information:

If one were to ask 'how is a person to realize these empowerments and directly encounter their meanings?', the answer is that if one attains the flask empowerment then one must understand that the whole of the container-like world with its organismic life forms, comprising the five fundamental forces, the psychophysical groupings, the operational presuppositions and their operational fields and so on, have been (Being's) spontaneous thereness in (the form of a configuration of deiform energies (*lha'i dkyil-'khor*). If one does not understand it in this manner but takes the world and the living beings in it at their face value, one has not realized the flask empowerment. Similarly, the demarcation between realizing and not realizing the mystery empowerment hinges on whether or not one understands that whatever is spoken by oneself or others, as well as (one's) breathing, are the way in which Being 'voices' itself (*sngags*, Skt. *mantra*). So also, the demarcation between realizing or not realizing the third empowerment hinges on whether or not one understands that all the feelings and sentiments as well as the crowd of dichotomic notions in one's biologically evolved, ego-centered mind (*yid*) are the systemic pristine awareness (of Being's ensconcement in the thing-itself that we are). (Lastly,) the demarcation between realizing or not realizing the fourth empowerment hinges on whether or not one is absolutely certain that all the above is Being's meaning-rich gestaltism as (an expression of Being's) ec-static intensity. Once one has made the request for obtaining these four empowerments, their meaning must seep into one's being; those of highest intelligence deeply feel and understand (*rtogs*) their meanings; those of mediocre intelligence sort of savor and relish (*myong*) them; and those of ordinary intelligence get an intellectual glimpse (*go-ba*) of them. Therefore, it is not enough to merely ask for the empowerments and then think that one has realized them.

36. By way of a gloss the printed text adds:

Details concerning the configurational settings, utensils, methods of performing the empowerments and so on with respect to the four different empowerments can be learned from each of their rituals; however, the commitments with respect to meticulously observing the rules relating to food and drink as well as to one's life-style and to one's never becoming amiss with them have to be strictly followed as detailed in both the Old and New versions of the Mantrayāna.

37. The printed text in a gloss states them to be those who have not adopted a perspective as presented by a philosophical system (*grub-mtha'*).

38. This is a reference to the well-known Pratītyasamutpada that marks a strictly rational and reductionist approach to an individual's problematic situation and his life-world.

39. *rigs-gsum*. They are technically known as

    1. *de-bzhin gshegs-pa'i rigs*
    2. *rdo-rje rigs*, and
    3. *padma'i rigs*.

The meaning of the term *rigs* extends from a concrete sociocultural dimension to a proto-representational background that is an experiencer's mode of being-in-the-world and of belonging-to any of its many regions of concern, none of them necessarily being a definable object, but rather being 'realization challenges' that express themselves through guiding images that somehow have a magnetic pull, not in the least, through their compelling beauty.

The three 'realization challenges', to the extent that they emphasize the individual's belongingness are

1. the individual's belongingness to mankind's overall evolu-

tionary experimentation, finding, in the words of Erich Jantsch (1976, p. 7), 'confirmation *a posteriori* through *vindication* (and not *a priori* through certainty and prediction)', and termed the individual's 'belongingness to the force that is on its way to the beingness-of-Being' (*de-bzhin gshegs-pa'i rigs*). It is explicated in *Tshig-don*, p. 225 as follows:

> Since those who have had the Buddha-experience (*sangs-rgyas*) in the past, have gained this experience (*sangs-rgyas-pa*) by their vision of Being's ec-static intensity (*rig-pa-nyid*) [as their very being] and so, in and through this beingness-of-Being (*de-bzhin*), have gone (*gshegs*) to the level of Buddhahood, (one speaks of) *de-bzhin gshegs-pa'i rigs*,

and in *mKha'-yang* II, p. 380:

> Since (Being's) sheer lucency (*'od-gsal*), a coming-to-presence (*snang*) that yet remains an utter nothingness (*stong*), is the highway of all 'Buddhas' (one speaks of a) *de-bzhin gshegs-pa'i rigs*.

2. The individual's belongingness to Being's indestructibility or Being's exact symmetry limit, meaning that each individual is the whole and yet only part of it—*rdo-rje rigs*. Its explication (*loc. cit.*, p. 225) is as follows:

> Since the very ec-static intensity does not step out of itself into something other than itself and also does not change (*'pho-'gyur med-pa*), when and where a living being may be born, (it is spoken of as) *rdo-rje rigs*.

3. The individual's belongingness to an existential purity that marks his integrity and cannot be defiled, similar to a lotus flower (*padma*) that, though growing in water, is not soiled by it. Its explication (*loc. cit.*, p. 225) is as follows:

> Since (Being's ec-static intensity) is not marred by any shortcomings, although it resides in samsara, it is spoken of a *padma'i rigs*.

Since these three kinds of belongingness belong to the infancy of the evolutionary process, the guiding images through which they express themselves are the beautiful mythic figures of Mañjuśrī (the one of sweet beauty), Vajrapāṇi (the one who holds the universe in his hand), and Avalokiteśvara (the one looks down on mankind with deep compassion).

40. These are existence, non-existence, both existence and non-existence, and neither existence nor non-existence.

41. *rigs lnga*. They belong to an advanced level in the individual's evolutionary experimentation. To the extent that the individual's belongingness is emphasized, they are the same as those mentioned in note 48, to which two other aspects of belongingness are added, suggesting an increase in complexity. They are the individual's belongingness to an enormous (inner) wealth—*rin-po-che'i rigs*, explained in *Tshig-don*, p. 225 as follows:

> Since in Being's ec-static intensity (the wealth of Being's) capa-

bilities and capacities are spontaneously there, (one speaks of it) as *rin-po-che'i rigs*,

and the individual's belongingness to the dynamics of Being that expresses itself in actions that further mankind's evolution—*las-kyi rigs*. Its explication in *Tshig-don*, p. 225 makes it abundantly clear, these actions are not the inconsiderate actions (*las*) of ordinary persons, but benignant actions (*'phrin-las*) originating on a higher level that presents the whole. Thus:

Since in Being's ec-static intensity Being's benignant activities are spontaneously there, (one speaks of it) as *las-kyi rigs*.

On this advanced level the guiding images, in addition to a compelling beauty, carry with them the character of majesticness. They are referred to as the Victorious Ones (*rgyal-ba*), the regents of the various regions of concern. They are the well-known images of Vairocana, Akṣobhya, Ratnasambhava, Amitābha, and Amoghasiddhi.

42. *rigs brgya*. They are the same as the five mentioned in note 50, seen in their interconnectedness such that each *rigs* is a set of five *rigs* ($5 \times 5 = 25$), each of which has the traditional three gestalts (*chos-sku*, *longs-sku*, *sprul-sku*), augmented, as it were, by a fourth gestalt expressive of a pristine awareness dynamics (*ye-shes-sku*), thus $25 \times 4 = 100$.

43. *rang rig*. In rDzogs-chen thought this term signifies Being's auto-excitation. It is impossible to express the dynamics indicated by this term, in the English language. At the risk of 'using too many words' one can elaborate by stating that *rang* refers to Being (or any living system) as 'it itself' and *rig* to Being's (or any living system's) capacity of getting into an 'excited' state. This excited state is always the system's 'own' (*rang*) excitation and intensity of this excitation. The term *rang-rig*, as used by rDzogs-chen thinkers, must not be confused with its Yogācāra connotation of 'introspection'.

44. *ye-grol*. This term, too, presents considerable difficulties. First of all, *ye*, rendered by 'primordiality' points to a 'beginning' before there was a beginning that started with the first symmetry break in the original unity and led to a time- and space-binding. 'Primordiality' has no substantial reference, nor does it denote an objectifiable object. The term *grol* has a verbal connotation, it is not a quality word or adjective, accidentally modifying some object, but rather what Alfred North Whitehead meant by the subjective form of a relational activity, a vector feeling-tone.

45. *gnad*, Skt. *marman*. 'Cardinal charge' is an attempt to convey the notion of vitality, without falling into the trap of some vitalism. The term for which there is no equivalent in any Western language, may be paraphrased as 'that which makes something tick'. In Indian medicine it is used with reference to those points in the body which, when hit, result in instant death.

46. This work may have been lost; it is not in the *Collected Works* (*gsung-'bum*), photostatically reproduced and published by Sanje Dorje in 1974.

47. The author of this work is Śrīsimha, the 'Chinese scholar/abbot' (*rgya-nag-gi mkhan-po*). It has been included in the *Bi-ma snying-thig*, vol. 2, pp. 376-87, by Klong-chen rab-'byams-pa.

48. *loc. cit.*, p. 378.
49. *loc. cit.*, p. 378 for the first two verse lines and p. 381 for the remaining ones.
50. *yon-tan ltar snang*. The implication is that the perceptual immediacies, however valuable their experience may be, are not Being's creative possibilities themselves. The perceptual immediacies (*mngon-shes*) occur within the framework of one's commonplace realities and are marked by a temporary suspension of the subject-object division. Being's creative possibilities (*yon-tan*) have no such restrictiveness, they reflect or express the dynamics of the whole and as such are intertwined with their understanding (*rtogs*). Perceptual immediacy is a static notion, understanding and creative possibilities are dynamic ones. Perceptual immediacy does not resolve the dualism which may be seen as a symmetry break in the original unity of lived through experience. An instructive account of what understanding is about has been given by Klong-chen rab-'byams-pa in *Theg-mchog* II, p. 124:

    It understands (*rtogs*) the cognitive domains (of the senses, *yul*) as Being's dynamic field-like expanse (*dbyings*);

    it understands the being born and passing away (*skye-'gro*) as Being's *Gestaltung*-process (*sku*);

    it understands Being's lighting-up (in what becomes the phenomenal, *snang-ba*) as (the play of) light frequencies (*'od*);

    it understands the having come-to-presence and its self-emancipatory dissipation (*shar-grol*) as having no demarcation line between them (*ris-med*); and

    it understands one's appreciative discrimination (*shes-rab*) as Being's ec-static intensity (working through it in us, *rig-pa*).

    (The German word *Gestaltung* has been used to emphasize the dynamic character of what is implied by the Tibetan term *sku* which, though rendered as Gestalt, is always understood as a process structure.)
51. This statement is directed against the objectivist's claim that truth is an absolute notion. Truth (*bden-pa*) is always relative to one's understanding of one's world that evinces a hierarchical organization. The realization that truth is relative to one's understanding has found its clearest expression in the Buddhist idea of the Two Truths (*bden-pa gnyis*) which are not only complementary to but also interactional with each other (*bden-gnyis dbyer-med*). See *Yid-bzhin mdzod*, pp. 643, 647; *Theg-mchog* I, p. 97.
52. *sems-phyogs*. The 'mentality' section (*sems-sde*) of the rDzogs-chen teaching is divided into two major branches. The one is termed *sems-yin*, claiming that our experienced reality *is* mentation, the other is termed *sems-phyogs* claiming that our experienced reality is 'mentation-related' or 'mind-dependent'. For further details see *Grub-mtha'*, pp. 353ff.
53. *bar-do*. This word is here used as an umbrella term for a number of experiences that have a distinct process character. See also my *The Creative Vision*, *s. v.*
54. *dran-pa*. The reason for rendering this term in the above manner has been given in my *The Jewel Ornament of Liberation*, p. 230.

55. Both the blockprint and the photostatic reprint of a handwritten copy add by way of a gloss: 'At this time perceptual immediacies are bound to occur'.
56. *mnyam-pa-nyid*. The rendering of this term by 'self-consistency' has been prompted by the consideration that it conveys its dynamic character, while the 'identity' is a static concept.
57. They are gain and loss, fame and disgrace, slander and praise, happiness and misery.
58. The full name of this teaching and practice is *phyag-chen lhan-cig-skyes-sbyor*. It goes back to sGam-po-pa (1079-1153) and became the central topic in the teaching of sGam-po-pa's disciple Phag-mo grub-pa (1110-70).

In his *Collected Works* (*gsung-'bum*), vol. *Da*, fol. 3a sGam-po-pa states:

> *phyag-rgya chen-po* (Mahāmudrā) means that all that is subsumed under the headings of samsara and nirvana has, (from the viewpoint of its) primordiality (a beginning before there was any beginning, *ye-nas*) been a spontaneous presence (*lhun-gyis grub-pa*), (Begin's) possibilizing dynamics that is like the (open) sky (and as such) an pristine awareness that is an all-time (operation), and a singular non-duality. It is a stream flowing uninterruptedly.
>
> *lhan-cig-skyes-sbyor* (Sahajayoga) means that, since it is the linking-up of one's representational thinking (*rtog-pa*) that has come-into-existence with the quaternary of (Being's) gestaltism (*sku-bzhi*), it is not considered to be an all-time (operation); it is a stream that stops (once the linkage has been effected).

More explicit is his account in vol. *Ki*, fols. 16b f.:

> With what is what has come-into-existence being linked up? (What is called) ec-static cognitive intensity (*rig-pa*) and (what is called) openness/nothingness (*stong-pa*) have come-into-existence together, but this (togetherness) is not like something as such and something different from it. When (what is referred to as) ec-static intensity (*rig-pa*), radiance (*gsal-ba*), and bliss (*bde-ba*) is being linked up with the openness/nothingness (that is Being, *stong-nyid*), this is what is meant by *lhan-cig-skyes-sbyor*.
>
> This practice involves two tools: (i) vision (*lta-ba*) and (ii) appreciative discrimination (*shes-rab*).
>
> (i) Vision has to do with four functional properties of (a living system): the functional property of it being cognitive (*shes-pa'i mtshan-nyid*), the functional property of being distinct (*khyad-par-gyi mtshan-nyid*), the functional property of being effectuating (*byed-pa'i mtshan-nyid*), and the functional property of it being a pure fact (*ngo-bo-nyid-kyi mtshan-nyid*).
>
> Here, cognitiveness (*shes-pa*) is such that in the beginning it is not something that has come-into-existence as something or other, that in between (its onset and end) it is not something that abides anywhere, and that, lastly, it does not end anywhere; it has neither color nor shape. (All this is what is meant by) it being dissociated

from conceptual-propositional limitations, dissociated from any concretizability, and not being something non-existent. (The fact of its) being without origination is (referred to as) *chos-sku,* its being without ending as *longs-sku,* its non-abidingness as *sprul-sku,* and its non-concretizability into it being the pure fact of some thing as *ngo-bo-nyid-kyi sku.* This definition (of cognitiveness) in terms of a gestaltism quaternary (is meant to point out that) it is not something non-existent, but that in its radiance and ceaselessness it is an uninterruptedly flowing stream and as such abides through all times.

Distinctness (*khyad-par*) means that this very cognitiveness that is not some thing or other comes-to-presence in a variety of divisive concepts. This very coming-to-presence abides in its facticity of not being some thing or other.

Effectuating (*byed-pa*) means that although the possibilizing dynamics (that is the system's cognitiveness) comes-to-presence in a variety of divisive concepts, there is no creator involved, and the variety of divisive concepts as the presencing of the possibilizing dynamics also does not involve a creator.

Pure fact (*ngo-bo*) means the experiencing of this reality as (Being's) pure field-like expanse.

(ii) Appreciative discrimination involves listening (*thos-pa*) to the spoken word, thinking about (*bsam-pa*) what it means, and through creative imagination (*sgom-pa*) developing (this meaning) which, in turn, involves four tuning-in phases (*rnal-'byor*).

The undistractedness of the ec-static intensity [that is, to know that whatever comes-to-presence and whatever is inspected is mind/mentation] is the tuning-in to a peak experience (of concentratedness, *rtse-gcig*). If in this experience concepts pertaining to representational (dichotomic) thinking should turn up one should meet them (as friends) and go along with them. When thus these concepts have become the way, one should not try to do away with them, but be thankful to them. This is the tuning-in to a thematization-free experience (*spros-bral*). By continuing undistractedly in this vibrant dimension the external phenomena turn out to be just bits and pieces, and this is the tuning-in to an experience of the one-flavoredness of the many (*du-ma ro-gcig*). When by familiarizing oneself with this experience the ec-static intensity is there in all its nakedness [not shrouded by any concepts] and when this familiarity with it reaches its destination the *chos-sku* is attained. This is the tuning-in to the no-more-meditation experience (*sgom-med*). These, then, with the tool of vision point out the tool of appreciative discrimination.

(The passages in brackets are glosses in the text.)

A detailed presentation of the *phyag-chen lhan-cig-skyes-sbyor* practice has been given by the Sixth Zhwa-dmar Karma-pa Chos-kyi dbang-phyug (1584-1630) in his *Phyag-chen lhan-cig-skyes-sbyor-gyi- zab-khrid,* in which on pp. 485ff. he gives a detailed explanation of this technical term.

59. The source for the claim that the phenomenal (that which lights up,

snang-ba) *is* mind/mentation (*sems*) seems to go back to a statement in the *Ngo-sprod spras-pa* (in: *Ati*, vol. 2, pp. 77-109), p. 107, which was thoroughly misunderstood by the literalists. The passage in question runs as follows:

> Indeed, by encountering everything phenomenal (*snang-ba*) as mind/mentation (*sems*) one gets an in-depth understanding of (the working of) mind/mentation; by encountering mind/mentation as (being) nothing (*stong-pa*), one seals this nothing with bliss; by encountering this nothing as an ec-static intensity (*rig-pa*) this very ec-static intensity (becomes) the non-duality of (Being's) field-like expanse and its (pervasive) pristine awareness.

As Klong-chen rab-'byams-pa elaborates (*Theg-mchog* II, pp. 276f., 343, 346; *gNas-lugs*, pp. 34f.; *Grub-mtha'*, pp. 352f.), people have taken this statement at its face value and have overlooked its purpose of undermining the naive idea that the external world is something apart from its experiencing it, that it furthermore aims at breaking the inordinate attachment to it, and that the one being the other (*snang-ba=sems=stong-pa=rig-pa*) is by the literalist's own standards mutually contradictory.

60. *rnam-rtog chos-sku*. This expression is frequently used in Mahāmudrā works. Against the literalist's misunderstanding Padma dkar-po (1526-92) plainly states that it is meant metaphorically. See his *rNal-'byor bzhi'i bshad-pa don-dam mdzub-tshugs-su bstan-pa*, fol. 11a.
61. This term is, for instance, used by Padma dkar-po in his *Phyag-rgya chen-po rnal-'byor bzhi'i bshad-pa nges-don lta-ba'i mig*, fol. 2a.
62. It seems that an anti-intellectualism has been as rampant at the time of rTse-les sNa-tshogs rang-grol as it is still today among the various cultist groups.
63. With this transformative vision a transition from the purely structurally conceived level of the human body to a more 'image-schematic' one has been effected. The images are the 'Victorious Ones'—victorious because they have overcome the rigidity of structure and now as 'regents' (*rgyal-ba*) over the various regions of concern that constitute the 'configuration' of the individual's multifaceted being-in-his-world, have approximate autonomy the ultimate autonomy resting with the 'king' (*rgyal-po*) who is Being's (the human system's) ec-static cognitive intensity (*rig-pa*).
64. So also *Bla-yang* II, p. 246 and *Zab-yang* II, p. 139.
65. Six lamps are also listed in *Zab-yang* II, pp. 138f. Altogether there are nine 'lamps'. See Documentation/Glossary under *sgron-ma*.
66. For further details see *Bla-yang* I, pp. 462f.
67. This is a reference to the intricate pattern detailed in the *gSang-ba snying-po*. See my *Matrix of Mystery*.
68. *sku lnga*. This expression has found different interpretations according to the context in which it occurs. Here it refers to the gestalt character of the five 'regents'.
69. *rigs gcig*. This term is synonymous with *rgyu gcig* as used in the *gSang-ba snying-po* and points to the homology of the mind. To illustrate what is

meant by this statement: a sentient being (*sems-can*) and a Buddha (*sangs-rgyas*) evolve by homologous principles related to their common origin (here termed *rigs gcig*). There is no 'ascent' from the level of a sentient being to that of a Buddha, in the strict sense of the word, although language speaking in terms of 'higher' and 'lower' suggests the idea of an ascent (while tacitly implying the possibility of a descent). Figuratively we may speak of an ascent to a new level, but at the same time should remind ourselves that, in the words of Erich Jantsch (1980, p. 296), "a new level does not mean an 'ascent', but an enrichment of the ensemble of possibilities of expression and the dimensions of its autonomy." Thus, a 'Buddha' is a person who lives his possibilities, while an ordinary person lets these same possibilities wither away.

70. The paraphrase of the highly technical term *thig-le* by 'organizing principle and information package' attempts to bring out two of its most important aspects. Its complexity, cryptically referred to by the statement that it operates on both the 'higher-order' level of reality (*don-dam*) and the 'lower-order' level of reality (*kun-rdzob*), has been detailed in *Theg-mchog* II, pp. 372f.; *Tshig-don*, p. 256.

71. Throughout the intellectual history of Buddhism a controversy has raged with regards to which works deal with the 'definite' meaning (*nges-don*) and which were merely 'suggestive' (*drang-don*).

72. For a detailed account of the developing stage (*bskyed-rim*) see my *The Creative Vision.*

73. There is a subtle difference between the triad of *brda don rtags* and the more frequently used *dpe don rtags*. While *brda* emphasizes the symbolic character of the image for the thing-under-consideration (*don*) and the indication of its dynamic presence (*rtags*), the word *dpe* is used to emphasize its illustrative character.

74. Psychologically speaking this is an 'archetypal image'.

75. *rtsa.* The word 'chreod' has been coined by Conrad H. Waddington to describe the canalization of development. This is precisely what the *rtsa* are doing.

76. The rendering of the technical term *rlung* by 'motor-activity' and/or 'motility' is far from satisfactory. What was understood by the Buddhists is best summed up in *mKha'-yang* II, p. 126:

    When the creative dynamics of (Being's) pristine awareness comes to the fore out of the vibrant dimension of (Being's) openness/nothingness, light in five hues originates. Since in it the creativity of (Being's) ec-static cognitive intensity is present, (in this transition from a virtual state into an actual state) it becomes (a subject's) grasping (*'dzin*) of the five hues (as its objects). This grasping is called *rlung*; it is the creative dynamics in (Being's) resonance as an inner radiance rushing outward.

77. This expression is used here synonymously with *thig-le* as an organizing principle. As such it initiates its own movement (*rlung*) setting up its own lines of development (*rtsa*). The lengthy term *bkod-pa byang-chub-kyi sems* is used by Yon-tan rgya-mtsho in his *Nyi-ma'i 'od-zer*, p. 237,

where he comments on 'Jigs-med gling-pa's *Yon-tan mdzod*, vol. 2, p. 340 (*bkod-pa'i byang-sems*).

78. *'khor-lo*. Usually four such dynamic regimes are discussed in the Buddhist context. Sometimes, as here, a fifth such regime is added. They reflect a hierarchy and are, figuratively, located in the perineum, navel, heart, throat, and head regions. There is, however, no fixed number.
79. See also above note 76.
80. The imagery is highly revealing. The 'lamps' as well as the 'light chreods' (*'od-rtsa*) are related to the working of the system's pristine awareness (*ye-shes*) which certainly has a cognitive quality, but this very quality is as much cognitive as it is a 'feeling-tone'. The experiencer senses or feels it with every fiber of his being.
81. *rdo-rje sems-dpa'*. According to *Theg-mchog* I, p. 323 and II, p. 131 this 'mythological' term is synonymous with *rig-pa*.
82. *gyen-'greng*. This term is not found in any dictionary. Primarily, or so it seems, it is an architectural term, but here it is used in the context of a lived through experience and by no means refers to any 'objective' datum. Like other such architectural terms (see *rtsibs-shar* in note 105 and *gru-chad* in note 91) it describes what Edmund Husserl has called 'live body events' (*Leibesvorkommnisse*) which occur as functional correlations to specific types of bodily feelings of motion or kinaesthesias, as Husserl calls them. As such they are the live body's self-presentation which involves what is commonly called 'behavior', patterns fed and sustained by what is imprecisely referred as 'emotions', the live body itself being the mansion or palace as the 'material' system that manages the processes of these emotions. Hence, when the live body is felt and conceived of as a 'mansion' (*gzhal yas-khang*), its kinaesthesias give rise to their 'architectural' connotations and envisionings. The 'emotion' presented by a vertical post is 'passion-lust' (*'dod-chags*).
83. *rtsibs-shar*. This term is descriptive of rafters that are not concealed by any coverings, but are jutting out. As a 'live body event' it presents the emotion of 'irritation-aversion' (*zhe-sdang*).
84. The impulses (*lu-gu-rgyud*) are the gestalt (*sku*) of the ec-static intensity (*rig-pa*), which figuratively is the 'king' (*rgyal-po*). He has to be kept 'prisoner', because getting up from his throne would amount to an abdication of autonomy. Thus Klong-chen rab-'byams-pa states (*Zab-yang*) I, p. 290:

    In the enclosure of light (as Being's) lighting-up by (and for) itself
    The continual (welling up of) impulses (of) the effulgence of (Being's) ec-static intensity, the king,
    Has to be kept prisoner so that he can neither shake nor move.
    At the time (when this takes place) Being's auto-excitation (in its ec-static intensity, *rang-rig*) has entered the auto-luminescence of its three effulgences (*gdangs gsum*).

    As he then goes on to elaborate, the three effulgences reflect the triune dynamics of Being.
85. The photostatic copy (pp. 453f.) contains the following passage that is missing in the printed edition and may well be an unmarked gloss:

Thus, the 'all-at-once' (*gcig-'char*) individual who experiences this in one flash since his creativity is already fully developed, is a superior type. The 'step-by-step' (*rim-gyis-pa*) individual, for whom this experience comes gradually to the extent as his feeling and understanding grow within him and the indications become present, is a type of mediocre capacity. As for the *thod-rgal* individuals, since in some cases it arises even though they have not really made it a felt experience, while in other cases it does not arise even though they have (tried to) make an experience of it, there is a great (diversity in terms of) high and low, increase and decrease. And since whatever (experience) comes to them does not necessarily correspond with how it is felt and experienced or with the indications for it, they are considered to be the lowest type.

86. On the two pristine awareness modes mentioned here see above note 37. The 'three pristine awareness modes' (*ye-shes gsum*) are, strictly speaking, a 'triune pristine awareness mode' illustrating the dynamics of Being as a symmetry transformation process summed up by the three terms of facticity (*ngo-bo*), actuality (*rang-bzhin*) and resonance (*thugs-rje*). Thus, Klong-chen rab-'byams-pa states (*Zab-yang* I, p. 300):

Facticity — a superdiaphaneity (and) openness/nothingness;
Actuality — a spontaneous thereness having an effulgence; and
Resonance — an ec-static intensity having a creative dynamics
Abide in the manner of a triune pristine awareness mode.

See also *Theg-mchog* II, p. 520; *mKha'-snying* I, pp. 344. 347; *mKha'-yang* I, p. 463.

87. This unusual image has found a detailed explanation in the *Lha-rgyud rin-po-che dbang-gi 'khor-lo* (in: *rNying-rgyud*, vol. 5, pp. 92-112), p. 92:

When a tortoise capable (of moving about)
Is placed in a metal basin,
It is unable to crawl about
Because the metal basin is slippery and
So are the feet of the tortoise.
Similarly, through the empowerment by the creativity in (one's) ec-static cognitive intensity
Whatever has lit up (as the phenomenal) dissipates and (one's) craving for the phenomenal turns back (on itself).

A few verse lines later on the text takes up the image of a tortoise again and states:

Just as when a tortoise has drawn in its legs
So when the flickering (of what is to become mentation) has passed, (one's) ec-static cognitive intensity is freely operative deep within (one's self).

88. The actions performed by body, speech and mind.
89. These are: the wheel (as the orbiting of the royal authority), the state jewel, the queen, the minister, the elephant, the horse, and the army commander.
90. These are: the jewelled umbrella, a pair of golden fishes, a (full) vase,

an exquisite lotus flower, a white conch-shell with whoorls turning to the right, a curled noose, the standard of victory, and a golden wheel.

91. *gru-chad.* In the *bTags-pas grol-bar bstan-pa Bu-gcig-gi gsang-'grel* by dGa'-rab rdo-rje (included by Klong-chen rab-'byams-pa in his *Bi-ma snying-thig* I, pp. 73-271), p. 195, this term is explained as *yul-gru-tsam* 'a certain region'. The term *chad* 'cut off' implies a dead end. Architecturally this term means a butt-end; as a live body event it presents the emotion of 'delusion-bewilderment' (*gti-mug*).
92. *bcud-du 'dril-ba.* On this expression see *Theg-mchog* I, p. 126; *Grub-mtha'*, p. 392; *Thig-le kun-gsal*, p. 127; *rDzogs-pa chen-po thig-le gsang-ba de-kho-na-nyid nges-pa'i rgyud* (in: *rNying-rgyud*, vol. 5, pp. 515-25), p. 517.
93. So also *Grub-mtha'*, p. 386.
94. A gloss states that these refer to the barrier-free approach (*khregs-chod*) and the final-leap approach (*thod-rgal*).
95. A gloss states that the *sngon-'gro* or preliminary practices are meant.
96. *ngo-sprod bzhi.* These 'encounters with the beingness of Being' come in various nuances of which the four referred to here, are the ones specified in *mKha'-yang* III, p. 134:

    (1) Whatever lights up (as the phenomenal, when coming out of a 'state' of composure) is not something that can be pinpointed as being this or that, but is like last night's dream;

    (2) In the ec-static intensity that may present itself in any guises there is nothing to be accepted or rejected and it is without pitfalls and obscurations, but is like water and its waves;

    (3) The 'march' of the vortex in which there is no subjective appropriation of Being's facticity that is not something objectifiable, is like a storm raging through the air; and

    (4) Although there is a lighting-up in a variety (of phenomena) there is no subjective belief in it as being this or that, but is like a play of phantasms.
97. A gloss states that the *khregs-chod* is meant.
98. A gloss states that the *thod-rgal* is meant.
99. From here on the quotation differs from the version preserved in the *rNying-rgyud*.
100. A gloss states that 'the lighting-up of vibrations that grow and spread into higher and higher regimes' (*nyams gong-'phel*) is meant.
101. A gloss states that this refers to the 'lighting-up that constitutes Being's ec-static intensity having reached the limits of its scope' (*rig-pa tshad-phebs*).
102. A gloss states that this refers to the 'lighting-up (in whose experience the experiencer) has done with Being's possibilizing dynamics' (*chos-nyid zad-pa*).
103. A gloss states that 'three countless (*asamkhyeya*) aeons' are implied. 'Countless' is the name of a number amounting to the number ten raised to the fifthieth potency.
104. *Rig-pa rang-shar*, pp. 778f.
105. The intricate interplay between 'joys' and 'pristine awareness modes' in

the context of phases of concentration with strong sexual overtones has been detailed in *mKha'-yang* II, pp. 285ff.

106. These Treasures (*mdzod*) are Klong-chen-rab-'byams-pa's major works: *Yid-bzhin mdzod, Theg-mchog mdzod, Tshig-don mdzod, Grub-mtha' mdzod. Chos-dbyings mdzod, gNas-lugs mdzod,* and *Man-ngag mdzod.*

107. *Collected works*, vol. 2, pp. 139-233.

108. On p. 482 in the photostatic edition the text continues:

> Once again to sum up, the indications and the measure of the effectiveness of the (experience of) the lighting-up of Being's possibilizing dynamics in the immediacy (of its perception) are that the experiencer is not interested in anything else but the experiencing of this dynamics; the indications and the measure of the effectiveness of (the experience of) the lighting-up of vibrations that grow and spread into higher regimes is that the eight worldly concerns (see above note 69) have become annulled; the indications and the measure of effectiveness of (the experience of) the lighting-up of Being's ec-static intensity having reached the limits of its scope is that perceptual immediacies as well as changed body/mind patterns are bound to occur. However, there is no point to expatiating (on this by resorting to) dry verbiage. The measure of effectiveness shows (itself) in (one's) dreams and is also displayed in one's life-style. One will recognize it without further ado.

Obviously this insert was meant as a gloss, but was not marked as such.

109. *Ati*, vol. 3, pp. 197ff.; quoted in *Theg-mchog* II, p. 150; *Tshig-don.* p. 315.

110. See above note 50.

111. Probably the same as Yongs-'dzin Blo-'gros rgyal-mtshan.

LITERATURE REFERENCES

A. Works in Western Languages

Boss, Medard (1979), *Existential Foundations of Medicine and Psychology*. New York: Jason Aronson.

Casey, Edward S. (1976), *Imagining. A Phenomenological Study*. Bloomington: Indiana University Press.

Cole, K.C. (1984), *Sympathetic Vibrations*. New York: Bantam Books.

Deleuze, Gilles and Felix Guattari (1987), *A Thousand Plateaus*. Minneapolis, University of Minnesota Press.

Guenther, Herbert V. (1975-76), *Kindly Bent to Case Us*. 3 vols. Emeryville, CA: Dharma Publishing.

Guenther, Herbert V. (1983), "The Dynamics of Being: rDzogs-chen process thinking". In: Eva K. Dargyay, ed. (1983), *Canadian Tibetan Studies* 1. Calgary, Alberta: Society for Tibetan Studies.

Guenther, Herbert V. (1984), *Matrix of Mystery: Scientific and Humanistic Aspects of rDzogs-chen Thought*. Boulder & London: Shambhala.

Guenther, Herbert V. (1986), "Being's Vitalizing Core Intensity", *Journal of Naritasan Institute for Buddhist Studies*, No. 10, (1986), 75-112.

Guenther, Herbert V. (1987), *The Creative Vision*. Novato, CA: Lotsava.

Guenther, Herbert V. (1989), *From Reductionism to Creativity: rDzogs-chen and the New Sciences of Mind*. Boston: Shambhala Publications, Inc.

Hegel, Georg Friedrich Wilhelm, *The Phenomenology of Mind*, J.B. Baillie, trans. (New York: Muirhead Philosophical Library, 1931).

Heidegger, Martin (1982), *The Basic Problems of Phenomenology*. Translation, Introduction, and Lexicon by Albert Hofstadter. Revised edition. Bloomington & Indianapolis: Indiana University Press.

Herbert, Nick (1987), *Quantum Reality*. Garden City, New York: Anchor Books.

Jantsch, Erich (1975), *Design for Evolution*. New York: George Braziller.

Jantsch, Erich (1980), *The Self-organizing Universe*. Oxford: Pergamon Press.

Jantsch, Erich, ed. (1981), *The Evolutionary Vision: Toward a Unifying Paradigm of Physical, Biological and Sociocultural Evolution*. Boulder, Colorado: AAAS Selected Symposium 61.

Kraus, Elizabeth M. (1979), *The Metaphysics of Experience*. New York: Fordham University Press.

Levin, David Michael (1988), *The Opening of Vision: Nihilism and the Postmodern Situation*. New York: Routledge.

Schrag, Calvin O. (1969), *Experience and Being*. Evanston, Ill.: Northwestern University Press.

Strasser, Stephan (1977), *Phenomenology of Feeling*, Pittsburgh: Duquesne University Press.

Zaner, Richard M. (1964), *The Problem of Embodiment. Some Contributions to a Phenomenology of the Body*. The Hague: Martinus Nijhoff.

B. Tibetan Works (by known authors)

Klong-chen rab-'byams-pa

mKha'-yang

=*mKha'-'gro yang-tig*

In: *sNying-thig ya-bzhi*, Vols. 4-6.
New Delhi, 1971

Grub-mtha'

=*Theg-pa mtha'-dag-gi don gsal-bar byed-pa grub-pa'i mtha' rin-po-che'i mdzod*
Sde-dge ed., Delhi, 1983

Chos-dbyings

Chos-dbyings rin-po-che'i mdzod-kyi 'grel-pa lung-gi gter-mdzod
Sde-dge ed., Delhi, 1983

Theg-mchog

=*Theg-pa'i mchog rin-po-che'i mdzod*, 2 vols.
Sde-dge ed., Delhi, 1983

gNas-lugs

=*sDe-gsum snying-po'i don-'grel gnas-lugs rin-po-che'i mdzod*
Sde-dge ed., Delhi, 1983

Bi-ma

=*Bi-ma snying-thig*

In: *sNying-thig ya-bzhi*, Vols. 7-9
Bla-yang
=*Bla-ma yang-tig*
In: *s Nying-thig ya-bzhi*, Vol. 1
Man-ngag
=*Man-ngag rin-po-che'i mdzod*
Sde-dge ed., Delhi, 1983
Tshig-don
=*gSang-ba bla-na-med-pa'i 'od-gsal rdo-rje snying-po'i gnas-gsum gsal-bar byed-pa'i tshig-don rin-po-che'i mdzod*
Sde-dge ed., Delhi, 1983
Zab-yang
=*Zab-mo yang-tig*
In: *sNying-thig ya-bzhi*, Vols. 10-11
Yid-bzhin
=*Theg-pa chen-po'i man-ngag-gi bstan-bcos yid-bzhin rin-po-che'i mdzod*
Sde-dge ed., Delhi, 1983
mKhan-po Yon-dga' v. Yon-tan rgya-mtsho
sGam-po-pa v. Collections
'Jigs-med gling-pa
Yon-tan
=*Yon-tan rin-po-che'i dga'-ba'i char*
In: *The Collected Works of Kun-mkhyen 'Jigs-med gling-pa* (*Ngagyur Nyingmay Sungrab*, Vol. 30)
Gangtok, 1971
rNam-mkhyen shing-rta (commentary on the above)
In: *The Collected Works of Kun-mkhyen'Jigs-med gling-pa* (*Ngagyur Nyingmay Sungrab*, Vol. 30)
Gangtok, 1971
Padma dkar-po v. Collections
Padma-las-'brel-rtsal
Nam-mkha' klong-yangs
in: *mKha'-'gro yang-tig*, vol. 2
New Delhi, 1971
gNad-gsum sgron-me
in: *mKha'-'gro yang-tig*, vol. 3
New Delhi, 1971
Zhva-dmar Chos-kyi dbang-phyug

Phyag-chen lhan-cig-skyes-sbyor-gyi zab-khrid
Paro, 1979
Yon-tan rgya-mtsho (mkhan-po Yon-dga')
Nyi-ma'i 'od-zer
Nyi-zla'i sgron-ma
=*Yon-tan rin-po-che'i mdzod-kyi 'grel-pa zab-don snang-byed nyi-ma'i 'od-zer*
Gangtok, 1969
Rong-zom Chos-kyi bzang-po
bKa'-'bum
n.p., n.d.
gSang-snying 'grel-pa
n.p., n.d.
Vairocana v. Collections
Śrīsiṃha
Byang-chub-sems khyung-chen-gyi rgyud
in: *rNying-rgyud*, vol. 1
Thimbu, 1973
Khyung-chen mkha'-lding
in: *Bi-ma snying-tig*, vol. 2
New Delhi, 1971

C. Tibetan works (by unknown authors)

Kun-bzang klong-drug
=*Kun-tu bzang-po klong-drug-pa'i rgyud*
In: *Ati*, vol. 2, pp. 111-214
Kun-bzang thugs-kyi me-long
=*Kun-tu bzang-po thugs-kyi me-long-gi rgyud*
In: *Ati*, vol. 1, pp. 233-280
sGron-ma snang-byed
in: *Bi-ma snying-thig*, vol. 2, pp. 2-159
sGron-ma 'bar-ba'i rgyud
In: *Ati*, vol. 1, pp. 281-313
dGongs-pa zang-thal
=*rDzogs-pa chen-po dgongs-pa zang-thal*
In: *Smanrtsis Shesrig Spendzod*, Vols. 60-64
Leh, 1973
sGra-thal 'gyur-ba
=*Rin-po-che 'byung-bar byed-pa sgra-thal 'gyur chen-po'i rgyud*
In: *Ati*, vol. 1, pp. 1-205

Ngo-sprod spras-pa'i rgyud
=*Ngo-sprod rin-po-che spras-pa'i zhing-khams bstan-pa'i rgyud*
In: *Ati*, vol. 2, pp. 77-109
Nyi-zla kha-sbyor
=*Nyi-ma dang zla-ba kha-sbyor-ba chen-po gsang-ba'i rgyud*
In: *Ati*, vol. 3, pp. 152-233
Thig-le kun-gsal
=*Thig-le kun-gsal chen-po'i rgyud*
In: *rNying-rgyud*, Vol. 5, pp. 124-289
Thig-le gsang-ba' brda'i rgyud
In *rNying-rgyud*, vol. 5, pp. 482-485
rDo-rje sems-dpa' snying-gi me-long
=*rDo-rje sems-dpa' snying-gi me-long-gi rgyud*
In: *Ati*, vol. 1, pp. 315-388
Nor-bu phra-bkod-kyi rgyud
=*Nor-bu phra-bkod rang-gi don thams-cad gsal-bar byed-pa'i rgyud*
In: *Ati*. vol. 2, pp. 1-75
sNang-srid kha-sbyor bdud-rtsi bcud-thig 'khor-ba thog-mtha' gcod-pa'i rgyud
In: *rNying-rgyud*, vol. 5, pp. 525-601
Mu-tig phreng-ba
=*Mu-tig phreng-ba zhes-bya-ba'i rgyud*
In: *Ati*, vol. 2, pp. 417-537
rDzogs-pa chen-po nges-don thams-cad 'dus-pa ye-shes nam-mkha' mnyam-pa'i rgyud
In: *rNying-rgyud*, vol. 8, pp. 124-478
rDzogs-pa chen-po lta-ba thams-cad-kyi snying-po'i rgyud
In: *rNying-rgyud*, vol. 8, pp. 58-101
rDzogs-pa chen-po lta-ba ye-shes gting rdzogs-kyi rgyud
In: *rNying-rgyud*, vol. 3, pp. 33-65
rDzogs-pa chen-po thig-le gsang-ba de-kho-na-nyid nges-pa'i rgyud
In: *rNying-rgyud*, vol. 5, pp. 515-525
Yi-ge-med-pa
=*Yi-ge med-pa'i rgyud chen-po*
In: *Ati*, vol. 2, pp. 215-244
Ye-shes gsang-ba sgron-me rin-po-che man-ngag-gi rgyud
In: *rNying-rgyud*, vol. 4, pp. 1-24
Rig-pa rang-shar
=*Rig-pa rang-shar chen-po'i rgyud*
In: *Ati*, Vol. 1, pp. 389-855

Rin-chen spungs-pa'i rgyud
=*Rin-chen spungs-pa yon-tan chen-po ston-pa rgyud-kyi rgyal-pa*
In: *Ati*, vol. 3, pp. 73-114
Seng-ge rtsal-rdzogs
=*Seng-ge rtsal-rdzogs chen-po'i rgyud*
In: *Ati*, vol. 2, pp. 245-415
lHa-rgyud rin-po-che dbang-gi 'khor-lo
In: *rNying-rgyud*, vol. 5, pp. 92-111

D. Tibetan Collections

Ati
=*rNying-ma'i rgyud bcu-bdun* 3 vols.
New Delhi, 1973-77
sGam-po-pa, *Collected Works* (handwritten copy)
n.p., n.d.
rNying-rgyud
=*rNying-ma'i rgyud-'bum* 36 vols.
Thimbu, 1973
sNying-thig ya-bzhi 11 vols.
(author: Klong-chen rab-'byams-pa)
New Delhi, 1970
Padma-dkar-po, *Collected Works* 24 vols.
Darjeeling, W.B. 1973-75
rTse-le sna-tshogs rang-grol, *Collected Works* 5 vols.
New Delhi 1974
Vairocana, *rGyud-'bum* 8 vols.
In: *Smanrtsis Shesrig Spendzod*, vols. 16-23
Leh 1971

E. Sanskrit works

Abhidharmakośa
Critically edited by Swami Dwarikadas Shastri
Bauddha Bharati, Varanasi, 1970
French translation by Louis de la Vallée Poussin
Paris: Paul
Geuthner (1923-31)
Abhisamayālaṅkāra
Eds. Th. Stcherbatsky and E. Obermiller
Leningrad: Bibliotheca Buddhica (1929)
Uttaratantra
Ed. E.H. Johnston
Patna: Bihar Research Society (1950)

INDEX

of Technical terms Tibetan

SANSKRIT INDEX

INDEX

OF NAMES AND SUBJECTS